Manipulatory Politics

Robert E. Goodin

The common belief is that power is evil. Of course it is not, Robert Goodin points out. Sometimes we are ethically indifferent to the exercise of power, and other times we actually approve of it. But when it involves manipulation, it is evil, and it is the notion of manipulation that Goodin focuses on in this book.

Analytically, manipulation has two components: it is both deceptive and un-welcome. From an ethical point of view, a manipulatory practice is more worrisome the more persistent or distributively biased it threatens to be. With these criteria in mind, Goodin surveys various techniques of manipulatory politics; lying, laying linguistic traps, rhetorical trickery, symbolic rewards, political rituals, and the rigging of "obvious" solutions to problems. Goodin provides numerous vivid examples of all of these techniques from his unusually wide reading of history, biography, contemporary political studies, philosophy, anthropology, and sociology.

Altogether, he finds twenty distinct modes of manipulation, of which only three pose any serious threat. However, he points out that there is always the worry that we are being manipulated through some mechanism that no one notices, and he expresses the hope that his discussion will help uncover these.

"There is a continuing fascination wi power, and this book in my judgme carries the subject to a greater level sophistication."
—Brian Barry, University of Chicag

D1087810

Robert E. Goodin is lecturer in government at the University of Essex and the author of *The Politics of Rational Man.*

MANIPULATORY POLITICS

MANIPULATORY POLITICS

ROBERT E. GOODIN

NEW HAVEN AND LONDON, YALE UNIVERSITY PRESS

Designed by James J. Johnson
and set in VIP Baskerville type.
Printed in the United States of America by
Vail-Ballou Press, Binghamton, N.Y.

Library of Congress Cataloging in Publication Data

Goodin, Robert E
  Manipulatory politics.

  Includes index.
  1. Political ethics.   2. Power (Social sciences)
I. Title.
JA79.G64   172   79-27682
ISBN 0-300-02463-0

10 9 8 7 6 5 4 3 2 1

'They that govern most make least noise. You see when they row in a Barge, they that do drudgery-work, slash, and puff, and sweat; but he that governs sits quietly at the Stern, and scarce is seen to stir.'

John Selden, 'Power, State', *Table-Talk*
(London: E. Smith, 1689).

CONTENTS

PREFACE

WHAT FOLLOWS LAYS FOUNDATIONS FOR empirical political studies with a sharper evaluative focus. The ultimate aim is decidedly empirical. But evaluative retooling proves to be a necessary preliminary, and here I shall confine myself to that preparatory task of cataloguing various modes of political manipulation and assessing them from a moral point of view. I am not concerned to document the existence or antics of power elites in general or even to estimate the frequency of their manipulatory practices. I should think that they are fairly common—otherwise I could not have found so many examples to illustrate my discussion—but firm conclusions on empirical questions must await a full-scale enquiry organized along rather different lines. The present enterprise is both more limited and more limiting. I am simply trying to decide which methods of manipulation would be ethically worrisome if there were cohesive elites dedicated to the deceptive exercise of power. The workload of empirical researchers attempting to document them is considerably lightened by my finding that only a few of the most frequently discussed classes of cases need worry us. At the same time, however, I offer reasons for believing that some of the most worrying forms of manipulatory politics have yet to be revealed, thus requiring a continuing theoretical sensitivity on the part of empirical students of political power relations.

These are themes to which I have been returning for some time. I owe a collective debt to colleagues at various institutions—Nuffield College, Oxford; Strathclyde; Maryland;

Oslo; and Essex—for valuable advice in many cases and for even more valuable indulgence in many others. Special contributions to one or more of the following chapters have been made by Murray Edelman, John Madeley, John Pocock, Richard Rose, Jim Sharpe, David Spitz and Mike Taylor; Brian Barry, Herman van Gunsteren and Geraint Parry have read and commented most helpfully on the entire manuscript. I am grateful to them for all their advice, to my Leiden friends for originally encouraging me to think of this as a book, and to Marian Neal Ash for seeing it so smoothly into print.

CHAPTER ONE ⚶ POLITICAL THEORY WITH A POINT

1.1 WHAT'S WRONG WITH POWER?

ALL SEEM AGREED THAT POLITICS is the science of power, but each generation's perspective is shaped by its own peculiar experiences. For the children of the Great Depression, politics was the study of distribution—Lasswell's 'who gets what, when and how'. For Cold Warriors, politics was the study of force and counterforce, *pace* Morgenthau. And, for those touched by Watergate and the other great public scandals of the 1970s politics will inevitably be the study of dirty tricks.

This latest shift of focus is most fortuitous. It recalls almost forgotten themes of the Old Masters, from Machiavelli to Marx. It forces political scientists to look, as we have too rarely done before, to the work in our brother disciplines of anthropology and sociology. Most of all, it forces us to bring values back into our science. The phrase 'dirty tricks' is hardly a neutral one. It pointedly reminds us that political events require not only prediction and explanation but also evaluation and, quite often, moral condemnation.

I say 'reminds' because this seems quite in keeping with the fundamental traditions of the continuing enterprise that is the 'power debate'. The point of talking about power is (and, I take it, always has been) that it blends the empirical and the normative in a particularly constructive fashion. The reason empiricists talk of power instead of administrative procedures or voting trends, for example, is that the one presumably has evaluative significance the others lack. And the reason philosophers talk of social power rather than the mind-body problem or the identity of indiscernibles is that the one has clear practical significance in a way others do not. We have always valued the study of social power precisely because it promised to provide this sort of bridge between our factual and normative concerns.

Once it seemed that all paths—evaluative as well as descriptive—lead to an emphasis on power. Individual freedom (the obverse of power) is, after all, a recurring theme in normative discourse; and for empirical researchers power is to politics as money is to economics, the elemental force driving the machine. A wonderfully symbiotic relationship developed, with philosophers analysing the concept of 'power' in ever greater detail and empiricists searching for its manifestations with ever increasing rigour. But, as I shall show, the research effort has gone astray precisely because the concept of 'power' is ethically ambiguous. From the simple fact that power is being exercised no moral conclusions follow. Sometimes it is good that power is exercised, and sometimes it is wicked. With this realization, the empirical findings of power concentrations cease to carry any very clear evaluative implications. If our empirical studies are to lead to moral conclusions, we shall have to look elsewhere for an ethical anchor.

Evaluatively focused empirical studies make special demands of both political scientists and political moralists. The reforms required of the empirical scientist are perhaps the more apparent. His task, as it is ordinarily understood, is the prediction and explanation of political behaviour. 'Power' is an undeniably useful concept for that purpose. A strictly mechanistic model reducing political outcomes to the vector sum of opposing political forces may be a little too simple. (Indeed, it leaves untouched the really hard part of the job, *viz.*, specifying and quantifying the various 'forces'.) But however incomplete this model, it at least offers a natural starting point.

In our eagerness to explain and predict, however, we will have built a model of power politics which ignores morally significant distinctions between different ways of exercising power. You might get a man's money either by taking it forcibly from him or by persuading him to give it to you; you might change a legislative outcome by buying off legislators or by assassinating them or by voting them out of office. These distinctions do not much matter to the empirical political scientist. For the purposes of his predictions, he is interested only in the magnitudes and directions of opposing forces. He needs to differentiate alternative ways of exercising power only insofar as they differ in the force they carry. For the moral evaluation of the power act, however, it clearly matters whether the outcome was produced by pressure or persuasion, by bribery or the bullet or the ballot.

In a way, however, these scientific researchers must be forgiven. When focusing on 'power' they are simply mimicking emphases of political philosophers themselves. They go searching for concentrations of social power in full confidence that, if and when they find them, they will have revealed something ethically important about their societies. By listening to philosophers who are concerned to sort out the notion of power *per se,* however, empirical analysts have taken a false cue. Power is not necessarily evil, and, since it is not, no normative conclusions follow immediately and necessarily from its discovery. Political scientists structure their research in the way they do because they think they can piggyback on well-established philosophical conclusions. In truth, all the evaluative work remains to be done. And there are good reasons for insisting that it should be done before the fact rather than afterwards: otherwise researchers have no way of knowing where to direct their scientific attentions or even how to reccognize an important discovery should they stumble across one.

From a philosopher's point of view, the preoccupation with power might be traced to the desire to tidy up muddles arising from the confused use of concepts. The many and varied usages of 'power' are both confused and confusing. But the notion of power also suffers fundamentally from ethical ambiguities. I would argue that 'power' *per se* is ethically neutral. 'Power' might be either 'legitimate' or 'illegitimate'—the fact that we can attach either adjective is terribly revealing. Abstracted from the particular contexts that allow application of these qualifiers, the notion of 'power' seems to be entirely lacking in ethical overtones.

A particularly important source of the ethical ambiguities surrounding the concept of 'power' is the fact that people are often *glad* to have power exercised over them. Consider the following four cases: (1) Sometimes, in anticipation of momentary weakness of will, a person binds himself (either literally, as Ulysses, or more figuratively) so as to prevent backsliding he would later regret. In the interim, power is being exercised over him (or, at least, over the self temporarily inhabiting the body). But few would find that objectionable. (2) Other times a person voluntarily restricts his future freedom of action in connection with bargaining games. This constitutes an infringement of his power, if we take a broad understanding of power as the range of actions he might freely perform. But social theorists from Hobbes to Schelling have shown why individuals should rationally welcome opportunities for binding themselves in such situations. (3) The commitments one makes to one's family and friends are further constraints upon one's freedom of action—one gives friends and lovers a measure of power over oneself—yet none would presume that one is worse off for having yielded such power. (4) Or, again, a person sometimes happily yields to the dictates of authoritative spokesmen for groups to which he is committed. As I have written elsewhere, 'Practicing Catholics doubtless welcome papal guidance on matters of morals and religion. That does not make papal statements any less exercises of power, but it does suggest that not all power is necessarily objectionable.' Taken together, these examples indicate a fairly wide range of cases wherein the exercise of power might not be immoral at all.[1]

Now, it certainly is true that the words, '*A* has power over *B*', are typically said scoldingly. But that is only because we have, and usually are anxious to use, other more precise words such as 'authority' or 'persuasion' to describe exercises of power we regard as justifiable. We are typically unable or disinclined to make any such fine distinctions between types of morally offensive power play, and are content to leave the more general term 'power' to describe them. Thus Peters correctly observes that ' "power" usually has meaning by contrast with "authority" '—or, more precisely, 'authority' has meaning by contrast with other forms of 'power'. But that does not prove his claim that, therefore, 'power' is not 'a generic term of which "authority" is just one species.'[2] For a parallel case, imagine a discussion among exhibitors at a dog show. They have very elaborate terminology for differentiating various types of thoroughbred—Great Dane, Norwegian Elk Hound, Irish Wolf Hound, etc. Among these people, 'dog' is a re-

1. Jon Elster, *Ulysses and the Sirens* (Cambridge: Cambridge University Press, 1979). Thomas Hobbes, *Leviathan*, Ch. 14; Thomas C. Schelling, *The Strategy of Decision* (Cambridge: Harvard University Press, 1960). A. K. Sen, 'Rational Fools', *Philosophy and Public Affairs*, 6 (1977): 317–44. R. E. Goodin and S. G. Beackon, 'The Powers That Be and The Powers That Do: An "Economic" Approach', *European Journal of Political Research*, 4 (1976): 175–93. See similarly Dorothy Emmet, 'The Concept of Power', *Proceedings of the Aristotelian Society*, 54 (1953–54): 1–26 at 14, and Felix E. Oppenheim, *Dimensions of Freedom* (New York: St. Martin's, 1961), p. 92.

2. R. S. Peters, 'Authority', *Proceedings of the Aristotelian Society, (Supplement)*, 32 (1958): 207–40. Peter Bachrach and Morton S. Baratz, *Power and Poverty* (New York: Oxford University Press, 1970), p. 32, cf. p. 21, likewise suppose that 'authority' cannot be a form of 'power' because '*A* and *B* are in agreement as to ends [and] *B* will freely assent to *A*'s preferred course of action'; but would *A* not think it odd that, having been authorized by *B* to act as his agent, he lacks the power to do so precisely because he has the authority?

sidual, a term of derision assigned sneeringly to beasts lacking a pedigree. Thus we could well imagine a dog-owner correcting a young visitor, 'Clement is *not* a dog; he is a Great Dane.' Following Peters's logic, such usage would prove that 'Great Dane' is not a variety of 'dog' or at least is not acknowledged to be so in our ordinary language! This is clearly false, and so too is Peters's conclusion regarding the relationship between 'power' and 'authority'. A politician's insistence that he be said to rule by 'authority' rather than 'power', far from proving that the two are unrelated, instead makes sense only if we understand how dangerously closely the two *are* related.

Other efforts at circumscribing the notion of 'power' very narrowly, and denying that any of these acceptable instances of power are part of the concept at all, similarly amount to little more than linguistic legislation. Another very common move, for example, is to insist that the 'power of persuasion' cannot be a form of power at all precisely because we hold it in high regard. Ordinary language, however, simply does not support any such distinction. The two concepts 'power' and 'persuasion' substitute freely for one another in phrases such as 'he has powerful arguments' and 'he has persuasive arguments'.[3] In ordinary language, the 'power of persuasion' is indeed treated as an aspect of social power. Yet it is also clearly regarded as an aspect which is ethically unobjectionable.

All these ambiguities combine to make 'power' a promis-

3. Robert Bierstedt, 'An Analysis of Social Power', *American Sociological Review*, 15 (1950): 730–38 at 731. Stanley I. Benn, 'Power', *Encyclopedia of Philosophy*, ed. Paul Edwards (London: Collier-Macmillan, 1968), 6: 425–27. Some may say that the reason we do not mind that '*A* has powerful arguments' is that it is the arguments that are powerful, not the man. But similarly with '*A* has powerful armies': the armies are what are powerful, but this we do mind very much. The crucial fact the critic would have overlooked is that the armies and the arguments are under *A*'s control and serve *A*'s interests. They are not neutral resources lying around for anyone to pick up. Rather, they are at *his* service.

ing candidate for philosophical analysis aimed at tidying up the sorts of muddles they can cause. But concepts muddled all this badly cannot form a very secure base for ethically significant empirical enquiries. For those purposes it would be far better to seize upon a word with stronger and clearer ethical implications than those offered by the concept of 'power'. At this juncture, tradition would have us turn to a search for conditions rendering the exercise of power permissible. We would probe such concepts as 'authority' or 'legitimacy'. But we would also find, all too soon, that the familiar and intractable disputes of classical political philosophy have all been reintroduced in only a slightly different guise. Not much progress can be expected by concentrating on this positive side of the power relation—questions of what makes power morally legitimate and the like. I shall instead undertake the less orthodox task of exploring the negative side of the power relation, attempting to identify what makes power morally offensive. The following two sections isolate a concept of 'manipulation' which seems to present the nastiest face of power and which is of special moral interest for that reason. Avoiding manipulation is, of course, only a very minimal requirement of the Good Society. But, as several others have recently demonstrated, such minima are likely not to be achieved unless they are identified formally and insisted upon firmly.[4]

1.2 THE CONCEPT OF 'MANIPULATION'

'Manipulatory politics' can be regarded as a subset of the larger class of 'power politics', provided that phrase is broadly

4. Barrington Moore, Jr., *Reflections on the Causes of Human Misery* (Boston: Beacon Press, 1972). Douglas W. Rae, 'A Principle of Simple Justice,' and James Fishkin, 'Tyranny and Democratic Theory', *Philosophy, Politics and Society*, 5th Series, ed. Fishkin and Peter Laslett (Oxford: Blackwell, 1979), pp. 134-54 and 197-226 respectively.

construed. A person exercises power through influence and authority as well as orders and threats, and this is the region in which manipulation works. On a restricted understanding of power (such as Weber's, for example), manipulation might be excluded because it is not a means of 'overcoming resistance'. Rather, it is a means of *undermining* resistance, which any reasonable interpretation of the power phenomenon must of course include.

Manipulation is a slice out of the centre of this broader concept of 'power'. On the one side, the notion of 'manipulation' is bounded by flagrant exercises of power. Sometimes people get others to do what they want them to do by making absolutely blatant threats or offers. There can be no question that these count as clear cases of power politics, but it is highly questionable that so conspicuous an exercise of power can count as manipulation. On the other side, the notion of 'manipulation' is bounded by trivial exercises of power. Sometimes other people's power causes an individual to perform an action which he nevertheless does not mind doing and, indeed, would not *ex ante* have minded doing had he been asked. We are comfortable enough talking of the 'power' involved in such situations: one person is still bending another to his will, even if he encounters no resistance in so doing. But I doubt that we would feel equally comfortable in talking of 'manipulation' in such cases. The concept of 'manipulation', then, is circumscribed in these two ways: it is power exercised (1) deceptively and (2) against the putative will of its objects.[5] Each of these aspects is morally objectionable in its own right. Together, they guarantee that manipulation constitutes the evil

---

5. Joel Rudinow, 'Manipulation', *Ethics*, 88 (1978): 338-47 at 338-39, suggests similar boundaries for the concept: 'Most people ... would distinguish manipulation from persuasion, on one hand, and from coercion, on the other.'

core of the concept of 'power', which I shall argue more fully in the following section.

1.2.1 *Manipulation as Unknown Interference*

The first aspect of my definition of 'manipulation' is the implication of subtlety. In the strongest sense, 'manipulation' is something which actually happens invisibly. A puppeteer, for example, manipulates his marionette with wires his audience cannot see. A masseur manipulates his client's sacroiliac without exposing the vertebrae to view.

Sometimes the term is stretched to cover cases where the processes are more open to inspection. A mathematician is said to manipulate an equation even though it is written on the chalkboard for all to see. When a technician is said to manipulate an electron microscope, there is no suggestion that a sleight of hand is involved. But even in these more attenuated usages the implication of profound subtlety persists. Indeed, it would seem that it is by virtue of this implication that we extend the term 'manipulation' to cover such cases at all. Were the mathematician performing a straightforward operation on a straightforward equation, or were the 'technician' working merely with a magnifying glass, we would not be inclined to say they were 'manipulating' anything at all.[6]

In social contexts, 'manipulation' has especially strong connotations of something sneaky. The *Oxford English Dictionary* defines the relevant sense of 'to manipulate' as meaning 'to manage by dexterous contrivance or influence'. And the implication of deviousness so apparent in ordinary language

6. Ibid., p. 339. Our reactions to the stilted language of the instruction manual accompanying an ordinary household appliance suggest much the same point. When the manufacturer writes, 'Manipulate dial X until . . . ', we get the distinct impression that he is just bragging about the complexity of his product. Otherwise he would have stated simply, 'Turn dial X until. . . .'

is not lost in the more specialized discourse of professional
students of politics. Herbert Goldhamer and Edward Shils, in
their early attempt to distinguish 'Types of Power and Status',
comment that 'in the case of manipulation there is no recognition by the subordinated individual that an act of power has
been effected.' Felix Oppenheim describes as the paradigm
case of political manipulation something which is similarly
sneaky: 'Y purposely influences X's activity, but purposely
conceals this fact from him. X complies in the mistaken belief
that he is acting in his own interest.' Or, again, Christian Bay
proposes a taxonomy in which 'manipulative power' contrasts
with 'coercive power', which is exercised through distinctly
unsubtle threats of sanctions for noncompliance.[7]

    Although this connection between 'manipulation' and 'de-
ception' is well established in both ordinary language and
professional discourse, some do object to it. Joel Rudinow, for
example, offers the following counterexample: Imagine a
wino seeking admission to a hospital's mental ward. The duty
officer, seeing that he is perfectly healthy and supposing he is
just looking for a bed for the night, refuses. The wino replies,
'If you don't admit me, I'll threaten to throw myself off the
City Water Tower; I'll create such a fuss that you will have to
admit me.' The doctor is intransigent, and the wino carries
out his threat. In due course, two policemen bring him back
to the hospital, saying that they have 'rescued' him from a
suicide attempt and suggest that he be admitted for observation. In this case, our intuition is that manipulation has occurred; but clearly the doctor is not being deceived. Rudinow

    7. Herbert Goldhamer and Edward A. Shils, 'Types of Power and
Status', *American Journal of Sociology*, 45 (1939): 171–82 at 172. Oppenheim,
Dimensions of Freedom, p. 95. Christian Bay, *The Structure of Freedom* (Stanford:
Stanford University Press, 1958), p. 259. See similarly Bachrach and Baratz,
Power and Poverty, p. 31.

supposes that this proves that manipulation need not entail deception.[8] But the crucial question in this case is *who* or *what* is being manipulated. My prime candidate would be the police, who *are* deceived by the wino's pseudo-attempt at suicide. (They would not suggest admitting him for observation unless they were deceived.) In some sense the 'rules of admission' are also being manipulated. They too are 'deceived', in the sense that they are incapable of taking cognizance of certain relevant facts about the case (i.e., those arising from the doctor's earlier encounter with the wino). The doctor, who knows precisely what is going on, strikes me as the least plausible candidate for the staus of 'object of manipulation'. Thus, the person who is not being deceived in this case is not being manipulated; and we describe the case as involving manipulation by virtue of the fact that some others are being deceived. Rudinow's example fails to drive a wedge between deception and manipulation.

Others might offer more general objections to this connection. Some may protest my assertion that, for manipulation to occur, those subject to it must not know that they are being manipulated. This, they may say, is not the way we ordinarily talk about manipulation. In a way, of course, they would be right. By the time we start talking about manipulation at all, the act has already been exposed. But when we do speak of manipulation, either in the past tense ('I was manipulated') or in the second or third person ('You/they are being manipulated'), the implication is always that the manipulation was unbeknownst to its object at the time of the act. When we tell someone, 'You are being manipulated', we think we really are telling him something he does not already know. That is why we do not feel silly in saying to someone, 'You are being

8. Rudinow, 'Manipulation', p. 340.

manipulated', in the same way as we would feel foolish in saying, 'You are eating', of which he is presumably perfectly well
aware.[9]

Others might concede the connection between deception
and manipulation but argue that it is merely a contingent, not
an analytic one. For example, politicians can manipulate the
economy for partisan advantage only so long as voters do not
realize that the economic boom during the run-up to the election is artificially induced and cannot be sustained in the
post-election period. As soon as voters discover the trick it
ceases to work. J. K. Galbraith asserts that, more generally,
'People need to believe that they are unmanaged if they are to
be managed effectively.'[10] Consequently, most of the cases of
successful political manipulation will also, *ipso facto,* be cases
of successful deception. There is no denying this contingent
connection between the two phenomena. There is, however,
also a more fundamental analytic bond which might most effectively be isolated by focusing on *un*successful attempts at
manipulation. Imagine two situations, one in which *A* attempts to influence *B* secretly and another in which *A* at-

9. 'You are eating' might not be a silly remark if addressed to a compul-
sive eater, who gobbles down food without thinking or perhaps even noticing.
This suggests that psychological manipulation might fit this larger pattern of
deception rather than requiring separate analysis as Rudinow, 'Manipulation'
supposes. At the very least, the manipulator in such cases is *bypassing* (if not,
strictly speaking, deceiving) the rational, thinking self when playing upon
another's weaknesses.

10. William D. Nordhaus, 'The Political Business Cycle', *Review of Economic Studies,* 42 (1975): 167–90. Richard E. Wagner, 'Economic Manipulation for Political Profit', *Kyklos,* 30 (1977): 395–410. J. K. Galbraith, *The New
Industrial State* (London: Hamish Hamilton, 1967), p. 218. William E. Connolly, *The Terms of Political Discourse* (Lexington, Mass.: D. C. Heath, 1974),
p. 98, suggests a similarly contingent connection: 'When some manipulate
others effectively, both the recipients and third parties will find it difficult to
grasp the role played by the manipulator. Interested in denying power, elites
of power favor exactly the forms most difficult for recipients or third parties
(for instance, journalists and social scientists) to identify with confidence.'

tempts the same openly. Both fail. In the former case we would say (by virtue of the effort at deception) that A attempted to manipulate B, whereas in the latter case we would only say that he tried to influence him. The Vichy regime for example is fairly described as a 'puppet' government, with the implication that it was manipulated, as is the way with all puppets, precisely because it pretended (however disingenuously) to be a government of Frenchmen by Frenchmen. Forthrightly military governments of occupation would never be described as 'puppets' being 'manipulated' from the outside precisely because they make no pretence to independence. They frankly admit that they act under orders from outside, and such an open display of power cannot be described as 'manipulative' in the full sense of the term.

1.2.2 *Manipulation as Unwelcome Interference*
It is a general feature of manipulation that, being an act of power, it alters the ordinary course of events. When we manipulate an instrument we move its dials. When we manipulate a committee agenda, we alter what would otherwise have been the order of business.[11] Similarly, when we manipulate people we cause them to do something they would not otherwise have done—which is to say, manipulation of human agents runs contrary to their putative will.

This, I believe, is a superior way of formulating an aspect of the concept of 'manipulation' for which many recent commentators have been groping. Their various alternatives state the point either too strongly or too weakly. One overly robust analysis comes from advocates of individual autonomy who regard any influence one person exerts over another as im-

11. And when we 'manipulate' a social decision rule by strategic voting, we cause it to produce an outcome other than it would ordinarily have produced. Allan Gibbard, 'Manipulation of Voting Schemes', *Econometrica*, 41 (1973): 587–601.

permissible interference deserving to be called 'manipulative'. Construed in this way, however, 'manipulative power' would 'include the mutual influence exerted in the best of marriages or friendships, in collaboration toward joint tasks, and indeed in probably all social interaction.'[12] Condemning all such influence as 'manipulative' is both morally peculiar and also unfaithful to conventional usage. In ordinary language, 'manipulation' is used to specify a special kind of 'influence', i.e., as a qualifier of that term rather than as a synonym for it.

Appreciating this fact, most commentators proceed to define 'manipulation' by seeking the differentia setting it apart from other members of the genus 'influence'. One suggestion is that 'manipulation' is influence accomplished by distorting or withholding information. This is the way Dahl distinguishes 'manipulative persuasion' from 'rational persuasion'. Before him, Merton similarly resolved the 'moral dilemma' presented by *Mass Persuasion* in the context of the 1943 War Bond marathon radio broadcast: 'Mass persuasion is not manipulative when it provides access to pertinent facts; it is manipulative when the appeal to sentiment is used to the exclusion of pertinent information.'[13]

---

12. Bay, *Structure of Freedom*, p. 320. The sort of broad usage Bay criticizes is found, for example, in Douglas H. Parker, 'Rhetoric, Ethics and Manipulation', *Philosophy and Rhetoric*, 5 (1972): 69–87, which expands the concept so incredibly that even the phrase 'invited manipulation' can make sense.

13. Robert A. Dahl, *Modern Political Analysis*, 3rd ed. (Englewood Cliffs, N.J.: Prentice-Hall, 1976), pp. 45–46. Robert K. Merton, *Mass Persuasion* (New York: Harper, 1946), p. 186. Peter Abell, 'The Many Faces of Power and Liberty', *Sociology*, 11 (1977): 3–24 at 10, combines these first two moves, defining 'manipulation' as influence decreasing the 'autonomy' of the manipulated and operationalizing 'autonomy' in terms of 'information provision'. Lawrence Stern, 'Freedom, Blame and Moral Community', *Journal of Philosophy*, 71 (1974): 72–84, phrases a similar point slightly differently, equating 'manipulation' with 'subverting or by-passing another person's rational or moral capabilities for the sake of some result.' See also Connolly, *Terms of Political Discourse*, pp. 89, 93–94.

There is a striking but misleading resemblance between this distinction and the analysis in Section 1.2.1 of manipulation as unknown interference. Since manipulation must be deceptive, certain information (i.e., that the manipulation is underway) must be withheld. But that only calls for concealment after the fact. It says nothing about the mechanism by which the manipulation now being concealed was itself originally accomplished. Specifically, there is no necessary presumption that the manipulation was, in the first instance, accomplished by withholding or distorting information. Here again there is likely to be a contingent connection—manipulation will probably be easier to conceal if accomplished by fiddling information—but that tells us nothing about the *concept* of 'manipulation' as such.

The analysis of manipulation as withholding or distorting information proves to be unduly narrow. It builds one particular method of manipulation into the very definition of the term, excluding other methods which are equally important. The relative weakness of the mechanisms discussed in Chapter 2 compared to the strengths of those discussed in subsequent chapters is evidence of this. But for now it might suffice to consider the case of 'gerrymandering', the manipulation of political boundaries for electoral advantage. Once accomplished, of course, such manipulation must be hidden from the public. But the original act of manipulation requires no withholding of information, only the skillful drawing of boundaries so as to bunch opponents and spread supporters. Indeed, schemes for eliminating such manipulation call *not* for revelation of suppressed information but rather for suppressing more still, making certain facts (party strengths, addresses of incumbents, etc.) inaccessible to those redrawing electoral boundaries.[14]

14. Bruce Adams, 'A Model State Reapportionment Process', *Harvard Journal on Legislation*, 14 (1977): 825–904 at 866–67.

An alternative which errs in the opposite direction, offering too broad an analysis of manipulation, is enshrined in the *Oxford English Dictionary* suggestion that 'to manipulate', when used disparagingly, means especially 'to treat unfairly or insidiously *for one's own advantage*' (emphasis added). This is clearly the sort of thing Galbraith has in mind when he complains that manipulation of preferences vitiates the cherished notion of 'consumer sovereignty'. If, as he argues, 'the individual's wants, though superficially they may seem to originate with him, are ultimately at the behest of the mechanism that supplies them', then the rationale for respecting the outcome of choices in economic (or political) markets would be seriously undermined.[15]

Although the word 'manipulation' is often used in this way, such an analysis crucially depends upon conflating two distinct notions—'serving the manipulator' on the one hand and 'abusing the manipulated' on the other. These are often equated in contemporary commentaries. Bay, for example, pointedly confines his objections to 'special interest' manipulation of a person, defined as that 'which serves other interests at the expense of his own'. But, of course, it is possible for other interests to be served at no cost to his own. Galbraith, too, ignores this distinction, not bothering to provide reasons for supposing that what advantages producers necessarily disadvantages consumers. He ignores the possibility that consumers were genuinely indifferent between alternative consumption bundles or that they actually welcomed the advice.[16]

15. J. K. Galbraith, 'Economics as a System of Belief', *American Economic Review (Papers and Proceedings)*, 60 (1970): 472.

16. Ibid. Bay, *Structure of Freedom*, p. 97, cf. p. 320. Jack H. Nagel *The Descriptive Analysis of Power* (New Haven: Yale University Press, 1975), pp. 105–06 weakens the Galbraith–Bay condition too much, however. Where they maintain that A has manipulated B if and only if (1) A has shaped B's preferences and (2) A benefits from this change in B's preferences, Nagel

What Galbraith describes might still be termed 'manipulation' simply by virtue of the 'unknown interference' criterion. 'Hidden persuaders' are always manipulative in that sense. But Galbraith seems to have been grasping for more—and to have missed this second dimension of 'manipulation' in a way that neo-Marxists, for example, do not. They succeed where he fails precisely because they *do* provide reasons for supposing that what serves one class necessarily disserves another.[17]

It is tempting to follow the lead of neo-Marxists and phrase the point in terms of 'interests', so manipulation necessarily works agains the interests of those being manipulated. This, however, would make it impossible to manipulate someone in his own interest: if the interference really were in his interest, it could not count as manipulative. Again, this is simply not the way we ordinarily use the word. We are perfectly comfortable speaking, for example, of manipulating a stubborn old uncle to invest in sound stocks or to go for an annual physical examination. What makes these acts manipulative is not that they are contrary to his interests (for surely they are not) but rather that they are contrary to his will. Or, more precisely, they are contrary to his *putative* will: since the manipulation deceives our old uncle, he does not notice the interference and hence does not resist it; but although we are not actually forcing him to do something

---

requires only the first condition exist. This specification is equally open to the objection that B might not mind—and might, indeed, welcome—A's intervention. In that case it would hardly seem manipulative, assuming of course that A's consent to the intervention were truly 'informed consent' and not itself manipulated.

17. Abba P. Lerner, 'The Economics and Politics of Consumer Sovereignty', *American Economic Review (Papers and Proceedings)*, 62 (1972): 258–66. Herbert Gintis, 'Consumer Behavior and the Concept of Sovereignty', *American Economic Review (Papers and Proceedings)*, 62 (1972): 267–78 and 'A Radical Analysis of Welfare Economics and Individual Development', *Quarterly Journal of Economics*, 68 (1972): 572–99.

against his will, we are causing him to do something contrary
to what he would have willed in the absence of manipulation.

Manipulation, then, involves bending another's will. When
saying that he has been manipulated, we are basically asserting the truth of a counterfactual proposition, *viz.*, that in
the absence of the intervention we describe as 'manipulatory' he would have behaved (and, indeed, have willed) differently. Validating such counterfactual propositions is, of
course, one of the more difficult steps in any analysis of social
power relations. Some commentators despair of the problem
as being fundamentally indeterminant; and even those supposing that there is a single right answer to the question,
'What would he have done otherwise?', acknowledge the extraordinary difficulty in proving precisely what that might be.
By tying the concept of 'manipulation' to the putative rather
than the actual will of those being manipulated, this analysis
evokes all these familiar difficulties. So much the better, I
would argue. The problem of validating counterfactual
propositions about 'what he would have done otherwise'
seems so central to the notions of 'power' and 'influence' that
we would be profoundly suspicious of any analysis of constituent influence-terms which fails even to acknowledge this
difficulty. But while it does not evade any of these familiar
problems, neither does the present analysis of manipulation
raise any peculiar new problems along these lines.

Defining 'manipulation' as action contrary to an individual's putative will seems a far more adequate formulation of
the point imperfectly appreciated even in the *Oxford English
Dictionary*. Manipulation must work against the putative will
of those subject to it. Withholding or distorting information is
one way of producing this result, but it is not the only way.
The fact that a scheme works to the advantage of manipulators correlates in a rough-and-ready way with its working against the putative will of those being manipulated. But

these are contingent connections. The *analytic* link to which all these observations point is best phrased in terms of the putative will of those being manipulated.

1.2.3 *Manipulation and Cognate Notions*

In addition to successfully manipulating others, one may also *attempt* to manipulate them. In addition to *being* manipulated, one may also *feel* manipulated. The core notion is, in each case, that of manipulation itself, defined in terms of what it would be to succeed in the attempt to manipulate someone else. One person manipulates another when he deceptively influences him, causing the other to act contrary to his putative will. Attempts at manipulation may of course fail, as in the case of the Vichy regime; would-be manipulators are then forced to fall back upon more conspicuous instruments of social control. But it counts as an attempt at manipulation by virtue of the fact that the attempt was aimed at exercising deceptive influence.

In the case of feeling manipulated, too, the core notion is that of 'manipulation' itself. 'Feeling manipulated is feeling (believing) that one is (or has been) the object of someone else's successful attempt to manipulate.'[18] Feeling, after the fact, that you have been manipulated is both more common and more easily fitted into the present analysis. The person who now feels manipulated had, at the time, been deceived. Now he possesses information unavailable to him at the time, and based upon these new facts he sees the manipulatory acts for what they were and feels he has been manipulated. Feeling manipulated at the moment you are being manipulated is somewhat more difficult to understand. On the present definition, manipulation must be deceptive—a person who is being manipulated must be unaware of the fact at the mo-

18. Rudinow, 'Manipulation', p. 338.

ment of manipulation. This makes it impossible to be manipulated (which implies ignorance of the fact) and at the same time to feel manipulated (which implies awareness of the fact). But actually it seems that when someone says, 'I feel I am being manipulated', he typically displays (and, indeed, claims) much less than full awareness. Instead, he is simply reporting a feeling 'deep in his bones' that someone is up to something funny. Usually he cannot pinpoint how or by whom the manipulation is being accomplished.[19] Feeling manipulated, in this sense of a dim perception of the fact, is consistent with the definition of 'manipulation' itself offered earlier in this section.

1.3   MANIPULATION, THE UGLIEST FACE OF POWER

I want to argue that this concept of 'manipulation' isolates the evil core of the concept of 'power'. In so doing, I am crucially making certain presuppositions about the sorts of ethical grudges we harbour against social power. Specifically, I am supposing that we object (when we do) not merely to the obnoxious outcomes that usually follow from a power play. Were the results all that offended us, 'oppression' or 'domination' or 'exploitation' or some other concept pointing to ethically unacceptable end-states would fully capture the evil core of 'power'. But I do not think that our moral judgements are

19. Sometimes a person might say, 'I feel manipulated', meaning that he is the conscious but unwilling agent through which one person arranges to manipulate another. This might be the case in Rudinow's example of the doctor and the wino, discussed above: the wino manipulates the rules of admission to the hospital through the doctor. But for fully conscious intermediaries (such as the doctor) to say that they themselves feel manipulated is to speak loosely, or perhaps elliptically. They should complete the statement, saying more precisely that they feel they are *being used* for manipulating *(other)* people.

so straightforwardly consequentialistic as that suggests. We are not indifferent between two equally good (or bad) outcomes, one produced by free and open discussion and the other by brainwashing. The process by which the results are produced plays an independent role in our moral reckoning. We often have independent, and not merely derivative, objections to the techniques by which power is exercised; and this is what must be explained in any account of the evil core of the concept of 'power'. Unlike the end-state notions of 'oppression', 'domination' and 'exploitation', the concept of 'manipulation' points to the evils of processes. Whereas a focus on end-states would reduce us to banalities ('power is evil when put to evil uses'), the focus on 'manipulation' allows us to isolate the particularly disagreeable features of the process by which power is exercised. Of course, the 'power' cluster contains many other process-notions besides 'manipulation', among them 'intimidate', 'terrorize', 'force', 'coerce', etc. The burden of this section is to argue that, among all these concepts describing processes for exercising power, 'manipulation' is the most morally offensive.

Part of the reason we use the word 'manipulation' so consistently disparagingly in social contexts is that there is an element of deception built into the notion. Whatever we have to say against exercises of power in general, it surely goes double for sneaky exercises of power. A blatant power play, if not quite honourable, is at least honest. Political manipulation does not even display this virtue. This is primarily what sets it off from—and makes it so much more objectionable than—other process-notions of 'intimidating', 'terrorizing', 'forcing' or 'coercing' people. Unpleasant as they all are in other respects, these processes can at least boast as their saving grace that they are open and aboveboard. They are ways of overcoming a person physically rather than of deceptively subverting his powers of reasoning, as in the case of manipulation.

This element of deception, then, seems to make manipulation more immoral than alternative processes for exercising political power.[20]

Morally speaking, the distinction between manipulative and non-manipulative power plays is parallel to that between 'cheating' someone and merely 'beating' him. What makes us object to cheating is not just that in so doing the cheater moves outside the rules of whatever game he is playing—there is no reason to prefer one game or one set of rules to another—but rather that he is deceiving others in pretending to play according to rules which he then proceeds to violate. Cheating has as its defining characteristics to 'deceive, trick, deal fraudulently'. That is what makes cheating someone so much worse than beating him. That, too, is one of the things that makes manipulating someone so much worse than just exercising power over him.

Manipulation is also ethically unobjectionable because its very definition eliminates a source of the ethical ambiguities that surround the concept of 'power'. Recall the examples from Section 1.1. A person sometimes welcomes power being exercised over him, as in the cases of Ulysses facing the sirens or the

20. Some might defend this aspect of manipulation, arguing that precisely because its influence is hidden the person being manipulated is spared the temptation to put up necessarily futile resistance. Deception is a kindness. It is bad enough that he should be dominated and exploited, the argument goes; he should not also have to bear the further costs of a hopeless fight against the inevitable. One reply to such an argument might echo existentialist assertions that it is crucial to one's dignity that one struggle against one's situation, however hopeless the fight. Manipulation, by obscuring the forces against which one should be struggling, deprives one of the opportunity to resist and is therefore fundamentally degrading. But there is no need to look this far for an adequate reply to defenders of deception. Surely it is enough to notice that deception is an overreaction to the problem. The costs deception spares us are not costs of *knowing* that we are being pushed around. If they were, we could be spared them by being denied that knowledge. Rather, they are costs of fighting against hopeless odds to prevent being pushed around. All we need to spare us *these* costs is the sense to concede where we cannot win.

good bargainer or the father or the Roman Catholic. There can be little doubt in any of these cases that the person's freedom of action is restricted—that power is exercised over him—but ethically there is something far less objectionable about power which is exercised by one's leave than about power which is exercised against one's will. Even if it is exercised in a sneaky manner, the sort of power which one would (had he known of it) welcome still seems less objectionable than would the other sort of power exercised in an equally deceptive manner. The excuse that 'I am just helping him realize his will' can sometimes be offered for exercises of power. Manipulation, however, has been defined in such a way as to eliminate the possibility of any such excuse for it. By definition, a manipulator is never just helping the person he manipulates realize his pre-existing will. Rather, his actions are always contrary to the putative will of the person he manipulates.[21] Thus, manipulation is necessarily nasty in a way that simple power plays need not be.

In calling 'manipulation' the evil core of power, I am implying that the pair of features I have associated with it exhaustively explains our objections to manipulation in particular and to power plays more generally. Others would dispute this claim, insisting that something more must be involved. One example is Larry Blum who, investigating the

21. This is how Rudinow, 'Manipulation' (p. 347) explains 'the typical moral reaction to manipulation. To attempt to manipulate someone is to attempt to elicit his behaviour without regard for—and with a will to interfere with—his operative goals. Insofar as a person regards the selection of goals as rightfully within his sphere of autonomy and the freedom to pursue his goals as a *prima facie* right, it is little wonder that he finds attempts to manipulate him objectionable.' But such objections would apply to any attempt to influence people, making 'manipulation' no worse than 'coercion', as Rudinow himself acknowledges.

Manipulators often *shape* the will of those they manipulate. But not all action shaping people's wills necessarily amounts to manipulation. For it to count in that category, the influence would also have to be deceptive. Often—as in the case of education—it is not.

parallel notion of 'using' people, concludes that our objections to the practice cannot be reduced to more basic objections to deceiving or hurting them. Blum proves his point by offering some examples to show that we might 'use' people in morally questionable ways without hurting them and other examples to show how we might 'use' people without deceiving them. From these, Blum concludes that there must be something more than deceiving and hurting underlying our objections to using people.[22]

I would suggest instead that what these results really demonstrate is that our opposition is *overdetermined:* either deception or harm is in itself sufficient for producing our objections. Where the one is present the other is unnecessary; and where the one is absent the other may still suffice. This would explain Blum's examples. He drops the conditions one at a time, finding that we object to using (or manipulating) people even when no deception is involved and even when no one is hurt. But that only proves that neither is a necessary condition—it does not prove that neither is a sufficient condition. If, as I suppose, each is independently sufficient, then Blum's results are easily explained: one condition generates our objections whenever the other is missing. To eliminate this possibility Blum would need convincing cases in which we object to using people even though neither deception nor harm is involved in a single example.[23]

22. Larry Blum, 'Deceiving, Hurting and Using', *Philosophy and Personal Relations,* ed. Alan Montefiore (London: Routledge & Kegan Paul, 1973), pp. 34–61. None of his examples are particularly 'clean' ones, it should be noted; many bear an alternative interpretation to the one Blum suggests.

23. John R. S. Wilson, 'In One Another's Power', *Ethics,* 88 (1978): 299–315, similarly suggests that our ethical objections to Blum's examples are overdetermined. He isolates two immoral features, entrapment (the treacherous or deceptive acquisition of power) and exploitation (the use of such power for selfish ends). The latter formulation runs afoul of the same criticisms I make of Galbraith and the *Oxford English Dictionary* in Section 1.2.2.

Blum does not actually suggest what else it is that might be missing from my explanation of why manipulation is morally objectionable. Those who do would draw attention to the fact that the sort of 'objective attitude' toward fellow men which we so resent combines 'manipulation' with 'calculation'.[24] The latter, they suggest, is also a source of moral concern. But surely what matters to the moral evaluation of calculating behaviour is the end toward which your calculations aim. If one were calculating so as to produce the most possible benefits for others, or if one were calculating so as to discharge one's duties most effectively, then there would be nothing wrong with calculating. Indeed, then calculating would be an indispensable element in moral action. Therefore, calculation *per se* seems not to be morally objectionable. What makes it so is the cause in aid of which we are calculating, what our calculations include and what they leave out. When combined with the goal of manipulating others, calculation of course is evil; but the evil is derivative and not intrinsic. Thus it seems that our moral objections to manipulation can be fully explained in terms of the two features of that concept which I have identified, and our objections to power plays more generally can be traced to the same two sources.

Before concluding my discussion of the ethical status of manipulation, I must comment on the source and the strength of our objections to the practice. The *source* of the objections can be confidently traced to 'ideal-regarding' principles of political action. 'Want-regarding' principles, which deal in the more comfortable terms of preferences, desires and satisfactions, simply cannot be stretched far enough to cover this case. It certainly is true that most people want not to be manipulated, and that this provides a want-regarding reason for opposing manipulation. But that only argues against

24. Stern, 'Freedom, Blame and Moral Community', building on P. F. Strawson, *Freedom and Resentment* (London: Methuen, 1974), esp. Ch. 1.

unsuccessful attempts at manipulation. People do not mind being manipulated if they do not know they are being manipulated, and if they do not mind there is no basis for objecting to the practice on want-regarding grounds.[25] Since our considered moral judgements indicate that manipulation is all the more repugnant for having succeeded, the want-regarding explanation of our objections to manipulation must fail.

As regards the *strength* of our ethical objections to the practice, I must say straightaway that they are not absolute. Suppose Hitler's astrologer deliberately misconstrued the signs so as to recommend the release of thousands of Jews from the concentration camps. His actions would certainly count as manipulation; they would surely be morally laudable nevertheless. Still, manipulation would seem to be a *prima facie* evil. The moral presumption must always be set against it. And, even if this presumption is overridden on any given occasion, that does not change the fact that we have been forced to do evil in order to do good.[26]

25. Brian Barry, *Political Argument* (London: Routledge & Kegan Paul, 1965), pp. 70–71. Indeed, Adrian M. S. Piper, 'Utility, Publicity and Manipulation', *Ethics*, 88 (1978): 189–206, purports to prove that the most familiar want-regarding principle, utility-maximization, would even under the best conditions require secret manipulation of other people.

Advocates of want-regarding explanations might grasp at the straw of 'fear', as suggested by Robert Nozick in *Anarchy, State and Utopia* (Oxford: Blackwell, 1974), pp. 65–71. The argument would be this: people fear discovering that they have been manipulated, even if they never are or never discover that they have been; and want-regarding principles should prohibit anything engendering such fears. But prohibiting manipulation is not necessarily the best way to stop people fearing it: we could instead prohibit discussions or reports of manipulation; or we could require citizens to undergo brainwashing to put the idea out of their heads altogether.

26. Distinguishing 'rational persuasion' from 'manipulation', Connolly, *Terms of Political Discourse* (p. 94) suggests, 'There is a moral presumption against the latter that does not obtain for the former'. But saying that there is a presumption does not imply that it cannot be overridden. Surely it can, as Terrence Ball emphasizes in his reply to Felix Oppenheim, "'Power" Re-

1.4   Rational vs. Psychological Models of Manipulation

The aim of this book, as I have described it, is to lay foundations for empirical studies with a sharper evaluative focus.
Partly this is a matter of selecting proper concepts. Examining
'manipulation' is preferable on these grounds to the study of
the more ethically ambiguous phenomenon of 'power'. But an
equally important part of this task lies in choosing the right
way to study these phenomena: we must orient our investigations in such a way as to enable us to do something about any
evils we may uncover. The point of studying ethically significant phenomena is not just to understand or even to pass
judgement but is rather to evaluate them, which carries with it
strong implications of being prepared to act upon the conclusions of the evaluation.

All this is by way of preface to my justification for choosing to study manipulation in rationalistic terms rather than in
the more familiar psychological ones. Crudely stated, the

---

visited', *Journal of Politics*, 40 (1978): 589–608; and Oppenheim, in his rejoin-
der, concedes the point.

Some, such as Michael Walzer, 'Political Action: The Problem of Dirty
Hands', *War and Moral Responsibility*, ed. M. Cohen, T. Nagel, and T. Scanlon
(Princeton: Princeton University Press, 1974), pp. 62–82 at 73, interpret moral
rules more severely. Instead of a presumption being overridden, which
means that the action is fully justified, Walzer no more than excuses the failure. 'When [moral] rules are overridden, we do not talk or act as if they had
been set aside, canceled or anulled. They still stand and have this much effect
at least: that we know we have done something wrong even if what we have
done was also the best thing to do on the whole in the circumstances.' Hitler's
astrologer, for example, would be obliged to argue that the same Jews could
not have been freed in other ways—by persuading Hitler to like Jews, by
mounting a raid on the camps, etc.—and after the fact he should feel guilty
for deceiving Hitler, even though he was morally justified in doing so. Robert
Nozick, 'Moral Complications and Moral Structures', *Natural Law Forum*, 13
(1968): 34–35, would even require the deceptive astrologer to pay Hitler re-
parations!

psychological model pictures man as responding automatically to certain sorts of symbolic stimuli. Man is 'wired' much as a puppet. Manipulating him is a simple matter of pulling the strings by playing on the right symbols to trigger the desired response mechanism.[27] The strongest form of this claim—that man is nothing more than a stimulus-response mechanism—is utterly implausible. To explain the behaviour of a person, we must refer to his reasons for choosing to behave as he does as well as to the causes that drive him one way or another.[28] But manipulating people by playing on their psychological weaknesses is particularly offensive precisely because man is such a mixed bag of reason and compulsions. Clearly it is worse to bypass reason in a person capable of exercising reason than it would be to pull the psychological levers of someone who is utterly incapable of exercising independent judgement in any case. We are taking advantage of the worst side of someone who has a better side, whereas if the stimulus-response model were entirely correct fewer apologies would be required since men do not have a better side than that which we manipulate.[29]

It must be conceded that psychological manipulation is the most morally offensive variety. But, unfortunately, it is also the variety we can do least about. That is not to say that

27. Rudinow, 'Manipulation', builds his case for the paradigmatic status of psychological manipulation on more specialized literature, such as: Ben Bursten, *The Manipulator* (New Haven: Yale University Press, 1973), and H. R. St. Clair, 'Manipulation', *Comprehensive Psychology*, 7 (1966): 250–55.

28. Charles Taylor, *The Explanation of Behaviour* (London: Routledge & Kegan Paul, 1964). Martin Hollis, *Models of Man* (Cambridge: Cambridge University Press, 1977).

29. Stern, 'Freedom, Blame and Moral Community'. Vance Packard, *The Hidden Persuaders* (London: Longmans, Green, 1957), pp. 258–59, maintains similarly that 'playing upon hidden weaknesses and frailties ... inherently involves a disrespect for the individual personality', and that this is what we have against manipulation. John Wilson, 'In One Another's Power', similarly suggests that some sorts of power to exploit psychological vulnerabilities, such as that power lovers yield to one another, simply ought not be used.

psychological compulsions are strictly unalterable. It has been one of the emphases of stimulus-response theorists that, just as man is programmed by his experiences, so too can he be reprogrammed. But this is hardly a hopeful message. There is little anyone, by himself, can do to overcome his own psychoses. Reprogramming will almost inevitably be imposed from without, often deceptively and probably against the (current) will of its object. That is to say, even character-building will usually have to be manipulative. And there is no guarantee that those licensed to perform this task would necessarily use their powers to create a more autonomous man capable of living without just the sort of manipulative intervention in which they are engaged.

Rationalistic approaches to manipulation are preferable for evaluative studies, then, not because they point to a more morally important side of the phenomenon (they do not) but rather because they point to a side of the phenomenon more subject to our control. In rationalistic terms, too, manipulation is seen as a matter of bypassing reason. But in the rational model this is done by tricking people rather than by playing on deeper psychological drives. Reason is always operative— it is just being fooled, misled or distracted. Whereas overcoming psychological manipulation would seem to require mass therapy, rational manipulation can often be overcome through simple exposure of the tricks. Once we know 'how to lie with statistics', for example, we can no longer be led astray by deceptive statisticians.[30] Simple analysis of how the tech-

30. Darrell Huff, *How to Lie with Statistics* (New York: Norton, 1954). While people who know the tricks may not be deceived by the false statistics, they may still be bullied into accepting them. In one of her first official acts, Prime Minister Margaret Thatcher cut taxes, whereupon she promptly introduced a new 'cost of living' index aimed explicitly at reflecting these tax cuts; see *The Guardian*, 12 July 1979 and 13 July 1979, p. 4, for reports. The trick was absolutely transparent—nobody was fooled or, therefore, manipulated—although in some abstract impersonal sense the statistics were being manipulated rather like the hospital rules were manipulated by the wino.

niques work will, then, do much to overcome many forms of rational manipulation. And, where that is not enough, the analysis will at least point to practical next steps. Therefore, this is the approach I have chosen to pursue in the balance of this book.

1.5   THE EMPIRICAL STUDY OF MANIPULATION

In an incredible confession-in-passing, W. J. M. Mackenzie remarks that, while 'it is easy to invent situations which will generate problems for the moral philosopher, ... most theorists would set manipulation aside' for the purposes of empirical science.[31] As a report on the theoretical predilections of the profession, this characterization is accurate enough. Such an attitude is, however, outrageously inappropriate. One reason is quite simply that such an emphasis ignores what I have shown to be of greatest ethical concern. Even from the narrow perspective of empiricists themselves, however, this attitude is not justified. Ignoring manipulation, they would be ignoring something of great importance in explaining and predicting political outcomes.

On a fairly mundane level, manipulation is just too important a phenomenon to leave out of our descriptions of political interaction. Yet this is exactly what political scientists ordinarily do. The accepted procedure for locating centres of power, at least among Dahl's dominant school, is to look for fights and to see who wins them. Since manipulation is influence wielded deceptively, there is no fight and hence (on this model) no power in play.

Deeply embedded in this (typically liberal) analysis of social power is the rococo presumption that opposing parties will fight out their differences openly on the field of honour.

31. *Politics and the Social Sciences* (Harmondsworth: Penguin, 1967), p. 225.

Eighteenth-century field marshals learned better; and those engaged in domestic intrigues are surely at least as clever. Power plays are far more successful if accomplished deceptively. You stand a far better chance of getting your way if others do not notice that you are doing something to them that they should be resisting. Once long ago political scientists appreciated these truths. Charles Merriam, the mastermind of the American behavioural revolution, has written, 'Power is not strongest when it uses violence, but weakest. It is strongest when it employs the instruments of substitution and counter attraction, of allurement, of participation rather than of exclusion, of education rather than annihilation. Rape is not evidence of irresistible power in politics or in sex.'[32] But the lesson seems to have been forgotten by contemporary political scientists, who are always looking for a fight.

The implication is that, even for purely descriptive purposes, it is vitally important for political scientists to study mechanisms of manipulation. Unless they understand how political agendas are set and how political routines are rigged and how systematic biases are mobilized, political scientists will enjoy little success in predicting political outcomes. They must predict 'non-decisions' as well as decisions, to borrow Bachrach and Baratz's wonderfully ambiguous phrase.[33] Thus, the neglect of political manipulation is outrageous even from the point of view of the orthodox political scientist who is simply trying to predict well. To accomplish that task, he must study power in all its forms.

Manipulation is not only of descriptive importance, how-

32. *Political Power* (New York: McGraw-Hill, 1934), Ch. 6.
33. Peter Bachrach and Morton S. Baratz, 'The Two Faces of Power', *American Political Science Review*, 56 (1962): 947–52, critiques Robert Dahl, *Who Governs?* (New Haven: Yale University Press, 1961). They are critiqued in turn by Steven Lukes, *Power: A Radical View* (London: Macmillan, 1974), who exposes a 'third face of power'.

ever. Such a notion is also more appropriate for the sort of theoretical constructs required for true scientific understanding of politics. These theories must be couched in terms of 'monotypic' concepts, each having a single set of mutually compatible implications, rather than of the 'polythetic' concepts typically found in ordinary language. The concept of 'power', as it is ordinarily used, seems to be particularly polythetic, i.e., to have a great many potentially contradictory implications. No concept with such logically messy properties can provide a firm basis for a truly scientific theory of politics. A more refined concept is required. Ultimately this means that we must build a 'technical' language related to ordinary language but distinct from it. To generate the concepts of that technical language, however, we must look for inspiration to ordinary language. We must start with those messy concepts and strip them down, 'abducting' (to use Peirce's term) one of the multiple senses to produce a concept refined enough to function effectively in our technical language.[34] Shifting from the concept of 'power' to the less ambiguous subcategory of 'manipulation' constitutes a step in this direction, although it must be admitted that it still may have properties entirely too polythetic for it to play this technical role perfectly.

Empirical political scientists have these many reasons for focusing upon manipulation. But this new focus will require some revision of their research strategies. Students of power in general have developed a variety of research options which are largely unavailable to students of manipulation. The 'reputational' approach, for example, uncovers the power elite by asking people in a community who has power there. It

34. Among those building on the lead of C. S. Peirce, see David Willer and Murray Webster, 'Theoretical Concepts and Observables', *American Sociological Review*, 35 (1970): 748–57, and Rodney Needham, 'Polythetic Classification: Convergence and Consequences', *Man*, 10 (1975): 349–69. I am grateful to Bill Stuart for drawing these to my attention.

works, however, only insofar as elites are somehow 'open' about their power. Power which is exercised secretly, as in the case of manipulation, is credited to the reputation of no one. Indeed, acquiring a reputation for manipulating people would surely undercut one's future capacity for succeeding in such manoeuvres. The 'decisional' approach reveals power through an examination of actual political decisions and who has influenced them. But again the very essence of manipulation is that this influence will have been hidden. The 're-source' approach ascribes power to people in proportion to their control over power resources. However, we must have some understanding of how the process of exercising power operates in order to know what resources will be instrumental.[35] More abstract approaches to the study of manipulation are not likely to prove any more fruitful. Manipulation is essentially a matter of tricking people. Any attempt at deducing *a priori* a list of tricks that might work politically would, I should have thought, be about as hopeless as attempting an exhaustive list of tricks that Houdini might try. Trickery is simply not something that lends itself to such analysis.

All told, we find ourselves back in a pre-scientific stage of 'thick description'. Before we can study the problem of manipulation in any systematic way, we need to build up a larger stock of examples, described in depth but with theoretical overtones.[36] The strategy is intentionally borrowed from social anthropologists, for we are investigating an unfamiliar

35. For examples see Willis D. Hawley and Frederick M. Wirt, eds., *The Search for Community Power* (Englewood Cliffs, N.J.: Prentice-Hall, 1968).

36. The term is from Clifford Geertz, 'Thick Description: Toward an Interpretive Theory of Culture', *The Interpretation of Cultures* (New York: Basic Books, 1973), Ch. 1, who in turn borrows it from Gilbert Ryle, 'Thinking and Reflecting' and 'Thinking Thoughts and Having Concepts', *Collected Papers* (London: Hutchinson, 1971), 2:480-96, and 446-50, respectively. But the best description of the process is by John Beattie in *Other Cultures* (London: Cohen & West, 1964), Ch. 3.

'culture' of manipulation—using the word 'culture' in a distinctly non-metaphorical sense. By its very nature, manipulation must be carried out by one group according to shared and settled rules against another group which does not understand those rules.

It is not enough to be told the bottom line of the arguments, that there is a 'mobilization of bias' or a 'non-decision'. We need to know how it happens. It is not enough to be told that there is a 'third face of power'. We need to see its features. It is not enough to allude to the processes of language or ritual. We need a fairly fully specified model of the various ways in which language and ritual might bias the political process. And it is not enough to be told in rich detail about the 'symbolic uses of politics'. Not all symbolic (or linguistic or ritualistic) tricks are equally objectionable or, indeed, even manipulative at all. The sort of descriptions I am calling for—and hope to be providing in subsequent chapters—are thick with both theory and detail. They afford clues not only to what happens but also to how it happens and why we react as we do. There is no presumption that my catalogue is complete, but at least it is a start. On the basis of this survey, I hope we might abstract some general properties of particularly worrying forms of manipulation and adduce clues for counterstrategies.

1.6 DIMENSIONS OF ETHICAL EVALUATION OF MANIPULATION

The evaluative aspirations of this book dictate a mixture of the empirical and the ethical. The chapters that follow are chiefly devoted to describing in some detail the features of more familiar modes of manipulation. At the same time, these practices must also be evaluated for their 'threat potential' to our more basic moral values. In order to systematize my conclusions in this regard, I shall attempt to ask a standard set of questions when evaluating mechanisms of manipulation. The first two of these questions simply query whether the defining features of manipulation are present:

  1. Is the interference deceptive?
  2. Is the interference contrary to the putative will of those subject to it?

Together, these two features define an instance of manipulation. However, not all instances of manipulation are equally worrisome from an ethical perspective. The evil of an act of manipulation will be mitigated, although not eliminated, if it is sufficiently short-lived, suggesting the further question:

  3. How persistent is the effect of the manipulation?

Finally, a mechanism of manipulation is clearly more troubling the more narrow its availability. Hence, a fourth question:

  4. Are any distributive biases inherent in the mechanism?

A technique is biased insofar as it can only be used by one group (typically those already in power) against others not similarly situated in the social hierarchy. A mechanism will be said to lack distributive biases either if it can be turned against those using it or else if it imposes severe constraints of some other sort upon those using it. There are two ways to justify a preference for manipulatory mechanisms to be unbiased in this sense. One rationale is couched in terms of deterrence: we prefer that manipulatory tools be equally available to all, not so that all may actually use them, but rather so that none will be tempted. Techniques which only I can use against you I will use with impunity. If there is instead the risk of the tables being turned, and the objects of my attempted manipulation becoming themselves the manipulators, I would be much more reluctant to make the attempt. This deterrence rationale depends, of course, upon everyone perceiving the possibility that the tables may be turned and upon everyone reacting rationally to that threat. They may not, and we may find ourselves in a situation of everyone manipulating everyone else. This brings us to the second justification of unbiased mechanisms of manipulation. In the murky world of second-best, it seems better that everyone be able to manipulate everyone else than for certain people to be able always to do the manipulating and others always to be subject to it. Both are inferior to the world in which no one manipulates anyone. But, if forced to choose, I think it is the world of reciprocal manipulation we would prefer to the world of unilateral manipulation.

To anticipate my conclusions, I shall show that most of the familiar modes of manipulation present fewer problems than commonly supposed. Either they fail to qualify as manipulatory at all, or else they lack the sort of persistence or distributive bias that would make them particularly disquieting. But while the familiar gives little cause for concern, the unknown might contain some real dangers. Chapter 7 discusses one form of manipulation which, although both perverse and pervasive, goes largely unnoticed. The next step in the study of political manipulation, I shall suggest, is to see how many more of these overlooked techniques are in common use. While my conclusions are reassuring as regards commonly discussed modes of manipulation, then, they are profoundly disquieting as regards the possibility that there are really serious forms of manipulation we have not yet even noticed.

CHAPTER TWO ❡ THE POLITICS OF LYING

> The people may as well all pretend to be lords of manors, and possess great estates, as to have truth told them in matters of government. . . . They have no right at all to political truth.
> Jonathan Swift[1]

FROM MACHIAVELLI TO WATERGATE, deceit and treachery are among the most constantly recurring themes in the literature of political manipulation. Much has been written by journalists and historians detailing the deceptions. Much has been written by moralists deploring the practice and hoping to help us guard against it. But in all these treatments several varieties of deceitful dealing are collected indiscriminately under the general heading of the 'politics of lying'. In what follows, I shall distinguish between these strategies and explore their peculiar strengths and weaknesses. Before this can be done, however, it is important to understand how deceit can ever succeed. Hence I preface my discussion of the politics of lying with an analysis of the rationality of ignorance, which makes us prey to liars.

2.1 PLAYING ON RATIONAL IGNORANCE

Often it can be eminently rational to act in ignorance. Individuals start any endeavour with strictly limited information. Further information is costly to acquire and still more costly to assess. Actors will rationally invest in additional information if and only if they expect that it will turn up something

---

1. Jonathan Swift, 'The Art of Political Lying', *Works*, ed. Thomas Roscoe (London: George Bell & Sons, 1880), 2:402–05.

important. To justify the expenditure, they must expect that decisions they will make on the basis of the improved information will be sufficiently superior to the decisions they would otherwise have made to repay (at least) the costs of acquiring it. The results that might reasonably be expected to come from further investigation are frequently not worth the price. Then it would be rational for people to 'take the plunge', making the best decision they can on the basis of the admittedly imperfect information already at hand.[2] In so doing, of course, they run the risk of making a mistake which could have been avoided had they perfect information. But in light of the costs of acquiring and processing all the relevant information they would, *ex ante,* be risks worth running. In short, it is often rational to err.

Four elements comprise the model of rational ignorance:

1. Citizens have imperfect information.
2. Citizens know they have imperfect information.
3. It is costly:
    a. to acquire more information and
    b. to assess more information.
4. The expected gains from further information are thought likely to be less than these costs.

Manipulators will attempt to play on one or more of these elements through any of four distinct strategies. The first is

2. Alternatively, they might choose to follow some rule of thumb, which is thought to offer the best general guidance on decisions of this 'type' without any presumption that it will produce optimal results in any particular instance. This is Herbert Simon's model of 'satisficing' as developed in *Administrative Behavior* (New York: Free Press, 1945). Variations on this theme include Anthony Downs's notion of 'rational ignorance' and political ideologies as a response, found in *An Economic Theory of Democracy* (New York: Harper, 1957), Ch. 11, and Aaron Wildavsky, 'Analysis of Issue-Contexts in the Study of Policy-Making', *Journal of Politics,* 24 (1962): 717-32.

actual *lying*, deliberate dissemination of untrue information. This strategy works straightforwardly on the first element in the model, reducing the stock of accurate information available to citizens by cancelling out some true information with lies tending to contradict it. The second strategy is *secrecy*, the deliberate withholding of information which tends to undermine official policy. This works not only on the first element in the model of rational ignorance (reducing the quantity and quality of available information) but also on the second (emphasizing to citizens that they lack much information that is relevant).[3] A third strategy is one of *propaganda*, the subsidizing of true but biased information. This strategy works on elements one (weighting the evidence favourable to a particular policy unduly heavily) and four (conveying the illusion that' citizens are in possession of all relevant information, making further enquiries a waste of resources). A final strategy is one of information *overload*, the intentional release of so much information that citizens will have trouble assimilating it all. This increases the costs to citizens of assessing all the information themselves, inclining them to rely upon official interpretations instead. This strategy, therefore, basically works on element 3b in the model of rational ignorance.

In choosing between these strategies, the manipulative politician must be sensitive to two potential costs. The first danger is that his distortions will be exposed and that he will be subject to whatever short-term penalties might come from being caught in a lie. A second and more daunting prospect is that his credibility will be compromised, which would reduce his future capacity to influence others through the communi-

3. Tibor Scitovsky, 'Ignorance as a Source of Oligopoly Power', *American Economic Review (Papers and Proceedings)*, 40 (1950): 48–53. William A. Niskanen, Jr., *Bureaucracy and Representative Government* (Chicago: Aldine-Atherton, 1971). Randall Bartlett, *Economic Foundations of Political Power* (New York: Free Press, 1973).

cation of information. Whether his reports are true or false, they will always be suspect. This might happen even if there is no incontrovertible proof of falsehood. Doubts are enough to undermine one's credibility.[4]

While the occasional lie may pay off, then, the manipulation of information as a sustained strategy of political rule seems a tricky business. The costs can be quite high, and in order to make lying an effective strategy politicians must find ways of minimizing its risks, either by learning to lie without arousing suspicions or by learning to preserve credibility even if caught. Below I shall examine each of the four strategies to see how well they meet these requirements.

2.2   LYING

The most straightforward instance of the politics of deception is lying itself, the communication of deliberate untruths. Perhaps the Gulf of Tonkin Resolution is the contemporary example with the most far-reaching consequences. This resolution, which President Johnson claimed gave him unlimited authority to pursue war in Vietnam, was railroaded through the Congress on the basis of false reports of an attack on American warships. Recent American history is peppered with lesser examples, ranging from the Eisenhower Administration's initial denial of aerial spying in the U2 affair, through the Kennedy Administration's denial of CIA complicity in the overthrow of Vietnamese President Diem, to the elaborate tissue of lies Nixon built to protect himself from the consequences of Watergate.[5]

Pervasive though it may be, deliberate lying is subject to a

4. Gordon Tullock, 'The Economics of Lying', *Toward a Mathematics of Politics* (Ann Arbor: University of Michigan Press, 1967), Ch. 9.
5. For a useful collection of anecdotes, see David Wise, *The Politics of Lying* (New York: Vintage Books, 1973).

most potent constraint, *viz.*, the prospect of getting caught in the act. There are elements in the logic of rational ignorance to make this a real threat. Citizen ignorance is rational only in limited quantities. It is perfectly rational for people to accept modest lies, even if they have their doubts about them, because the costs of learning the truth are likely to exceed the rewards. But as the tales become increasingly improbable it becomes increasingly apparent that the results of investigation will be worth its costs. Jonathan Swift, in his 1712 essay on 'The Art of Political Lying', advises that 'they shall not far exceed the common degrees of probability' and attributes 'the ill success of either party to their glutting the market, and retailing too much of a bad commodity all at once.'[6] Politicians must keep their lies down to believable proportions if they are to be believed, which seems to limit possibilities for political manipulation of this sort.

There are, however, reasons to doubt that lying politicians will get caught either certainly or swiftly. In the first place, the above model presupposes that the larger the lie the more suspicions will be aroused. Our daily experience surely belies this proposition—truth typically is stranger than fiction, at least in small bits and in the short term. Hannah Arendt rightly observes that this affords lying politicians considerable leeway: 'Lies are often much more plausible, much more appealing to reason, than reality, since the liar has the great advantage of knowing beforehand what the audience wishes or expects to hear. He has prepared his story for public consumption with a careful eye to making it credible, whereas reality has the disconcerting habit of confronting us with the unexpected, for which we were not prepared.'[7] Of course, the liar cannot

6. Swift, 'Art of Political Lying', p. 404.
7. Hannah Arendt, 'Lying in Politics: Reflections on the Pentagon Papers', *Crises of the Republic* (New York: Harcourt, Brace, Jovanovich, 1972), pp. 6–7.

keep this up forever—eventually he is caught in his own 'tangled web'—but in the short run at least the liar enjoys this natural advantage of having more plausible tales to tell.

The 'tangled web' model bears a striking resemblance to—and suffers the same flaws as—*caveat emptor*. Parallel to the present claim that citizens will learn from experience to distrust deceitful politicians is the familiar argument that there is no need for public regulation of product quality since consumers will learn from experience to distrust unreliable producers. This might work if purchases are modest in size and frequently repeated: if the last packet of razor blades gave you poor shaves, you will shift brands next month. But where consumers are making major investments in durable goods that are not soon replaced, there is less reason to suppose that consumer learning will suffice to ensure product quality. If you purchase an unsatisfactory automobile, you are probably stuck with it for several years regardless of your dissatisfaction. The punishment to be visited upon the producer is, at the very least, delayed. It might never be felt at all. In buying your next car you might be persuaded that the models have changed so dramatically that there is no reason to expect the Thunderbird to display the same flaws as your old Model T had done.[8]

The same objections might be made against the argument that citizens will learn by experience to distrust lying politicians. Perhaps it is inevitable that any big lie will eventually be exposed. Nevertheless, this may take a long time to accomplish. The politician might be out of office by the time his lie has been exposed, so the credibility gap he has created will penalize only his successors. Even if he is still in public life, enough time may have passed since the initial dishonesty that

8. Kenneth J. Arrow, 'Social Responsibility and Economic Efficiency', *Public Policy*, 21 (1973): 303–17.

he can assert that he is now a 'new' man, quite different from the scoundrel whose credibility has at last been undermined. Or, again, ancient lies might no longer matter much for policy. Chicago Mayor Richard Daley justified his order for police to shoot to kill black arsonists by reference to intelligence reports of a nationwide conspiracy to disrupt the cities, and his order for police to brutalize demonstrators at the Democratic National Convention of 1968 by reference to reports of a plan to assassinate all the leading candidates. These lies served their immediate purpose; and by the time they were contradicted (by the Mayor's own riot commission in the first instance and the Chicago Eight's grand jury in the second) no one was listening.[9] Furthermore, any really grand lie will probably have truly profound policy implications. Unless exposed immediately it may well lead the nation along an irreversible course. When the Gulf of Tonkin attack on American warships was finally exposed as a fraud, America was so deeply enmeshed in the war that the truth about circumstances surrounding American entry could do little to facilitate withdrawal from the Vietnamese war.

A final limit on the extent to which we can count on citizens catching politicians in their lies arises from the 'logic of collective action'. Socially useful knowledge is typically a public good which benefits everyone once anyone makes it available. Since there are costs entailed in providing it, and everyone would benefit equally from having the information available, everyone waits for someone else to undertake the research. The overall consequence is that no one does. A similar logic actually encourages politicians in their lying. The reason is that credibility risks are partially pooled. If a politician is caught lying, his stigma is to a large extent shared with

9. Mike Royko, *Boss: Richard J. Daley of Chicago* (New York: E. P. Dutton, 1971), pp. 166, 177–78.

the entire class of politicians—the public concludes not only that the particular individual lacks credibility but also that politicians in general are not to be trusted. This makes 'loss of credibility' a public evil, the converse of a public good, and as such it is overproduced for precisely the same reasons public goods are underproduced. Since no one politician bears the full costs of his deceptions, he produces more of them than he would have done had all the costs been internalized.[10]

Taken together, these arguments suggest a strong incentive for politicians to lie and little reason to expect citizens to trip them up. There are, however, two bases for hope that such manipulation may be avoided. Firstly, while ordinary citizens will not undertake the task of exposing lying politicians, there are nevertheless groups which might be relied upon to perform the task. Interest in and resources for exposing dishonest politicians are concentrated in a relatively few individuals. Newsmen and opposing politicians have special reasons for wanting to expose lies. Not only do they benefit in their capacity as citizens enjoying better government once the lies are corrected; they also enjoy the selective benefits of promotion and election respectively in consequence of their revelations. Such incentives are enough to persuade these especially well-placed individuals to provide the public good of information on lying politicians.[11] The same concentration

10. Mancur Olson, Jr., *The Logic of Collective Action* (Cambridge: Harvard University Press, 1965) and 'Ignorance and Uncertainty', delivered to the Philosophy of Science Association Conference, 1977. One of the most popular Republican pamphleteering slogans during Watergate was that 'it didn't start with Nixon'.

11. The conventional wisdom that television news programmes have 'minimal effect' on public opinion, popular in the 1950s and early 1960s, is now well on the way to being refuted. Michael J. Robinson, 'Public Affairs Television and the Growth of Political Malaise: The Case of "The Selling of the Pentagon"', *American Political Science Review*, 70 (1976): 409–32. S. William Alper and Thomas Leidy, 'The Impact of Information Transmission

of interest and resources speeds up the process of correcting lies, severely limiting the efficacy of the politics of lying. Finally, politicians will have strong personal incentives for distancing themselves from the deceptive practices of their opponents, either by confining their attacks to particular individuals or parties or by taking steps to prove their own veracity. Insofar as they succeed in narrowing the focus of their own attacks and in preventing others from widening their focus, opposing politicians will avoid overproduction of public distrust of the species in general.

Secondly, even if lies are difficult to expose, they can often be counteracted by other lies. Swift supposes that 'the properest contradiction to a lie is another lie', and that the power to propagate lies is well dispersed throughout the community.

> The right of inventing and spreading political lies is partly in the people; and their obstinate adherence to this just privilege has been most conspicuous, and shined with great luster of late years: it happens very often that there are no other means left to the good people of England to pull down a ministry and government they are weary of but by exercising this their undoubted right: the abundance of political lying is a sure sign of true English liberty: that as ministers do sometimes use tools to support their power, it is but reasonable that the people should employ the same weapon to defend themselves, and pull them down.

Some people, and some classes, are in a better position to spread lies, so the counter-lie strategy is not quite distribu-

---

through Television', *Public Opinion Quarterly*, 33 (1969–70): 556–62. Stephen Fitzsimmons and Hobart Osburn, 'The Impact of Social Issues and Public Affairs Television Documentaries', *Public Opinion Quarterly*, 32 (1968): 379–97.

tively neutral. But whispering campaigns and rumours in-
itiated by people of no prominence can sometimes have most
telling effects, which moderates whatever worries we might
have about lying as a mechanism for manipulation.[12]

2.3 SECRECY

2.3.1. *Withholding Information*

Historically, attacks upon deceptive politics have centered
upon the evils of secrecy and the virtues of publicity. Bentham's overblown prose is illustrative: in praise of publicity he
writes, 'The efficacy of this great instrument extends to
everything—legislation, administration, judicature. Without
publicity, no good is permanent; under the auspices of publicity, no evil can continue.' The British Government, operating
under the Official Secrets Act of 1911, continues to be among
the most devoted practitioners of secretive government. The
effects of such practices, however, can best be seen in
America, where newspapermen and political opponents are
much less reticent to 'go public' with senseless or mischievous
secrets. The practice of secret government was, at least until
recently, quite widespread in America. As of 1973, the De-
partments of State and Defense alone possessed an estimated
57,000,000 classified documents. Adding those in Central Intelligence Agency, National Security Agency, Atomic Energy
Commission and National Security Council files, the number
certainly exceeded 100,000,000. In addition, the National Ar-

12. Swift, 'Art of Political Lying', pp. 405, 403. On the power of rumour,
see: Warren A. Peterson and Noel P. Gist, 'Rumor and Public Opinion',
American Journal of Sociology, 57 (1951): 159–67; Tamotsu Shibutani, *Im-
poverished News* (Indianapolis: Bobbs-Merrill, 1966); Peter Lienhardt, 'The
Interpretation of Rumour', *Studies in Social Anthropology*, ed. J. H. M. Beattie
and R. G. Lienhardt (Oxford: Clarendon Press, 1975), pp. 105–31; and, for
examples from a primitive society, Raymond Firth, 'Rumour in a Primitive
Society', *Tikopia Ritual and Belief* (London: Allen & Unwin, 1967).

chives stores another 458,500,000 classified documents cover-
ing the period from World War II to 1954. There are 16,238
individuals (plus their subordinates) in the four major de-
partments and the White House adding to the stacks every
year. These secrets are not only numerous but are also used to
mean political advantage. Senator J. William Fulbright, during hearings on *The Withholding of Information by the Executive*,
complained bitterly that it is clear from the way such powers
are exercised that the Executive Branch regards Congress as
nothing but 'an appropriate object of manipulation'.[13]

The strategy of secrecy, although closely related to that of
lying, is characterized by a distinct benefit–risk profile. Lying
of course presupposes secrecy, in that the truth must be suppressed if untruths are to be believed. But it is commonly
supposed that secrecy is possible without actual lying. The
strategy here is simply to suppress information which if released would prove embarrassing to one's preferred policies.
Whereas lying works by disseminating falsehoods, the
strategy of secrecy distorts the informational base of decisions
by withholding true and relevant data.

Manipulative politicians might find this strategy more attractive for two reasons. Firstly, in the event of disclosure, the
credibility of a secretive politician is less at risk than that of a
lying politician. This is simply because he cannot be caught in
an actual lie. We still listen to someone who is known to tell
half-truths, whereas we are more inclined to ignore those
known to tell utter untruths. Secondly, a politician can reinforce the power that his secrets afford him. By leaking
tidbits—or simply by alluding to information too dangerous
to discuss in public—he undermines the confidence of ordinary citizens in the informational base of their own judge-

13. Wise, *Politics of Lying*, p. 162. Jeremy Bentham, 'Essay on Political
Tactics', *Works*, ed. J. Bowring (Edinburgh: W. Tait, 1843), 2:298–373, Ch. 2.

ment, thereby increasing their willingness to follow his lead. The practice has parallels in primitive societies. Among the Bella Coola of British Columbia and the Iatmul of New Guinea, someone who holds a privilege validated by a myth will, at his investiture, tell the public just enough of the myth to establish his legitimacy but keep the rest secret. In modern polities, deliberately leaking state secrets is absolutely endemic. Max Frankel, diplomatic correspondent for the *New York Times,* swore in an affidavit in the Pentagon Papers case that officials regularly leaked to him whatever they thought would serve a 'political, personal, bureaucratic or even commercial interest'. Even Allen Dulles, former Director of the CIA, queries, 'What good does it do to spend millions to protect ourselves against espionage if our secrets just leak away? Basically,' he concludes, 'I feel that the government is one of the worst offenders.'[14]

On the other hand, the costs of secrecy are immense even if they are reckoned merely in terms of the capacity of politicians to perform their tasks effectively. Secrets are organized in such a way as to facilitate their being effectively hidden, not used. There is no guarantee that those who 'need to know' will ever discover crucial facts lodged in secret files. Much in

14. T. F. McIlwraith, *The Bella Coola Indians* (Toronto: University of Toronto Press, 1948). Margaret Mead, *Continuities in Cultural Evolution* (New Haven: Yale University Press, 1964), p. 74. Max Frankel, 'The "State Secrets" Myth', *Columbia Journalism Review,* 9 (1971): 24. Dulles, *The Craft of Intelligence* (New York: Harper & Row, 1963), p. 237. Wise, *Politics of Lying,* Ch. 5 and 6, provides examples of leaks. Theoretical treatments include Scitovsky, 'Ignorance as a Source of Oligopoly Power' and Max Weber's analysis of specialized knowledge (and the power to protect it by keeping it secret) as the source of bureaucratic power. H. H. Gerth and C. Wright Mills, eds., *From Max Weber* (London: Routledge & Kegan Paul, 1948), pp. 233–39. For case studies of political secrecy more generally, see Edward A. Shils, *The Torment of Secrecy* (London: Heinemann, 1956), and Francis E. Rourke, *Secrecy and Publicity* (Baltimore: Johns Hopkins University Press, 1961).

contemporary history suggests the contrary. Judging from the experiences reported in the Pentagon Papers, Arendt concludes that 'one of the gravest dangers of overclassification' is that those 'who receive top clearance to learn all the relevant facts remain blissfully unaware of them . . . because they work under circumstances and with habits of mind that allow them neither time nor inclination to go hunting for pertinent facts in mountains of documents, 99½% of which should not be classified and most of which are irrelevant for all practical purposes.'[15] This problem would be severe enough were everyone conscientiously trying to further organization goals without regard to personal status or interests. In practice, it is considerably exacerbated because bureaucrats are playing politics. Consequently, they try to deprive a competitor of classified information he needs to do his job well, hoping thereby to render him inadequate to his task and undercut his position within the organization.

The secretive politician also bears costs parallel to those entailed in the loss of credibility for the lying politician. Once he is known to keep secrets, his future capacity to keep secrets is diminished. As Bentham notices, 'Suspicion always attaches to mystery. It thinks it sees a crime where it beholds an affectation of secrecy.' The allure of secrets is not just psychological but is justified strictly in terms of the model of rational ignorance. There is a natural presumption, often reinforced by the actual words of those entrusted with the secret, that if a piece of information is sufficiently important to be kept secret then the fact must matter tremendously for certain decisions. And, other things being equal, the more a fact matters the more inclined a rational actor would be to invest effort in discovering it. In primitive tribes, when elders rhetorically allude

15. Arendt, 'Lying in Politics', p. 30.

to 'something afoot' their listeners are quick to search out the secret. Similar norms pervade modern newsrooms.[16]

Having aroused our interest, then, the secretive politician must count on various ploys to keep us from pursuing the matter. Appeals to some sort of sacred principle are clearly the strongest guarantee of secrecy. In medieval times religious doctrine held that only princes ought be privy to the 'mysteries of state', and in contemporary America Nixon argued that 'executive privilege' is an equally sacred constitutional doctrine. Such claims, if accepted, certainly provide the desired cloak of secrecy. But in order to be accepted they *presuppose* secrecy. Bendix observes that 'before the early modern period . . . in Europe, kings, aristocrats and magnates of the church made claims against each other quite secluded from popular participation. Rulers even manipulated appeals to the transcendent powers without fear of seriously undermining their exclusive hold on authority. This seclusion of the political arena has disappeared', and with it has gone the capacity of rulers to manipulate the gods. Once people see that rulers are tailoring claims of 'executive privilege' or appeals to the 'mysteries of state' to their own personal or political advantage, then their claims under those principles are forfeited. Much the same might be said of the most popular secular cover, *viz.*, that 'national security' requires secrecy. This claim is usually an outright, and often transparent, lie perpetrated for bureaucratic advantage. Often the claim is *prima facie* suspect, as when the U.S. Migratory Bird Conser-

16. Bentham, 'Essay on Political Tactics', Ch. 2.1.1. Justice Potter Stewart argues similarly that 'secrecy can best be preserved only when credibility is truly maintained' in his opinion in *New York Times v. U.S.*, 403 U.S. 713, 729. Ethel M. Albert, "'Rhetoric", "Logic", and "Poetics" in Burundi', *American Anthropologist (Special Publication)*, vol. 66, no. 6, pt. 2 (1964): 35–54. Donald Brenneis, 'The Matter of Talk: Political Performances in Bhatgaon', *Language in Society*, 7 (1978): 159–70.

vation Commission or the Indian Arts and Crafts Board invokes authority to classify documents under an Executive Order of the President allowing classification only in the interests of national security. Even when the lie is not so obvious there is the prospect of leaks of secrets, which will be seen to have little to do with national security.

Still another reason secretive politicians might get caught in an actual lie is that the secrets, while pertaining to national security affairs, are not nearly so crucial to informed decision-making as politicians had long been claiming. Arthur Schlesinger quotes Dean Rusk as saying, 'I really don't know of any secrets which have a significant bearing upon the ability of the people to make their judgments about major issues of policy'; and Schlesinger adds his own testimony that '99 percent of the information necessary for intelligent political judgment is available to any careful reader of the *New York Times*, the *Washington Post* or the *Congressional Record*.'[17] Secretive politicians, however, must claim otherwise in order to justify keeping the secrets so crucial to their own status in the power hierarchy. Thus, the strategy of secrecy naturally degenerates into the politics of lying, with all the attendant hazards.

Since secretive politicians are absolutely reliant upon deception in this way, they are immensely susceptible to blackmail. There is always the danger that someone will 'blow

17. Ernst H. Kantorowicz, 'Mysteries of State', *Harvard Theological Review*, 48 (1955): 65-91. Reinhard Bendix, 'The Mandate to Rule', *Social Forces*, 55 (1976): 242-56 at 243. Raoul Berger, *Executive Privilege* (Cambridge: Harvard University Press, 1974). Wise, *Politics of Lying*, p. 95. Arthur M. Schlesinger, Jr., *The Imperial Presidency* (Boston: Houghton Mifflin, 1973), p. 361. Note similarly the report of the Pentagon's Task Force on Secrecy arguing that 'more might be gained than lost if our nation were to adopt—unilaterally, if necessary—a policy of complete openness in all areas of information'; their Final Report is reprinted in the Congressional Record, 23 May 1972, E 5675-8.

the whistle' on them, as in the famous case of Daniel Ellsberg
and the Pentagon Papers. This danger is increased the more
people there are privy to any given secret. In a modern
bureaucracy it is enormously difficult to restrict access to secrets. For example, former Undersecretary of State Nicholas
Katzenbach recalls that 'the tightest thing we had, the negotiations leading to the Paris peace talks in 1968, had a [super-
secret] flower code name. I never dared to tell the President
how many people knew. He had said that under no circumstances could it go over ten people. In fact over fifty people
knew.' In addition to those who 'officially' knew, there were
'numerous code clerks, teletype operators and communications personnel [who] also handle classified cables.'[18] With so
many people privy to such extraordinarily sensitive material,
leaks are an ever present threat.

2.3.2   *Co-optation*

The simple withholding of information seems an extremely dangerous strategy of manipulation. There is, however, a rather more complex strategy building upon institutionalized secrecy for far more devastating results. The
basic aim of this strategy is co-optation. As Samuel Brittan
writes of the British Civil Service, 'Outsiders, who have not
seen the confidential minutes of all the meetings and do not
know the stage which departmental thinking has reached,
have not the slightest chance of winning any battle of
memoranda against a minister's official advisers. They can
only hope to make an impact if they are taken into a department as antibodies and participate in the real discussions
where policy is made.'[19] In a system replete with 'official se-

18. Wise, *Politics of Lying,* pp. 112-13.
19. Samuel Brittan, 'The Irregulars', *Policy-Making in Britain,* ed. Richard
Rose (London: Macmillan, 1969), pp. 329-39 at 333. The variety of co-
optation discussed in this chapter plays on an information dynamic, whereas

crets' the only way people can participate effectively in public decision-making is to have information which can only come from the hands of officials entrusted with those secrets; and interveners are naturally disinclined to bite the hand that feeds them. Even if they are not forced to sign a British-style Official Secrets Act, subjecting themselves to prosecution for divulging information received in this way, interveners will still acquiesce to all sorts of policies they dislike for fear of being cut off from the information required to protect their interests in future decisions. Secrecy is crucial to this strategy, since the offer of otherwise unattainable information constitutes the bribe that tempts dissidents into the co-optive relationship. On this model, however, manipulation is not a direct consequence of secrecy itself, of withholding relevant facts, but instead results indirectly from secrecy forcing co-opted groups to moderate their demands.

---

the more widely discussed variety plays on a responsibility dynamic: when sharing decision-making power with a co-opted group, the Establishment also shares blame for policies made jointly with the co-opted; and this helps to keep them in line in the future. The present discussion presumes that people want to participate in decision-making for instrumental reasons, i.e., they want to influence policy. For a few people, participation might be an end in itself—they enjoy being 'in on the action' even if they never influence the outcome. They regard appointment to secretive councils of state as an 'affective symbolic reward' in itself, and (as Section 5.3 below argues) their choice in this matter must be respected. They cannot, strictly speaking, be co-opted.

For an example of someone being co-opted through the release of information, note Wise's explanation of why the *New York Times* failed to print a story about the CIA training of Tibetans for covert operations: 'The newspaper learned the nationality of the "Orientals" seen at Peterson Field [in Colorado] only from the high official who simultaneously requested that the story be killed. By taking the *Times* correspondent into his confidence, the official took a calculated risk, but he probably reasoned that this would make it ethically difficult for the newspaper to reveal that the men were Tibetans. The strategem is an old one, not unlike one boxer clinching with another, and the purpose is the same: to "tie up" the reporter so he cannot publish something.' *The Politics of Lying*, p. 261.

In one way, co-optation is a rather worrisome prospect. The strategy is available only to those already in policy-making roles. Simple secrecy of the sort discussed in Section 2.3.1 can be practiced by anyone, and how effective a strategy it will prove to be for them depends strictly upon how good a secret they have to keep and upon how well they can keep it. Thus 'secret societies' have traditionally been able to exercise considerable power by substituting tight-lipped loyalty for the intrinsic importance of the secrets being kept.[20] Co-optation, in contrast, can only be practiced by those in possession of 'official' secrets which, if they choose, they can share. The secrets on offer must be of direct and immediate use in influencing the policy-making process in order for dissident groups to be willing to sacrifice some of their demands to acquire them, and usually this sort of secret will be pretty well concentrated in the hands of established elites.

Doubts about the seriousness of co-optation centre instead upon the question of how much harm is done to the co-opted groups. In agreeing to be co-opted, they make a trade-off. Someone who has been co-opted has an influence upon policy which he would not otherwise have enjoyed, but to gain this influence he has been forced to pay the price of moderating his demands. Whether he would be better off making more extreme demands from the outside or less extreme ones from the inside depends upon how much he has to moderate his demands to get in and upon how much influence he has once inside the organization. If it is a good trade—if by being co-opted he could move the policy outcome measurably nearer his preferences—it is unclear what would be wrong with the trade. It certainly is unclear how the arrangement would be manipulative, since the co-optive arrangement is neither par-

20. Georg Simmel, 'The Sociology of Secrecy and Secret Societies', *American Journal of Sociology*, 11 (1906): 462 ff.

ticularly deceptive nor in the case just described contrary to the interests or putative will of the co-opted.

When calling co-optation 'manipulative', therefore, we must be thinking of something else that is going on behind the scenes. One thing that might make it manipulative is that the co-opted leaders are themselves fooled on one or more points. Perhaps their power within the organization is described to them in exaggerated ways, or perhaps their impact on policy from outside the organization is understated. But by co-opting these leaders, and providing them with heretofore secret information, we must be increasing the probability that they will discover the deception. This form of truly manipulative co-optation is consequently not likely to last very long. A more persistent mode of co-optive manipulation consists in providing co-opted group leaders with selective benefits for selling out their followers, and then offering them the veil of secrecy to hide that fact. But then the co-opted traitors are susceptible to 'whistle-blowers', just as are the keepers of any dark secrets.

A final consideration making co-optation an unrewarding mechanism for manipulation is the prospect of blackmail by those who have notionally been co-opted. When co-opting people we give them information they could not have obtained otherwise, and to retain their cooperation we must continue supplying this sort of privileged information. Yet for that information to be of value to us, either for co-opting them or keeping others in check, it is crucial that it remain confidential. Thus, in co-opting people by sharing our secrets with them we will have given them power over us. Should the co-opted individuals ever withdraw from the charmed circle and resume the role of outside challenger, they would be in a far better position to press their challenges with the information we have provided. Even if they never pursue the option, the threat of withdrawing gives those co-opted considerable power to blackmail their Establishment partners—especially in the early days of the pact, before they have come to share much responsibility for joint decisions. Secretive politicians can, then, secure power over others by offering to share information only if they are willing to give them a substantial measure of power over themselves. In all, it does not look like a very promising mechanism for manipulation. Modern politicians would do well to recall Francis Bacon's advice against a large group of advisers: 'As for cabinet councils, it may be their motto, *plenus rimarum sum*', or 'I am full of leaks.'[21]

2.4 PROPAGANDA

Propaganda is the flip side of secrecy. The latter withholds embarrassing information, while the former disseminates favourable reports. Propaganda, in the pure form at least, is distinguished from lying insofar as the information it spreads is accurate, as far as it goes. However, the propagandist's reports, while accurate, are crucially incomplete. The choice of information to be communicated is biased, with only that reflecting favourably upon the propagandist's cause being offered. In terms of the model of rational ignorance, this amounts to 'subsidizing' certain bits of information. The recipient's decision is biased insofar as information favourable to one outcome is made cheaper relative to that favouring other outcomes.[22]

21. 'Of Counsel', *Essays and New Atlantis,* ed. G. S. Haight (New York: Walter J. Black, 1942). Charles Peters and Taylor Branch, *Blowing the Whistle* (New York: Praeger, 1972). Ralph Nader, Peter Petkas and Kate Blackwell, eds., *Whistle Blowing* (New York: Grossman, 1972).

22. Randall Bartlett, *Economic Foundations of Political Power.* For examples see William Niskanen, *Bureaucracy and Representative Government* and, more

The first question we must ask of this model of political manipulation is whether the subsidy will have the intended effect. Certainly it is true that, in general, one buys more of a commodity the lower its price. But as Tibor Scitovsky observes, when decision-makers appreciate the depth of their own ignorance they often will take price as an indicator of quality. Cheap products are often shunned on the presumption that they must be of inferior quality. There are special reasons for supposing that cheap information will be shunned similarly. Insofar as people notice that their information is being subsidized, they will *discount* it. The greater the subsidy the greater the biases they must expect it to contain, and hence the less useful the information will be to people who want to make balanced and well-informed decisions.[23] The propagandist's trick can work only insofar as it remains hidden, and thus it seems susceptible to all the risks inherent in the politics of secrecy.

Furthermore, the biases introduced into the political system by subsidized information are only slight. The strategy is available to anyone, in the sense that anyone can subsidize information favourable to his case. Senator Edward Kennedy, for example, effectively rebutted the case for the anti-ballistic missile system by commissioning scientific studies critical of the scheme. There are biases arising from subsidized information, in that matching your opponent's subsidies constitutes an 'entrance fee' imposed for getting any new propositions into the political market.[24] But biases which can be

---

generally, J. A. C. Brown, *Techniques of Persuasion* (Harmondsworth: Penguin, 1963), esp. Ch. 5.

23. Scitovsky, 'Ignorance as a Source of Oligopoly Power'; Bartlett, *Economic Foundations of Political Power*.

24. Scitovsky, 'Ignorance as a Source of Oligopoly Power'.

overcome by the payment of typically modest fees are not really very severe ones.

2.5 OVERLOAD

The informational base of an individual's decision can be undermined as effectively by providing him with *too much* information as by denying him enough reliable data. Harary and Batell analyze this phenomenon under the heading of 'negative information', their paradigm case being increasing the number of alternatives that might possibly be true.[25] Additional information more generally can often simply serve to confuse the issue, undermining our confidence in our judgements about the probability of the various alternatives without actually adding new possibilities. Providing information will thus have undermined the decision just as effectively as withholding it does in the more familiar case.

This suggests a highly effective strategy for manipulating people through information management. This strategy, paradoxically, depends upon moves exactly opposite to those discussed in previous sections. In the place of secrecy this strategy recommends maximal disclosure; and in the place of lies this strategy recommends full and accurate reporting. The opportunity it sees for manipulation lies not at the level of fudging facts but rather at the level of interpreting them.

25. Frank Harary and Mark F. Batell, 'The Concept of Negative Information', *Behavioral Science,* 23 (1978): 264–70. Although 'overloaded government' has been widely discussed recently, most commentators regard it merely as an inevitable consequence of increasing social complexity. See, e.g., Anthony King, 'Overload', *Political Studies,* 23 (1975): 162–74, and James Douglas, 'Review Essay: The Overloaded Crown', *British Journal of Political Science,* 6 (1976): 483–505. Even those who see something manipulative about the strategy, such as Richard Rose and B. Guy Peters, *Can Government Go Bankrupt?* (New York: Free Press, 1978), do not focus upon this particular strategy of manipulation.

Once you have overloaded people with information, all of it both pertinent and accurate, they will be desperate for a scheme for integrating and making sense of it. Politicians can then step in with an interpretive framework which caters to their own policy preferences.

For the decision-maker (be he citizen or an official) the essential service the framework provides is to put data in perspective, to reduce the rich complexity to a manageable handful of variables. By reducing the list of alternative possible interpretations, the framework serves to reduce the 'negative information' provided by the overgenerous manipulator. Frameworks, then, work by filtering data—by getting certain bits of it discounted in the decision calculus. Barnet, for example, argues that the American 'National Security Managers ... exercise their power chiefly by filtering information that reaches the President and by interpreting the outside world for him'.[26] All political decision-makers require some such service in a highly complex world. The result achieved by the manipulators through such a strategy is much the same as that achieved by secretive politicians, who would never have released the information in the first place. But the techniques are significantly different, and their risks are nowise commensurable. The decision-maker learns to distrust those who have misled him, either explicitly by lying to him or implicitly by keeping secrets from him. The decision-maker who, using an interpretive framework, discounts information he later sees as important will tend to blame only himself for the oversight even though someone else might have originally suggested the framework to him.

From the point of view of those deploying it, this is a

26. Ralph Stavins, Richard Barnet and Marcus G. Raskin, *Washington Plans an Aggressive War* (New York: Vintage Books, 1971), p. 199. John H. Kessel, *The Domestic Presidency* (North Scituate, Mass.: Duxbury, 1975), Ch. 4, reports that the Domestic Council behaves similarly.

least-risk strategy of information-management. Someone
found advancing an ill-fitting interpretive framework might
be thought a fool, but he probably will not be called a liar. His
credibility is relatively secure. From the point of view of those
at whom it is aimed, the power of the manipulator's suggestion is likely to prove fairly compelling. The overload strategy
also affords the manipulator considerable leeway, at least in
the short term, to suggest any of a variety of schemes well
suited to his partisan purposes. Eventually, of course, ill-
fitting frames of reference will have to give way to well-fitting
ones as we are forced to confront realities which inadequate
schemata cannot explain. But this is a long-term constraint,
and the short-term pressures are in the opposite direction.
There is a strong tendency to discount information (and, indeed, the sources issuing the information) which is contrary
to the interpretive framework within which one is operating.
American foreign policy-makers, for example, persistently
ignored the remarkably accurate reports from the intelligence community denying the efficacy of the bombing of
North Vietnam. At some point, of course, accumulated
anomalies force reconsideration, but this point is likely to
come fairly far down the road.

The evils of this form of manipulation are mitigated once
again by the absence of any inherent distributive biases.
Interpretive schemata can be offered by any party to a political controversy, or by all parties simultaneously. Furthermore, politicians themselves typically become captive to
the schema they propagate for the benefit of the masses.
Partly this is a matter of consistency—if a politician or a party
offers a different framework for interpreting every event,
then none of them will stick. More important, manipulators
themselves need interpretive frameworks for dealing with
their world, and the more successful they are in constructing
schemata that others will find persuasive 'the more likely it is

that they will end by believing their own lies.' As Arendt observes, 'The trouble with lying and deceiving is that their efficacy depends entirely upon a clear notion of the truth that the liar and deceiver wishes to hide'; but in the process of lying the distinction is blurred, even in the mind of the liar himself. The 'interconnectedness of deception and self-deception' is well illustrated in the Pentagon Papers. American policymakers offered a system for interpreting events in Vietnam which rendered the Tet offensive a failure and the Cambodian invasion a success—and in the end they alone believed these absurdities. Abercrombie and Turner argue that, historically, 'just as the dominated classes do *not* hold the dominant ideology, the dominant classes *do*.... The dominant classes have been both the bearers and the recipients of orthodox religiosity, of conventional morality and conformist politics. While the shrift of the peasant was short and infrequent, the confessions of nobles under the guidance of spiritual directors was long and permanent.'[27] Interpretive frameworks promulgated for the benefit of others seem always to have posed greater threats to their promoters than to their recipients.

2.6 UNTRUTH AS A MODE OF MANIPULATION

A great variety of logically distinct strategies are often lumped together under the heading, 'the politics of lying'. Here I have

27. Arendt, 'Lying in Politics', pp. 31, 34. Daniel Ellsberg, 'The Quagmire Myth and the Stalemate Machine', *Public Policy*, 19 (1971): 217–74. Nicholas Abercrombie and Bryan S. Turner, 'The Dominant Ideology Thesis', *British Journal of Sociology*, 29 (1978): 149–70 at 159. Swift, 'The Art of Political Lying', p. 405, reports that even in the early eighteenth century 'the heads of parties ... believing their own lies ... has proved of pernicious consequences of late; both a wise party, and a wise nation, having regulated their affairs upon lies of their own invention.'

distinguished five: (1) lying proper; (2) secrecy, aiming at withholding information; (3) secrecy, aiming at co-opting potential opponents; (4) propaganda; and (5) information overload. The findings of this chapter with respect to each variety can now be summarized by reference to the standardized checklist described in Section 1.6:

1. Is the interference deceptive?

Both lying and keeping secrets are clearcut instances of deception, through commission in the first case and omission in the second. Insofar as the secrecy is aimed not so much at keeping secrets as at granting privileged access to them, on condition that those admitted will moderate their demands, the practice is only marginally deceptive: those co-opted can usually see perfectly well what they are doing; but perhaps those offering access to the official secrets might overstate their value, or perhaps those co-opted might then lie to their constituents about how hard they are pressing their claims behind closed doors. The propaganda strategy is only very slightly deceptive. It disseminates information which is perfectly true *so far as it goes* and is deceptive only in presenting an unbalanced account of those truths. The information overload strategy, if it is to work at all, quite probably has to be deceptive. The release of information itself is, of course, perfectly straightforward. Manipulation is accomplished by those responsible for the release of information then imposing a framework for interpreting the mass of unorganized data, and if people were to notice that the manipulator offers a framework tailor-made to his own policy preferences then they would be much less likely to accept it uncritically.

2. Is the interference contrary to the putative will of those subject to it?

In very intimate relationships there might be some things people would rather not know. But, considering the sort of information politicians typically lie about or withhold, it seems likely that people would rather know these truths and that keeping them from them is contrary to their putative wills. In the case of co-optation, the conclusion is not so obvious. People regret having moderated their demands; but in exchange they have acquired influence over policy, and on balance they may well prefer having been co-opted to continuing a fruitless fight from the outside. Again, propaganda —understood as the release of true but partial information—is only slightly contrary to the putative will of those subject to it. More true information is, in some sense, always better than less. In the case of deliberate information overload, however, it is likely that the deceptive imposition of a biased interpretive framework (with no acknowledgment of alternative possible frameworks) does indeed bias people's judgement in ways they would mind very much were they to realize what was happening.

Together, these first two criteria define an instance of manipulation. Of the five variants of the politics of lying, two (lying itself and withholding information) qualify clearly as manipulatory, and another (information overload) counts as a very probable example. Both the remaining variants are marginal cases: co-optation might be deceptive but is probably not unwelcome, and propaganda is only slightly either. Now I turn to two further criteria for determining the seriousness of the manipulation, focusing especially although not exclusively upon those three variants of the politics of lying which clearly qualify as manipulatory.

3. How persistent is the effect of the manipulation?

Lies probably have only a brief impact. Even if politicians do not trip themselves up with their own lies, their political opponents or the press reporters are likely to expose the lies or initiate counter-lies. Secrets, too, are likely to leak out fairly promptly. Manipulative forms of co-optation are equally likely to pass quickly, as those co-opted learn how valuable the shared secrets really are or as whistle-blowers expose their treachery to their constituents. Propaganda will have a large impact only in the short term, until people learn to recognize the slant and start correcting for it. Of the five variants, only the information overload strategy looks capable of exerting any really long-lasting influence.

4. Are any distributive biases inherent in the mechanism?

The distributive biases of lying and withholding information are trivial. Anyone can tell lies or keep secrets and, historically, spreading untrue rumours and forming 'secret societies' have been among the more effective strategies by which outsiders organize opposition to political power-holders. The strategy of co-optation may be slightly biased, in that only those already entrenched in the policy-making process have in their possession 'official secrets' which they can offer to share. However, the strategy can well backfire if those with whom they share the secrets threaten to 'go public' with them unless they get their way. This, it would seem, largely compensates for any distributive bias in the power to initiate co-optive relationships. The power to propagandize, too, seems available to anyone. Information overload is rather a more specialized skill, requiring not only dissemination of lots of information but also imposition of an interpretive framework. While this might be accomplished only by certain individuals, however, it is entirely likely that they will eventually become prisoners of their own constructions and pursue goals far less effectively in consequence, largely wiping out the distributive biases of the strategy as a whole.

Overall, it would seem that the information overload strategy alone poses much of a threat, and even that is mitigated by its uncertain distributive consequences. Lying and withholding information are clearly manipulatory, but they are neither persistent nor biased. Propagandizing is only marginally manipulatory and is equally marginal in these other respects. Co-optation, while rather more biased in its distribution, is equally marginal in all other ways.

CHAPTER THREE ¢ LAYING LINGUISTIC TRAPS

> We must forearm ourselves against the traps that language
> sets us. . . . Words are not . . . facts or things: we need therefore
> to prise them off the world, to hold them apart from and
> against it, so that we can realize their inadequacies and arbi-
> trariness, and re-look at the world without blinkers.
>
> J. L. Austin[1]

THERE IS A NAIVE VIEW THAT LANGUAGE, like the postal service, is a neutral conduit equally suited to conveying all messages that one might care to send through it. Once long ago
this was the predominant view. Today its band of adherents is
small and shrinking. The conventional wisdom has shifted
decisively in favour of an activist account of the role of language in our social life. In this account, two connections are
especially emphasized.

Language firstly constrains thought. Human behaviour is
(at least in part) intentional in nature. Insofar as language can
constrain thought it can constrain the formation of intentions
and thereby constrain behaviour itself. To some extent, of
course, the constraints of a shared language are necessary
ones, required if we are to be able to express our intentions at
all. But there is no guarantee that the constraints will be limited to those which are formally necessary to expression. Instead, there is every reason to suppose that the constraints
imposed by language will extend well beyond those limits.

Material from 'Laying Linguistic Traps' by Robert E. Goodin is reprinted
from *Political Theory*, vol. 5, number 4 (November 1977), pp. 491–504, by
permission of the Publishers, Sage Publications, Inc.

1. 'A Plea for Excuses', *Proceedings of the Aristotelian Society*, 57 (1956–57):
1–30.

Even if the constraints are so confined, they might still have significant implications for social action. By regulating the expression of intentions, language regulates formation of coalitions organized around a community of intentions. If some one individual succeeds in transcending linguistic constraints on his thought and manages to think linguistically proscribed thoughts, the language will still be inadequate for communicating them to others. Under the pressure of his innovatory use of words, of course, the language might grow and expand, eventually allowing him to communicate what he wishes. The original inadequacy of language will nevertheless have acted as a constraint, forcing him to waste time on the second-order activity of shaping linguistic tools he would have preferred to spend pursuing first-order political goals directly.

The constraints of language are imperfect ones, to be sure. If there is no direct path to the point you want to make, there is usually some roundabout way of coming to the same point. It is rare to find language ruling anything out, strictly speaking. But whereas deterministic phraseology might be inappropriate, talk of tendencies, proclivities and biases is entirely in order. The point remains that language might offer multiple opportunities for political manipulation of a particularly far-reaching kind.

3.1   IS LANGUAGE PARADIGMATIC?

The first task in exploring the manipulative power of words is to explain the nature of the link between language on the one hand and thought and action on the other. Postulates of some kind of a link are common enough; plausible theories accounting for the relationship are scarce. Social anthropologists recognize this as a variant of the Whorf hypothesis that language conditions thought.[2] But the Whorf hypothesis is just that—a hypothesis, a *de facto* empirical generalization largely bereft of theoretical underpinnings. Political theorists might regard the proposition as a mere application of Edmund Burke's more general doctrine that social action is, of necessity, constrained by respect for tradition and inherited collective habits. But the Burkean case rests precariously on functionalist foundations: tradition is powerful magic; a society that wants to survive can hardly afford to do without it, and one that has survived has probably made good use of it. This opens the Burkean argument to the spate of objections that have substantially discredited functionalism as a viable mode of social analysis.[3]

Quentin Skinner and J. G. A. Pocock offer instead an innovative argument based on an analysis of the nature of language itself.[4] Following the later Wittgenstein and J. L. Austin, they notice that one does indeed 'do things with words'. A word figures in many language games, and in some of them its meaning is far more than the picture it conjures up in the

2. Benjamin Lee Whorf, *Language, Thought and Reality* (Cambridge: MIT Press, 1956).

3. Edmund Burke, *Reflections on the Revolution in France* (London: J. Dodsley, 1790). Carl G. Hempel, 'The Logic of Functional Analysis', *Symposium on Sociological Theory*, ed. L. Gross (New York: Harper & Row, 1959), pp. 271-307. Ralf Dahrendorf, 'Out of Utopia', *American Journal of Sociology*, 64 (1958): 115-27. Gustav Bergmann, 'Purpose, Function and Scientific Explanation', *Acta Sociologica*, 5 (1962): 225-38.

4. Quentin Skinner, 'Meaning and Understanding in the History of Ideas', *History and Theory*, 8 (1969): 1-53, and '"Social Meaning" and the Explanation of Social Action', *Philosophy, Politics and Society*, 4th series, ed. P. Laslett, W. G. Runciman and Q. Skinner (Oxford: Blackwell, 1972), pp. 136-57. J. G. A. Pocock, *Politics, Language and Time* (New York: Atheneum, 1971), 'Verbalizing a Political Act: Toward a Politics of Speech', *Political Theory*, 1 (1973): 27-45, and *The Machiavellian Moment* (Princeton: Princeton University Press, 1975).

mind of the hearer. Words are sometimes 'performatives'
with 'illocutionary' or 'perlocutionary' force as when used to
plead, to pledge or to praise.[5] Crucially conjoined with this
activist analysis of language is the recollection of the conventionality of language. Utterances have meaning only because
there is some common, conventional understanding as to
what they connote.[6] Hence the close connection between language and action that characterizes the Skinner–Pocock thesis. Words are actors, essential participants in the organizing
of social activities. But some of the linguistic tools required for
organizing certain activities might be lacking, and, owing to
the necessary conventionality of language, organizers cannot
simply forge new linguistic tools as they are required. The
limitations of the language thus impose limitations on political
actors.

A large part of the reason this analysis is so immediately
appealing is, no doubt, that it basks in the reflected glory of
Kuhn's theory of scientific revolutions.[7] Pocock explicitly
suggests the analogy between languages and scientific paradigms which delimit the scope of 'scientific' concerns in a
thoroughly ascientific (not to say unscientific) way. Viewing
language as paradigm-writ-large implies that it performs the
same sort of structuring function.

5. Ludwig Wittgenstein, *Philosophical Investigations*, trans. G. E. M.
Anscombe (Oxford: Blackwell, 1958). J. L. Austin, *How to Do Things with
Words* (Oxford: Clarendon Press, 1962). J. R. Searle, *Speech Acts* (Cambridge:
Cambridge University Press, 1969).

6. Quentin Skinner, 'Conventions and Understanding of Speech Acts'
and 'On Performing and Explaining Linguistic Actions', *Philosophical Quarterly*, 20 (1970): 118–38, and 21 (1971): 1–21, respectively. Peter Mew, 'Conventions on Thin Ice', *Philosophical Quarterly*, 21 (1971): 352–56, suggests persuasive, but one suspects limited, exceptions. See more generally David K.
Lewis, *Convention* (Cambridge: Harvard University Press, 1969).

7. Thomas Kuhn, *The Structure of Scientific Revolutions* (Chicago: University of Chicago Press, 1962).

The existence of something in society which does just this seems absolutely undeniable. The question is simply whether this something is language. A more orthodox and reasonable suggestion is that there is a social paradigm—what is ordinarily called 'social theory' or even 'ideology'—which performs this task.[8] And, while the social paradigm is reflected in language, it is analytically distinct from it.

Consider for a moment the practice of normal science. The scientific paradigm is communicated through language —fancy symbols or everyday English or whatever— but no one would claim that it is the language that imposes the constraints on thought. Rather, it is the scientific paradigm that is the culprit.

Language, of course, is responsive to demands made on it. Suppose a language were originally neutral between various scientific theories, meaning that it is as easy to talk about one as the next in its terms. Now suppose one becomes installed as the dominant paradigm and the preeminent topic of scientific conversation. New distinctions required by that theory will inevitably find their way into the language, and at that point the language will begin looking biased. But there is surely a distinction between the language *reflecting* the paradigm and the language *being* paradigmatic.

The tendency for scientific language to be slanted in favour of the dominant paradigm appears to be merely an aspect of a more general phenomenon. It seems likely that linguistic biases in general reflect reality, and the need for people to talk about that reality, rather than the other way around. Eskimos have different words for making distinc-

8. Sheldon S. Wolin, 'Paradigms and Political Theories', *Politics and Experience*, ed. D. King and B. C. Parekh (Cambridge: Cambridge University Press, 1968), pp. 125–52. Claus Mueller, *The Politics of Communication* (New York: Oxford University Press, 1973), Ch. 3, follows Marxist orthodoxy in taking 'ideology' as the paradigm case of 'constrained communication'.

tions between kinds of snow (falling, packed, frozen, slushy, etc.) and Arabs have several words for distinguishing various kinds of sand, whereas English offers a single word in each instance. Surely this is because Eskimos see more snow and Arabs more sand and hence have more occasions for talking about them than do Anglo-Saxons. Similar explanations can be offered for 'the seventeen terms for cattle among the Masai of Africa, the twenty terms for rice among the Ifuego of the Philippines, the thousands of Arabic words associated with camels' or the seven words for bamboo among the Koyas of India.[9]

Much the same is true in the social realm. Linguistic biases reflect, for better or worse, what people are forced to talk about. In the slang of the underworld of Calcutta, there are forty-one words for 'police' and twenty-one for 'bomb', reflecting the more important features of daily life in that subculture. As social reality changes, however, so too does the language. Mid-nineteenth-century Russian offered 300 kinship terms, reflecting the 'great family' form of social organization then predominant. With the advent of the Soviet nuclear family, however, most of those terms have gradually fallen into disuse. Similarly one hypothesizes that in a feudal society there will be plenty of ways to talk about the lord–vassal relationship simply because that is a very important part of such a world. The situation was not structured (in the first instance, anyway) by language but rather by the military power of lords and knights and kings. The *de facto* distinctions between lord and vassal having been forcibly imposed, people will begin talking about the arrangement and the language will be thereby modified in precisely the same way sci-

9. Whorf, *Language, Thought and Reality*, p. 216. Peter Farb, *Word Play* (New York: Knopf, 1974), Chs. 8 and 9. Pocock tells me of a missionary who found that Hawaiians had about 22 different words for 'incest'—a common experience or a common preoccupation, I leave others to judge which.

entific language is modified once a dominant paradigm has been established. Thus, when Alexandre reports that some indigenous African languages are unsuited to talking about modern institutionalized politics, one presumes that that is because there are no such institutions in those societies to talk about. He neither offers evidence that these linguistic limitations hinder political institutionalization nor that they will fail to adapt to the fact of institutionalization once it gets underway.[10]

A variety of examples has been offered to show how linguistic distinctions shore up social ones. All can be interpreted plausibly in just this way. The thesis of Murray Edelman's 'Political Language of the Helping Professions' is that the power of psychiatrists and nurses over patients is bolstered by the suggestion that they are 'sick' and that medical professionals are 'just helping'. But surely it is just as plausible that psychologists have the power they do to put people in linguistic straitjackets by virtue of their power to put them in literal ones. Robin Lakoff similarly finds that language mirrors the social stereotype of women as the 'weaker' sex, but the ordinary way of interpreting this evidence would be that language bolsters a preexisting stereotype rather than creating it. Roger Brown and Albert Gilman, studying languages making the 'you'/'thou' distinction, find political radicalism associated with the less respectful 'thou' mode of speaking. But, again, it seems likely that political conversion antedated (and often, as in the case of French revolutionaries and George Fox's Soci-

10. Bhaktiprasad Mallik, *Language of the Underworld of West Bengal* (Calcutta: Sanskrit College Research Series No. 76, 1972). Paul Friedrich, 'The Linguistic Reflex of Social Change: From Tsarist to Russian Kinship', *Explorations in Sociolinguistics*, ed. S. Lieberson (Bloomington: Indiana University Press, 1967), pp. 31–57. P. Alexandre, 'Sur les Possibilités Expressives des Langues Africaines en Matière de la Terminologie Politique', *Afrique et L'Asie*, 56 (1961).

ety of Friends, even caused) linguistic conversion and not the other way around. Perhaps the clearest example is Claus Mueller's discussion of attempts by the totalitarian regimes of Nazi and East Germany to introduce propagandistic uses of words. There most clearly the police state predated and enforced linguistic revisions.[11]

Political scientists will find in the Skinner–Pocock talk of 'language' something akin to their treatment of 'routines'. All sorts of important issues are resolved through application of routinized procedures, and these procedures are far from being neutral between the alternatives under consideration.[12] But routines are inventions of men—sometimes identifiable individuals, sometimes collegial wholes—and to explain the cast they put on the issue one naturally examines the history of their origin. Geraint Parry and Peter Morriss, in their contribution to the 'community power' debate, notice that many power plays entail no actual decision but only the relentless workings of rigged routines. From that they do not conclude that routines rather than men are responsible for the outcomes and hence that no exercise of power is involved. Rather, they look behind the routine and see how it has simply ossified a past power imbalance.[13]

11. Murray Edelman, *Politics and Society*, 4 (1974): 295–310. Robin Lakoff, 'Language and Woman's Place', *Language in Society*, 2 (1973): 45–79. Roger Brown and Albert Gilman, 'The Pronouns of Power and Solidarity', *Style in Language*, ed. Thomas A. Sebeok (New York: MIT and Wiley, 1960), pp. 253–76. Richard Bauman, 'Aspects of Quaker Rhetoric', *Quarterly Journal of Speech*, 56 (1970): 67–74. Mueller, *Politics of Communication*, Ch. 1. See further David V. J. Bell, *Power, Influence and Authority* (New York: Oxford University Press, 1975).

12. Ira Sharkansky, *The Routines of Politics* (New York: Van Nostrand, 1970).

13. Geraint Parry and Peter Morriss, 'When is a Decision not a Decision?' *British Political Sociology Yearbook*, ed. I. M. Crewe (London: Croom Helm, 1974), 1: 317–36; see further Andrew S. McFarland, *Power and Leadership in Pluralist Systems* (Stanford: Stanford University Press, 1969), esp. Ch. 5.

The allusion to routines, besides providing a point of contact with orthodox political science, is also useful in reminding us of the power of institutional inertia. Routines, linguistic or governmental, may persist long after the objective conditions to which they were originally responses have passed away. The British notion of 'collective responsibility' of Cabinet Ministers was originally devised as a procedure by which the Cabinet could present a united front in confrontations with a powerful Sovereign. The routine continues to be used long after the power of the Sovereign has been curbed. The same inertia characterizes linguistic routines. Four centuries after the Copernican revolution, the Naval Observatory still reports the hour of the sunrise and sunset. In this instance, of course, the pattern of thinking about the heavenly bodies has changed even if some aspects of the language have not. But sometimes the linguistic inertia will surely help to prevent a paradigm-shift.

3.2 TYPES OF LINGUISTIC TRAPS

Even if the language is not itself the paradigm, there is no denying that it does embody it, reflect it and help bolster it. The crucial questions for linguistic trappers and quarry alike then become how the trap works and how to escape from it.

One alternative is a 'cage' model of linguistic traps. Pocock and Skinner are in many ways the clearest exponents of this

---

Pocock responds, 'Perhaps their vision is crudely dichotomous. The routine needn't be separated from the power—it *is* the power. It doesn't fully explain the power, but it doesn't follow that the power explains it.' But to ascribe (any) independent power to routines would be like writing a military history that explains the outcomes of battles (at least partly) by ascribing to bullets a mind of their own and partial power to change direction at will. At the very least, Pocock must appreciate that in order to be reproduced routines must rely upon a power beyond their own level.

model. Ordinary (i.e., non-revolutionary) language is for them what 'normal science' is for Kuhn. A language, like a scientific paradigm, defines what are the important questions and what counts as an adequate answer to them. In other words, it constructs barriers which, viewed from within, may seem to offer welcome protection from outside disturbances but which, viewed objectively, function more like a cage constricting the free movement of those confined within.

Pocock and Skinner may be the clearest exponents of the cage model. But they are hardly alone. Jeremy Bentham must be counted in their number, writing as he does in his treatise on *Evidence,*

> Improper terms are the chains which bind men to unreasonable practices. Error is never so difficult to be destroyed, as when it has its roots in language. Every improper term contains the germ of fallacious propositions; it forms a cloud, which conceals the nature of the thing, and presents a frequently invincible obstacle to the discovery of truth.

Something similar can be found lurking in the background of Marxist discussions of 'ideology', 'hegemony' and 'linguistic alienation'. The cage model is further reflected in T. D. Weldon's analogy between political principles and 'Keep Off the Grass' notices (each being a signal of bounds one is unprepared to transgress) and in W. B. Gallie's parallel analysis of how one can only work within and never across sets of 'essentially contested concepts'.[14]

14. Jeremy Bentham, 'Evidence', *Works,* ed. J. Bowring (Edinburgh: W. Tait, 1843), 6 and 7: Bk. 3, Ch. 1. Marxist treatments include: Herbert Marcuse, *One-Dimensional Man* (Boston: Beacon Press, 1964), Chs. 4 and 7; Ferruccio Rossi-Landi, *Linguistics and Economics* (The Hague: Mouton, 1975); and literature summarized by Mueller in *Politics of Communication.* 'Keep off

The cage analogy is peculiarly appropriate to the focuses of all these commentators. One encaged naturally finds his attention narrowed to—and hence focused on—the territory inside the bars. Consequently he becomes more familiar with it than he would have been had he remained free to wander widely. This is the point at which the analogy between scientific and linguistic paradigms seems especially strong for Pocock and Skinner: the details of normal science get worked out pretty fully; and the range of permissible speech acts gets pretty thoroughly explored. Similarly, interconnections within any one set of 'essentially contested concepts' tend to be exhaustively catalogued, etc.

Significantly, however, the elaboration of the paradigm has, according to the cage model, no necessary implications for the prospects of a paradigm-shift. Elaboration may undermine a paradigm. It may equally well reinforce it. There is no predicting with certainty which it will be. Talking in terms of contingent and probabilistic truths, however, it seems unlikely that elaboration can do anything except

---

the grass' analogies are offered by T. D. Weldon, 'Political Principles', *Philosophy, Politics and Society*, 1st series, ed. P. Laslett (Oxford: Blackwell, 1956), pp. 22–34, and Wittgensteinian relativism by Peter Winch, *Idea of a Social Science* (London: Routledge & Kegan Paul, 1958), and 'Understanding a Primitive Society', *American Philosophical Quarterly*, 1 (1964): 304–24. The radical relativism of W. B. Gallie, 'Essentially Contested Concepts', *Proceedings of the Aristotelian Society*, 56 (1955–56): 167–98, has been embraced by, e.g.: Steven Lukes, *Power: A Radical View* (London: Macmillan, 1974); William E. Connolly, *The Terms of Political Discourse* (Lexington, Mass.: D.C. Heath, 1974); Ronald M. Dworkin, *Taking Rights Seriously* (London: Duckworth, 1977), Chs. 4 and 5; and John Gray, 'On the Essential Contestability of Some Social and Political Concepts', *Political Theory*, 5 (1977): 331–48. But this extreme form of the cage-like linguistic trap model is discredited by various articles: Ernest Gellner, 'The Concept of a Story', *Ratio*, 9 (1967): 49–66; K. I. MacDonald, 'Is "Power" Essentially Contested?', *British Journal of Political Science*, 6 (1976): 380–82; and Barry Clarke, 'Eccentrically Contested Concepts', *British Journal of Political Science*, 9 (1979): 122–26.

strengthen the paradigm. The more bars the jailer adds to the cell the more likely one of them can be dislodged easily; but, then again, the more bars the denser they are and the less the chance of squeezing through any opening made by loosening just one of them. Likewise with scientific paradigms: the more detailed their claims the greater the risk that one will prove erroneous. But nothing is easier for the normal scientist than to concede particular points whilst reaffirming his faith in the larger theory.[15]

Much the same is true of language systems. As Pocock is anxious to emphasize, domination through linguistic trickery is a risky business, for there is always the chance of the other fellow turning the tables. But this is neither a necessary nor, one imagines, a likely scenario. The risk is real but decidedly slight, although perhaps it does increase cumulatively over time. It bears emphasizing, however, that the risk is not a gratuitous one. There is something of value to be gained from tightening the linguistic noose around the dominated, in light of which one might be willing to risk having the gambit backfire now and again.

Contrasting with the cage model of linguistic traps is a 'linguistic deprivation' model. On this account, the nefarious socio-political consequences arise less out of what language structures (for the benefit of some and to the disadvantage of others) and more out of what it leaves unstructured. What is left out of one's language tends to go unnoticed. For a mun-

15. Students of mass communication find that, when the weight of evidence strongly supports the main thesis, it is more persuasive to introduce arguments against it than to add still more in support. See C. I. Hovland, A. A. Lumsdaine and F. D. Sheffield, *Experiments on Mass Communication* (Princeton: Princeton University Press, 1949), esp. pp. 201–27. Peter W. Sperlich, *Conflict and Harmony in Human Affairs: A Study of Cross-Pressures and Political Behavior* (Chicago: Rand McNally, 1971), confirms that people seek out conflicting evidence in deciding how to vote.

dane example, the Navaho perceive no difference between the colours blue and green because their language makes no such distinction. For a more political example, a recent paper 'On the Myth of Social Equality in Iceland' suggests that Icelanders fail to notice substantial class differences because 'there is no vocabulary in the Icelandic language that adequately encapsulates a stratified notion of society. Specifically, there is no Icelandic term for "class".'[16]

The linguistic deprivation model grows out of—and is corroborated by—a variety of empirical studies. Among the most famous is Basil Bernstein's *Class, Codes and Control,* the thesis of which is that the docility of the English working class is largely a function of its less elaborated linguistic code. Similarly, Paulo Freire associates radical consequences with *The Pedagogy of the Oppressed,* and it is far from clear that they can be put down entirely to the revolutionary content of the curriculum. Simple instruction, teaching people to grasp complicated relationships and giving them linguistic tools to express those notions, might be as responsible for the revolutionary results as is Freire's own radicalism.[17]

Among theoretical treatments, perhaps the most sophisticated is that of Pierre Bourdieu. At the centre of his argument is a distinction between the 'universe of discourse' (which includes both heterodoxy and orthodoxy) and the

16. Roger W. Brown and Eric H. Lennebert, 'A Study in Language and Cognition', *Journal of Abnormal and Social Psychology,* 49 (1954): 454–62. For more recent evidence of the influence of language on colour coding see Brent Berlin and Paul Kay, *Basic Color Terms* (Berkeley: University of California Press, 1969). Thorbjørn Broddason and Keith Webb, 'On the Myth of Social Equality in Iceland', *Acta Sociologia,* 18 (1975): 49–61; it should be noted that these authors find other and stronger reasons for Icelanders to fail to notice class differentials.

17. Basil Bernstein, *Class, Codes and Control* (London: Routledge & Kegan Paul, 1971). Paulo Freire, *The Pedagogy of the Oppressed,* trans. Myra Bergman Ramos (Harmondsworth: Penguin, 1972).

'universe of the undiscussed' (or the 'doxa'). Bourdieu argues
that within the universe of discourse 'orthodoxy' can exist
only in opposition to 'heterodoxy', that is, 'by reference to the
choice made possible by the existence of *competing possibles.*'
This is the heresy the orthodoxy persecutes. But 'manifest
censorship' of this sort

> conceals another, more radical censorship: [it] masks in
> its turn the fundamental opposition between the universe
> of things that can be stated, and hence thought, and the
> universe of that which is taken for granted. The universe
> of discourse ... is practically defined in relation to the
> necessarily unnoticed complementary class that is consti-
> tuted by the universe of that which is undiscussed, un-
> named, admitted without argument or scrutiny.[18]

The manipulative possibilities offered by this model are
clearly far stronger than those offered by the cage model. If
something is represented in the language, though in a biased
way, then the bias is more apparent and consequently more
easily corrected. Irony has an especially important role to play
in this regard. Protesters say the name of the 'Defense Department' sarcastically to emphasize that its real function is
aggression; and they sneeringly refer to 'pacification', emphasizing that the peace thus attained is a peculiarly final one.
Among American slaves, Genovese finds similarly that

> words themselves often have directly opposite meanings,
> in accordance with the way in which they are pro-
> nounced, the gestures that accompany them, and the
> context in which they appear. Thus, the ba-ad nigger
> who appears frequently in the plantation literature was a
> very special sort of person to the slaves who might say Yo'

18. Pierre Bourdieu, *Outline of a Theory of Practice,* trans. Richard Nice
(Cambridge: Cambridge University Press, 1977), pp. 169–70.

a mighty *ba-ad* nigger with unquestionable delight whereas they would say Yo' a mighty bad *nigger* with extreme distaste.

It is far harder to turn the linguistic tables in these ways if the bias is achieved by leaving certain concepts out of the language altogether.[19]

Linguistic deprivation also offers a stronger form of manipulation in that it poses less danger of the manipulator getting caught in his own traps. With the cage model, this is a real threat. Pocock is fond of quoting Alice's Red Queen to the effect that 'when you've once said a thing, that fixes it, and you must take the consequences'. And politically significant examples of politicians getting caught in their own linguistic traps are not hard to find. Among the more impressive is President Johnson's insistent talk of America's 'pledge', 'obligation' and 'commitment' to South Vietnam. In so speaking, he was clearly raising the linguistic stakes: President Eisenhower's 1954 letter to President Diem, the source of the ostensible 'pledge', contains no verb stronger than 'to expect' or 'to hope'. Calling this letter a 'pledge', President Johnson was clearly trying to drum up support for his war policies through a linguistic sleight of hand. But by calling it a pledge Johnson *made* it a pledge, making it ever so much more difficult for him and his successor to withdraw.[20] Within the linguistic deprivation model, elites may well be immune to the

19. 'Turning the linguistic tables' is one of the central themes in Pocock, *Politics, Language and Time* and 'Verbalizing a Political Act'. For examples of the language of protesters see Arthur M. Schlesinger, Jr., 'Politics and the American Language', *The American Scholar*, 43 (1974); 553–62, and of slaves see Eugene D. Genovese, *Roll Jordan Roll* (New York: Random House, 1974), p. 436. For a more systematic account of 'Anti-Languages' see M. A. K. Halliday's article in the *American Anthropologist*, 78 (1976): 570–84.

20. Pocock, *Politics, Language and Time*, 24. Kenneth R. Johnson, 'The Rhetoric Surrounding the Vietnamese War', mimeographed (Department of English, Indiana University, 1967), pp. 6–7.

traps (of poverty of language) they set for the masses. They might talk in very subtle terms among themselves and at the same time leave the masses forever grasping for words to express their thoughts and feelings.

Both Bourdieu and Freire regard linguistic deprivation as being profoundly political. In its consequences it clearly is, giving power to some and withholding it from others. But for the deprivation to be truly political it must itself be the *consequence* of a power play, as opposed to being purely accidental. It is not enough merely that someone benefits from the biases thereby introduced. 'Deprivation' in the political sense implies that someone else is responsible for imposing the limitation, for withholding that which those deprived are seen as lacking. Certainly elites often do employ a more elaborate code in discourse among themselves, often with the intention of hiding their meaning from the masses. 'Among the Bemba' of northeastern Rhodesia, for example, 'much of the tribal ritual is secret', and if the advisory council should happen to 'meet in sitting on the open ground in the capital . . . they use archaic language on purpose, so that common people cannot understand.' In our own societies, too, 'many policy-makers have devised a form of communication in "code", that is, statements have specific meaning only to those who possess sufficient inside knowledge to penetrate beyond the superficial and cryptic character of public and published documents.' A prime example of such coded communications is the Plowden Report, described by Anthony Sampson as a 'revolutionary and critical document' discussing control of British public expenditure but written in an 'unknown tongue', effectively decoded (and ridiculed) by W. J. M. Mackenzie.[21]

21. Audrey I. Richards, 'The Political System of the Bemba Tribe—North-eastern Rhodesia', *African Political Systems*, ed. M. Fortes and E. E. Evans-Pritchard (London: Oxford University Press for International African Institute, 1940), pp. 82–120 at 111. Richard Rose, 'Introduction' and W. J. M.

Occasionally there is evidence that elites actively pre-
vented the masses from learning these codes, as in Genovese's
reference to American slaves being punished for trying to
speak 'proper' English. But usually no evidence of such
heavy-handed repression can be produced. In general it
would seem unlikely that elites would enjoy better success in
keeping linguistic secrets than any others; and Section 2.3
suggests that this success is extremely limited. Thus we should
not be surprised by the several instances of people employing
a suitably restricted code when addressing their social betters
but using a very subtle and elaborated code among their
peers. Use of a restricted code is often less a sign of linguistic
deprivation than of deference, grudging or otherwise. It is
the verbal equivalent of shuffling one's feet, slouching and
avoiding eye contact.[22]

Mackenzie, 'The Plowden Report: A Translation', *Policy-Making in Britain,*
ed. Richard Rose (London: Macmillan, 1969), pp. 273 and 273–82 respectively. Anthony Sampson, *The Anatomy of Britain* (New York: Harper & Row,
1962), p. 284.

22. Genovese, *Roll Jordan Roll,* p. 434. Paul Friedrich, 'Social Context and
Semantic Feature: The Russian Pronominal Usage' and Jan-Petter Bolm and
John J. Gumperz, 'Social Meaning in Linguistic Structures: Code-Switching
in Norway', *Directions in Sociolinguistics,* ed. John J. Gumperz and Dell Hymes
(New York: Holt, Rinehart & Winston, 1972), pp. 270–300 and 407–34 re-
spectively.

Conspiracy theorists might reply in either of two ways. Firstly, Bourdieu
certainly (and Freire probably) would argue that the power involved here is
structural, not *individual,* so the classical liberal's search for a culprit is misguided. Secondly, they might follow the lead of Ferruccio Rossi-Landi, 'Ideas
for the Study of Linguistic Alienation', *Social Praxis,* 3 (1975): 77–92 at 87–88:
'The ruling class increases the redundancy of the messages which confirm its
own position and attacks with noise, or if necessary with disturbance, the
codification and circulation of messages which could instead invalidate it.
The subordinate class is placed in the position of being able to decode with
particular ease and thus to consider as "real" or "natural" those messages
which are sufficiently redundant to overcome the noise or disturbance. . . .'
This latter strategy resembles that of propaganda and information overload
(Sections 2.4 and 2.5), and a variant will be discussed in Section 4.4.

3.3   REALITY AS A CONSTRAINT ON LINGUISTIC TRAPS

Underlying the linguistic deprivation model is something of a 'mirror theory' of language. Language can distort our perceptions of reality only by being incompletely reflective, only by being imperfectly silvered, as it were. There is in this analysis nothing of the 'picture' theory of meaning famous from Wittgenstein's *Tractatus* and later repudiated in his *Philosophical Investigations*. To refute the proposition that a word's meaning is simply the picture it conjures up in one's mind, one need only point to 'speech acts' with 'illocutionary' force: the lieutenant shouting, 'Charge!', is neither describing nor predicting but rather ordering; the bride saying, 'I do', is not simply describing her state of mind but also tying the marital knot. In both these cases the meaning of the utterance is not reducible to the images they bring to mind. The meaning of meaning is not at issue here, however. The present argument is that language can reflect (or, if you prefer, connect with or correspond to) something in reality. The order, 'Charge!', can have an impact on the soldier's actions only because there is such an action as attacking the enemy lines; and the words, 'I do', have an effect on the bride's behaviour only because there is the institution of matrimony.

Why the soldier obeys orders or why the bride is faithful to her vows is a separate question. Part of the answer might seem to turn on the force of the language used. 'Charge!' is a stirring battlecry and marriage vows do have a profound psychological impact. But for a full explanation of the power of the words we must look behind them, to the physical and psychological power of military discipline in the first instance and to the power of love in the second. Words mediate between underlying motives and action. It is inherent in the nature of such mediatory devices that attention might come to focus on the superficial manifestation—the word—rather than on the underlying motive. Thus, words might be used inappropriately and still evoke the same effect as when they are simply stand-ins for deeper motivating forces. When the lieutenant (call him Calley) orders a charge, his subordinates might neglect to check that the full weight of the military command stands behind the order. But this is just another manifestation of the ossification of routinized practices. One is in the habit of obeying one's superior because he is characteristically backed up by the chain of command. There are several ways of explaining habituated behaviour— as forgetfulness, as laziness or as economizing on one's time—which would avoid ascribing any independent power to the linguistic cue.

Suggesting that language might aspire to mirror reality obviously entails the claim that there is an external reality to be mirrored. Some bizarre philosophies deny just that proposition. There is a weaker and more plausible claim (historically associated with the names of Wilhelm von Humbolt, Ernest Cassirer, Ludwig Wittgenstein and Benjamin Whorf) which is well-captured in Peter Berger and Thomas Luckmann's title, *The Social Construction of Reality*.[23] The argument at least partially present in all these works concedes that there is some common objective reality which we all experience; but it insists that how we interpret it is governed by

23. J. L. Mackie, 'What's Really Wrong with Phenomenalism?' *Proceedings of the British Academy*, 55 (1969): 113-27. Wilhelm, Freiherr von Humbolt, *Linguistic Variability and Intellectual Development*, trans. G. C. Buck and F. A. Raven (Philadelphia: University of Pennsylvania Press, 1971). Ernst Cassirer, *The Philosophy of Symbolic Forms* (New Haven: Yale University Press, 1953). Edward Sapir, 'Conceptual Categories in Primitive Languages', *Science*, 74 (1931): 578. Wittgenstein, *Philosophical Investigations*. Whorf, *Language, Thought and Reality*. Peter L. Berger and Thomas Luckmann, *The Social Construction of Reality* (Harmondsworth: Penguin, 1967). See similarly Emile Durkheim and Marcel Mauss, *Primitive Classifications*, trans. and ed. R. Needham (Chicago: University of Chicago Press, 1963).

socially (or, to be precise, linguistically) dictated schemata. This thesis is borne out in studies of everyday experiences, such as the correlation between one's capacity to discriminate between colours and the linguistic pigeonholes available for labelling those distinctions.

The point remains, however, that we are experiencing the same reality, and some parts of the real world will impinge on us and make us take note of them whether or not we go looking for them. Thus, there will be data that do not fit into the socially constructed schema. So long as these deviant cases appear somehow marginal (occurring infrequently or in unimportant areas), they might not provoke challenges to the larger schema. But at some point they will likely become so frequent and central that they can no longer be ignored. If and when this happens, the deviations will surely provoke a reworking of the schema. Bourdieu argues in fairly abstract terms that, through 'culture contact' or social or economic crises, elements of the 'universe of the undiscussed' are shifted into the 'universe of discourse', and the linguistic deprivation trap is thereby destroyed. 'The critique which brings the undiscussed into discussion, the unformulated into formulation' is pointedly described as an 'objective crisis', producing this effect by 'breaking the immediate fit between subjective structures and the objective structures.' For a more concrete example, focus upon the Balinese notion of time. Geertz powerfully argues that ritual life on Bali is characterized by a static notion of time which also effectively underwrites the existing social hierarchy:

> Quarrels appear and disappear, on occasion they even persist, but they hardly ever come to a head. . . . Events happen like holidays. They appear, vanish, and reappear —each discrete, sufficient unto itself, a particular ma-

nifestation of the fixed order of things. Social activities are separate performances; they do not march toward some destination, gather toward some denouement. . . . Balinese social life lacks climax because it takes place in a motionless present, a vectorless now.

But Bloch, drawing upon Geertz's own evidence, shows that the Balinese also possess alongside static ritual notions of time a very ordinary linear notion of time used in everyday activities, such as planting and harvesting the rice crops. These linear notions of time, forced upon them by interactions with the 'real' world of rice rather than ritual, offer the Balinese a perspective from which they might critique static ritual time and the social structure such notions sustain. The Balinese have been slow to seize these possibilities, admittedly, but the possibilities exist nonetheless.[24]

Significantly, the revision of the schema is prompted by an honest concern to make it fit the facts. Whereas the function of a paradigm is to filter out certain data, the function of a schema, and the motivation for revising it, is to incorporate all the data insofar as is logically possible. A schema denies neither the existence nor the importance of conflicting data. And, unlike a paradigm-shift, there is nothing irrational

24. Bourdieu, *Outline of a Theory of Practice*, pp. 168-69. Clifford Geertz, 'Person, Time and Conduct in Bali', *The Interpretation of Cultures* (New York: Basic Books, 1973), pp. 360-411 at 403-4. Maurice Bloch, 'The Past and the Present in the Present', *Man* 12 (1977): 278-92. Martin Hollis, 'Reason and Ritual', *Philosophy*, 43 (1967): 231-47, and Steven Lukes, 'Some Problems about Rationality', *Archives Européennes de Sociologie*, 8 (1967): 247-64, argue for the possibility of understanding across cultures, at least as applied to the everyday world, in somewhat similar terms. The promised revision in the social schema, attempting to make it fit the objective facts better, may of course be thwarted by powerful forces in society, as illustrated in Robin Horton, 'African Traditional Thought and Western Science', *Africa*, 37 (1967): 50-71, 155-87.

about a schema-shift. The new schema is favoured precisely because it does better what all scientific theories are meant to do—explain the facts.[25]

3.4 METAPHYSICAL TRAPS

When we are talking about reality, language can mislead us only by imperfectly mirroring it, by being too sketchy a schema. We may reasonably expect that soon to be corrected. Often, however, we are not purporting to talk about facts of the world. Some of our language— and, presumably, much of our political theory—refers instead to ideas or values. Even if we follow empiricists and positivists in denying that any such 'metaphysical' propositions can ever aspire to the status of knowledge (defined as 'true belief'), we as social scientists cannot safely ignore the fact that people hold and act upon such beliefs. What keeps our language from entrapping our scientific theory is, as has been suggested, the insistent intrusion of reality. Abstract language avoids any such check, and consequently the cage model might be an appropriate one here.[26]

25. Robert Axelrod, 'Schema Theory: An Information Processing Model of Perception and Cognition', *American Political Science Review*, 67 (1973): 1248-66. Erving Goffman, *Frame Analysis: An Essay on the Organization of Experience* (New York: Harper & Row, 1974).

26. Hollis, 'Reason and Ritual', and Lukes, 'Some Problems about Rationality', similarly distinguish between experiences in the objective world (which everyone must share and, hence, of which cross-cultural understanding is possible) and experiences unconnected with the objective world (of which cross-cultural understanding is not necessarily possible). Charles F. Hockett, in 'Chinese versus English: An Exploration of the Whorfian Theses', *Language in Culture,* ed. H. Hoijer (Chicago: University of Chicago Press for American Anthropological Association, 1954), pp. 106-23 at 123, concludes, 'The impact of inherited linguistic pattern on activities is, in general, least important in the most practical contexts, and most important in such goings-

This analysis roughly corresponds to Wittgenstein's analysis of 'forms of life'. The device was designed with reassurance in mind: its original aim was to explain how we could understand others when they talk of very private sensations, like pain and anger. The basic idea seems to be that such sensations correspond to certain aspects of reality commonly experienced by all members of the life form. Everyone knows what pain is because everyone experiences it, and there are characteristic physiological reactions (grimacing, grinding the teeth) by which one learns to recognize it in others. But, as Wittgenstein soon discovers, the argument also cuts the other way. Some (e.g., religious) concepts correspond to nothing in this world. In the memorable words of President Eisenhower, everyone exercises his inalienable right of worshipping the God of his choice. When they worship different gods, people are not experiencing a common reality, so Wittgenstein's analysis must be construed as saying that different religions must constitute different 'forms of life'.[27] Similarly, the present account maintains that language is held in check by the constraints of the reality it is used to discuss, but that creates the possibility of flights of linguistic fancy when there is no attempt to mirror reality.

Of course, no language game—indeed, no statement within a language game—is either entirely abstract or wholly realistic. Quine has demonstrated that each statement con-

---

on as story-telling, religion, and philosophising—which consist largely or exclusively of talking anyway.' See further Hanna F. Pitkin, *Wittgenstein and Justice* (Berkeley: University of California Press, 1973), Ch. 5.

27. Ludwig Wittgenstein, *Philosophical Investigations* and *Lectures and Conversations on Aesthetics, Psychology and Religious Belief*, ed. C. Barrett (Oxford: Blackwell, 1966). Applications include: A. J. Watt, 'The Intelligibility of Wants', *Mind*, 81 (1972): 553–61; Pitkin, *Wittgenstein and Justice*, Chs. 6 and 7; and Herman van Gunsteren, *The Quest for Control* (London: Wiley, 1967), Ch. 4.

tains both analytic and synthetic components, but he also concedes that some statements are relatively more analytic than others. As Quine puts the point, the

> totality of knowledge or beliefs is a man-made fabric which impinges on experience only along the edges.... Recalcitrant experience can be accommodated by any of various reevaluations in various alternative quarters of the total system; but ... our natural tendency to disturb the total system as little as possible would lead us to focus our revisions upon these specific statements. These statements are felt, therefore, to have a sharper empirical reference than highly theoretical statements.... The latter statements may be thought of as relatively centrally located within the total network, meaning that little referential connection with any particular sense data obtrudes itself.[28]

Since the cage model of linguistic traps is appropriate only where language is relatively well sheltered from experience in this way, a straightforward test of the extent to which the model is needed to explain social behaviour is the extent to which language is relatively 'abstract' in this sense of being relatively 'sheltered'.

That, clearly, is an empirical question. Some generalizations can, however, be attempted without a full-blown empirical enquiry. One is that abstractness varies from one region of discourse to another. Religious and ethical language accounts for a large proportion of this well-sheltered core of propositions. Scientific talk is on Quine's 'experiential periphery'. Political theory stands somewhere in between.

28. W. V. O. Quine, 'Two Dogmas of Empiricism', *From a Logical Point of View*, 2nd ed. (Cambridge: Harvard University Press, 1961), pp. 20–46 at 42, 44.

No language game is cast entirely in abstractions. Even the most abstract mode of social discourse—religion—invokes claims of fact at crucial points in its arguments. Christian claims about the Resurrection entail empirical claims—that the stone really did roll back, etc.—and they remain empirical claims even if we cannot prove or disprove them at this historical distance. Similarly, Gilbert Ryle demonstrates to formalistically inclined philosophers that there are some 'Systematically Misleading Expressions', expressions which are 'couched in a syntactical form improper to the facts recorded and proper to facts of quite another logical form than the facts recorded.' Reference, notice, is back to the known *facts* about the objects under discussion.[29] Political theory, it would seem, relies even more heavily than metaphysics or formal philosophy on factual claims. Thus, while forced to concede the cage model a role in political life, we must make it a minor role only.

The linguistically oppressed are in the most serious strategic dilemma yet when confronted with cage-like traps in a world of pure abstractions. The effects of linguistic deprivation are easily overcome as the model is elaborated, which is an almost inevitable consequence of its confrontation with and application to the facts of the world. In dealing with cage-like linguistic traps in the real world, the oppressed need simply find them, signpost them and turn them to mean advantage, through sarcasm or whatever. But in the world of pure abstractions, cage-like linguistic traps might well go unnoticed. The most promising strategy available to those ensnared in such traps is the search for logical inconsistencies. The objective is only partially to expose the traps, which may

29. Roger Trigg, *Reason and Commitment* (Cambridge: Cambridge University Press, 1973). Gilbert Ryle, 'Systematically Misleading Expressions', *Proceedings of the Aristotelian Society*, 32 (1931-32): 139-70.

or may not result from the application of pure reason. The more important part of the goal is the discrediting of the entire system of abstractions in which such troublesome traps are likely to lie hidden.[30]

3.5   LINGUISTIC TRAPS AS A MODE OF MANIPULATION

Three variants of linguistic trap have been identified: (1) cage-like traps in the real world; (2) cage-like traps on a metaphysical plane; and (3) linguistic deprivation. This chapter has shown that political man finds himself linguistically 'wandering in the wilderness'. The best way to keep him politically passive is to keep him in *terra incognita* by denying him the linguistic equivalent of roadmaps. So far as political stage-managers are concerned, laying cage-like linguistic traps is a strategy that, as applied to the real world, can only pay off in the very short term. As soon as the cage-like traps are discovered they will become landmarks around which— and by which—the wanderers will learn to manoeuvre. Similar cages on a metaphysical plane, in contrast, entail few such risks and can usefully supplement the linguistic deprivation strategy.

Systematizing these conclusions by reference to the checklist suggested in Section 1.6:

1. Is the interference deceptive?

In all three cases it tries to be, although in most instances it stands little chance of success.

2. Is the interference contrary to the putative will of those subject to it?

Clearly, people would be better off if they were to possess

30. Alternatively, one might press directly for a paradigm-shift. In no case does one simply wait for successive elaboration of the model to expose its shortcomings. See Herbert Marcuse, 'Repressive Tolerance', *Critique of Pure Tolerance* (Boston: Beacon Press, 1970), on this point.

and act upon a more nearly complete understanding of their world. Insofar as their perceptions (and, *ipso facto,* actions) are shaped by any form of linguistic trap, they are probably acting contrary to their putative wills.

All three varieties of linguistic trap therefore seem to satisfy the definitional requirements for manipulation captured in these first two criteria. The next two questions concern the seriousness of the manipulation practiced. Here is where the three diverge, most falling away as inconsequential.

3. How persistent is the effect of the manipulation?

Cage-like linguistic traps in the real world have a very short life expectancy. They claim to capture reality, yet they fail to do so. This failure soon becomes apparent, releasing the quarry from the traps. When pitched on a metaphysical plane, where the claims are well-insulated from empirical disconfirmation, cage-like traps might well prove long-lasting. 'How long' depends strictly upon 'how insulated'; but since no language is completely isolated in this way, even metaphysical cage-like traps must eventually give way. The duration of influence of the third type of trap—linguistic deprivation—lies somewhere between these other two. Cage-like traps in the real world, explicitly embodying false claims about empirical reality, are easily overcome through sarcasm, etc. Linguistic deprivation makes similarly false claims, but it makes them implicitly and by omission. Consequently it will take a little longer for them to be exposed. But it will nevertheless be quicker work exposing these false claims about the empirical world than it will be exposing metaphysical traps which deny any connection with empirical reality.

4. Are any distributive biases inherent in the mechanism?

Only linguistic deprivation strategies seem to display any distributive bias, in favour of the 'teaching' classes responsible for framing and communicating the categories into which others are asked to fit experience. By and large, anyone can set cage-like traps of either sort. Furthermore, once they are set anyone might benefit from them. Often trappers will be found caught in their own traps.

All told, it seems that linguistic traps pose only modest threats of political manipulation. Cage-like traps in the real world are least worrying, being neither persistent nor distributively biased in their influence. Linguistic deprivation is somewhat more troublesome, being distributively biased. But it cannot be very long lasting, so its threat is substantially mitigated. Of the three types of linguistic trap, the metaphysical cage-like trap is doubtless most dangerous on account of its potentially persistent influence. But even with respect to this variety, the threat must be discounted on the grounds that distributive bias is largely lacking.

CHAPTER FOUR ❦ RHETORICAL TRICKERY

> It is one of the principal tenets of the Utilitarians, that sentiment and eloquence serve only to impede the pursuit of truth.... The strongest arguments, when clothed in brilliant language, seem to them so much wordy nonsense.... They do not seem to know that a fallacy may lurk in a syllogism as well as in a metaphor.
>
> T. B. Macaulay[1]

ELOQUENCE HAS LONG BEEN COUNTED among the most dangerous techniques of political rule. Spellbinders from Pericles to Hitler have exerted a maniacal influence over their listeners which often qualifies as manipulatory. People are swept away by stirring words before they know what is happening to them. Whipped into a frenzy, they are not themselves: they do all sorts of things quite out of character which, in calmer moments, they come to regret. In such cases, an orator's deceptive influence has caused people to act contrary to their putative wills, and manipulation truly has occurred.

Not all rhetorical appeals are manipulative in this way. Sometimes an orator actually manipulates—deceptively 'plays on'—the emotions of his audience. But upon other occasions his listeners realize fully well what they are doing—they are self-consciously going on an emotional binge, enjoying a rousing patriotic or religious appeal without suffering any illusion whatsoever that they are hearing a rational argument. The culture of Burundi offers a case in point. There 'reliance

---

1. T. B. Macaulay, 'Mill's Essay on Government: Utilitarian Logic and Politics', *Edinburgh Review*, 97 (March 1829); reprinted in Jack Lively and John Rees, eds., *Utilitarian Logic and Politics* (Oxford: Clarendon Press, 1978), p. 100.

upon appeals to the emotions as the chief technique of
rhetoric is taken for granted as right and natural'; indeed,
such performances are particularly appreciated, since 'practical and esthetic values take precedence over logical criteria in
all but a few classes of communication situation'. In Burundi,
people enjoy their rabble-rousing, but they recognize it for
what it is. When, as in legal proceedings, a logical outcome is
deemed particularly desirable, they prohibit the flowery
speech forms which are so prevalent in their ordinary
rhetoric.² People who succumb to rhetorical appeals in consequence of this sort of conscious aesthetic preference for pretty arguments over logical ones are hardly being deceived.
Therefore they are not being manipulated in terms of the
definition offered in Chapter 1.

On a great many occasions, however, people fall for
rhetorical tricks much less self-consciously. They really *are*
tricked, and then manipulation really has occurred. Sometimes the trick works because the orator's emotional appeals
are psychologically compelling; but such phenomena would
belong to the psychological model of manipulation which I
have (for reasons offered in Section 1.5) neglected in favour
of a rationalistic account. The aim of this chapter is to show
that there is some scope for a rationalistic analysis of the force
of rhetorical appeals. I shall argue that when audiences fall
for rhetorical tricks they often do so on the (mistaken) impression that they are succumbing to a sound, logical argument. Whereas psychological interpreters regard the logical
frame of the orator's argument as providing mere *rationaliza-*

2. Ethel M. Albert, '"Rhetoric", "Logic" and "Poetics" in Burundi: Culture Patterning of Speech Behaviour', *American Anthropologist (Special Publication)*, vol. 66, no. 6, pt. 2 (1964): 35–54. We must respect these aesthetic preferences in the same way we must respect affective symbols people enjoy, as
argued in Section 5.3 below.

tion for audiences to do what they were irrationally predisposed to do by the force of his rhetoric, I shall argue that the logical force of the argument can actually provide the *reasons* (i.e., motives) for their assent. Thus, my object is to illustrate the logical underpinnings of rhetorical appeals and the implications of this model for the assessment of political rhetoric as a mechanism of manipulation.[3]

4.1 RHETORIC AS IMPLICIT ASSERTION

Historically, 'rhetoric' has the two principal associations indicated by the first two *Oxford English Dictionary* entries. The first labels it 'the art of using language so as to persuade or influence others'. Aristotelian orthodoxy has indeed accustomed us to regard rhetoric as an inferior form of logic, producing 'persuasion' rather than 'proof', 'mere belief' rather than 'certain knowledge' in Platonic terms. A second feature of 'rhetoric' is that it is associated with 'elegance or eloquence of language characterized by artificial or ostentatious expression'. Rhetoric is stylized speech, and not merely in our own culture. In Papua New Guinea, Melpa speakers use 'veiled speech' in their formal oratory. In Madagascar, one engaged in ceremonial speech is obliged to 'wind his words', an allusive manner of speaking which 'demands the speaker have a command of a large repertoire of stylistic devices': examples and comparisons, proverbs and extended metaphors drawing

3. Chaim Perelman and L. Olbrechts-Tyteca, *The New Rhetoric,* trans. John Wilkinson and Purcell Weaver (Notre Dame, Ind.: University of Notre Dame Press, 1969), treat rhetoric as a less rigorous method of rational persuasion. Rhetorical tricks are thus a sub-species of the 'fallacies' in discourse and informal argumentation surveyed by J. L. Mackie in the *Encyclopedia of Philosophy,* ed. Paul Edwards (London: Collier-Macmillan, 1968), Vol. 3: 169–79.

on 'habits of plants and animals in the local environment . . .
to allude to some corresponding human behavior'.[4]

The relationship between these two features of rhetorical
language is ordinarily thought to be an emotive one. Stylistic
ornamentation makes an argument more appealing, and
hence more persuasive, although strictly speaking it does
nothing to alter its logical status. Here I hope to focus on a
less illogical aspect of the link between persuasion and 'veiled'
speech. The thrust of my thesis is that, through veiled speech,
one implicitly advocates propositions which might be accepted in that form which would be rejected had they been
put explicitly. The essence of rhetorical strategy as a logical
trick, then, is to 'smuggle in the goods' in one way or another.

4.1.1   *Hidden Presuppositions*

Consider the case of the 'rhetorical question'. It 'does not
require an answer, but is only put in the form of a question to
produce a more striking effect'. Once again, the *Oxford English Dictionary* entry suggests that the purpose is simply stylistic variation. But to a large extent this question-begging
typifies the *logical* underpinnings of the strategy of rhetorical
deception.

Often what is actually asserted is less debatable—and less
important—than what is *presupposed* by an assertion. Some
proposition *A* is said to presuppose another proposition *B* if

4. Aristotle, *Rhetoric*. Plato, *Gorgias*, 454–55. Andrew Strathern, 'Veiled
Speech in Mount Hagen' and Elinor Keenan, 'A Sliding Sense of Obligatori-
ness: The Polystructure of Malagasy Oratory', *Political Language and Oratory
in Traditional Society*, ed. Maurice Bloch (London: Academic Press, 1975), pp.
185–204 and 93–112 respectively. Similarly, 'crooked speech' is required
among the Ilongot of the Philippines according to Michelle Rosaldo, 'I Have
Nothing to Hide: The Language of Ilongot Oratory', *Language in Society*, 2
(1973): 193–223. Donald Brenneis, 'The Matter of Talk: Political Performances in Bhatgaon', *Language in Society*, 7 (1978): 159–70, also refers to the
preference for 'veiled talk' in certain situations.

and only if, in order for A to be either true or false, B must be true. Thus, the proposition 'Kepler died in misery' presupposes that 'Kepler died'; and the proposition that 'he who discovered the elliptic form of the planetary orbits died in misery' presupposes that 'someone first discovered the elliptic form of the planetary orbits'. If the first statement in each pair is asserted to be a true proposition, then that entails the truth of propositions that are presupposed. But the structure of the argument diverts attention away from the presuppositions and focuses it instead on the propositions which are being explicitly advocated. Sir George Cornewall Lewis, writing in 1832, remarks, 'It sometimes happens that people are satisfied of the truth of doctrines to which they were led by steps which they have forgotten;—that they believe the conclusion without remembering the premises.' In our own day, this principle has become the centrepiece of Herbert Marcuse's analysis of 'The Closing of the Universe of Discourse':

> the structure of the sentence is abridged and condensed in such a way that no tension, no 'space' is left between the parts of the sentence.... The word becomes *cliché* and, as *cliché*, governs the speech or the writing.... The analytic structure insulates the governing noun from those of its contents which would invalidate or at least disturb the accepted use of the noun in statements of policy and public opinion. The ritualized concept is made immune against contradiction.[5]

5. Herbert Marcuse, *One-Dimensional Man* (Boston: Beacon Press, 1964), pp. 86–88. George Cornewall Lewis, *Remarks on the Use and Abuse of Some Political Terms* (London: B. Fellowes, 1832), p. xxix. On the nature of 'presupposition' see: P. F. Strawson, *Introduction to Logical Theory* (London: Methuen, 1952), pp. 175–79; Max Black, 'Presupposition and Implication', *Models and Metaphors* (Ithaca: Cornell University Press, 1962), pp. 48–63; and J. L. Austin, *How to Do Things With Words* (Oxford: Clarendon Press, 1962), Lecture 4.

Explanations, whether of natural or social phenomena, usually take a highly elliptical form tending to bury many presuppositions in just this way. Asked why the house burned down, the fire marshal reports that the wiring was faulty. For him to detail all the other conditions with which that combined to constitute a sufficient condition of the fire—that it was a live wire, that the house was built of combustible materials, that the atmosphere contained sufficient oxygen to sustain the fire, etc.—would rightly be regarded as pedantic. Similarly, when the medical examiner explains a death by saying 'he had a heart attack', or the social historian the bread riots by saying 'they were hungry', there are many suppressed premises.[6] Asserting the truth of the explanation, of course, commits them to also asserting the truth of the presuppositions. But such assumptions typically go unexamined in discourse on all levels, ranging from the rigorously scientific to the casually practical.

This is, however, not simply an oversight. Instead, it is a necessary consequence of the way in which we fix our arguments in larger patterns of meaning (Wittgenstein's 'forms of life', or whatever) which carry with them various presuppositions, commitments and implications. This result is inherent even in the nature of deductive theory, against which the 'form of life' argument tends to rebel. Any such system needs some axioms, some unexamined principles taken as given, to serve as the foundation for the rest of the deductive system. This is true of scientific explanations of natural facts cast in a hypothetico-deductive mode. It is especially true of artificial systems of social rules. Within the logic of the normative system, any rule can only be justified in terms of some other higher-order rule. Unless the process is to lead to infinite re-

6. Carl G. Hempel, *Aspects of Scientific Explanation* (New York: Free Press, 1965).

gress or circularity (with rules justifying and being justified by each other in turn), the whole system must ultimately be based upon some *Grundnorm* which itself cannot be justified in terms internal to the system of rules. Thus, every time a mathematician uses Euclidean geometry, or a judge or bureaucrat says he is 'merely following the rules', he is implicitly asking us to assume premises for which he does not (and cannot) argue. Yet there is nothing fallacious, strictly speaking, about their appeal—'like arguments of a madman, they were correct and conclusive, if certain premises or principles were granted.'[7]

The need to gain assent for unspoken premises goes far toward explaining why orators must tailor their arguments to their audiences. This requirement of good rhetoric has long been recognized. Aristotle advises, 'Whatever the quality an audience esteems, the speaker must attribute that quality to the object of his praise....'; Vico agrees that the speaker 'must govern his speech in accordance with their opinions'; and the need for a fit between speaker and audience forms the basis for Perelman and Olbrechts-Tyteca's 'new rhetoric'.[8] Often this practice is thought advisable on grounds of individual psychology: the power of rhetorical persuasion is seen to be essentially akin to the (irrational) power of flattery. But now we can see important logical reasons that the argument must be tailored to the audience. Rhetorical arguments are crucially incomplete, requiring presuppositions which cannot

7. Lewis, *Use and Abuse of Political Terms,* vi. The *Grundnorm* approach, developed by Hans Kelsen, *General Theory of Law and State,* trans. Anders Wedberg (Cambridge: Harvard University Press, 1945), and H. L. A. Hart, *Concept of Law* (Oxford: Clarendon Press, 1961), Ch. 6, is rejected by Herman van Gunsteren, *Quest for Control* (London: Wiley, 1976), Ch. 4, in favour of a 'form of life' analysis.

8. Aristotle, *Rhetoric,* 1367b. Perelman and Olbrechts-Tyteca, *New Rhetoric,* pp. 5 and 23 (quoting Vico). See further Richard Whately, *Elements of Rhetoric,* 7th ed. (London: Parker, 1846), Pt. 2, Ch. 3, and Plato, *Gorgias* and *Menexenus,* 235d, calling rhetoric 'flattery'.

be established logically. Hence, the need to gain implicit assent to presuppositions makes it important for a rhetorical argument to play on the prejudices of an audience.

In everyday discourse, political rhetoric hides its premises in a variety of ways. One method is illustrated by the action of Americans renaming the old War Department the 'Department of Defense'. Of course, defence presupposes a threat—one can only defend *against* something. The implicit assertion is that someone is threatening the nation, but by being implicit, this assertion escapes the questioning it deserves. Similarly, advocating 'training programmes' (such as the Job Corps) for the unemployed presupposes that jobs are going begging for skilled labourers. The implicit assertion is that the cause of unemployment is lack of skills rather than any structural flaw in the economic system. Urging automobile drivers to 'Drive Safely' presupposes that human error is the cause of traffic mishaps. The implicit assertion is that the fault lies with operators rather than manufacturers of automobiles which are 'unsafe at any speed'.[9] The civil rights demand for 'freedom now' presupposes that there are oppressors, and the Berkeley demand for 'free speech' that some would deny it. In each of these cases, the explicit assertion presupposes various implicit ones—it can be true only if its presuppositions are—but the structure of the rhetorical appeal diverts attention from the question of the truth of these hidden premises. It encourages us to presuppose what, logically, we should be concerned to prove.

For a more sustained example of rhetoric as logical trickery, consider the American Declaration of Independence. Jefferson's purpose was to justify the colonies in separating from Great Britain, his strategy to argue that 'the colonists

9. Murray Edelman, *Political Language* (New York: Academic Press, 1977), pp. 16–17, 35.

were not rebels against established authority but rather a free
people maintaining long established and imprescriptible
rights against an usurping king'. Logically, the major premise
of the argument was that 'every "people" has a natural right
to make and unmake its own government', the minor premise
being that 'the Americans are a "people" in this sense'. Having
sketched the logical structure of the Declaration's argument
in this way, the noted American historian Carl Becker explains,

> The minor premise of the argument is easily overlooked
> because it is not explicitly stated in the Declaration. . . .
> To have stated it explicitly would perhaps have been to
> bring into too glaring a light certain incongruities be-
> tween the assumed premise and known historical facts.
> The role of the list of grievances against the king is to
> make the assumed premise emerge, of its own accord as it
> were, from a carefully formulated but apparently
> straightforward statement of concrete historical facts.[10]

4.1.2 Hidden Implications

Besides hidden premises, rhetoric also makes great play of
hidden implications. These are typically not implications in
the strong sense of logical entailment—they are not just conclusions of an argument which, though inescapable, one does
not spell out in their entirety. Were they, we would have no
reason for protesting them: if the argument for the explicit
proposition is a valid and compelling one, then that argument
also guarantees the truth of all the propositions (implicit or
otherwise) which are logically entailed by it. Rhetorical trickery is instead associated with 'implications' in the sense of

10. 'The Literary Qualities of the Declaration', *The Rhetoric of Speech*, ed.
Haig A. Bosmajian (Boston: D.C. Heath, 1967), pp. 132-47 at 138.

'insinuations' or 'oblique hints'. The connection is not one of logical entailment but rather of 'traditional association'.[11] The 'halo effect' still exists. 'Associated' propositions continue to bask in the reflected respectability of others with which they are linked and for which good reasons have been offered. But in the weaker case of extra-logical implication, the 'halo effect' is entirely unjustified, for there is no reason to see the propositions as being linked at all.

Sir George Cornewall Lewis, in his *Remarks on the Use and Abuse of Some Political Terms,* long ago exposed the mischief caused by sliding between distinct and logically unrelated senses of political words. The word 'right', for instance, can be used either as an adjective or as a noun. These are distinct notions and, as Lewis emphasizes, it is fallacious to slide between the two:

> *a* right may be *right* or *wrong, (i.e.* a claim given by law may be just or unjust, politic, or impolitic,) in the judgment of different persons. The necessity of a legislative sovereignty, or of a power of altering old and enacting new laws, is entirely founded on the supposition that *rights* may be wrong. . . . If the different senses of *right,* just pointed out, really coincided; that is, if all claims founded on justice and sound policy were legal rights, and all legal rights were founded on justice and sound policy, there would be no necessity for deliberative assemblies or legislative enactments, and the whole business of government might be confined to the administration of existing laws.

Among those misled by these hidden and logically groundless implications in the dual use of the word 'right' Lewis numbers

11. Black, *Models and Metaphors,* pp. 48–63, and Austin, *How to Do Things with Words,* Lecture 4.

Blackstone himself. In the *Commentaries* Blackstone defines 'municipal law' as 'a rule of civil conduct prescribed by the supreme power in a state, *commanding what is right, and prohibiting what is wrong.*' Justifying this definition, Blackstone fallaciously slides between the adjectival and the nounal 'right':

> it is first of all necessary that the boundaries of *right* and *wrong* [adjectival] be established and ascertained by law. And when this is once done, it will *follow of course* that it is likewise the business of the law, considered as a rule of civil conduct, to enforce *these rights* [nounal], and to restrain or redress these *wrongs*.[12]

Often the deceptions owing to a rhetorical slide between different and logically unrelated senses of an ambiguous term are unintentional. As Lewis allows, those committing such fallacies 'generally share in some degree in the delusions which they propagate'.[13] Euphemism is probably a more significant mechanism for intentionally smuggling hidden implications into an argument. For example, when classifying certain citizens as 'needy' (of income, education, physical or mental health, etc.) and charging public agencies with the task of 'helping' them, we are not just calling for provision of certain services. Implicit is also the suggestion that these are inadequate or inferior individuals who might reasonably be treated as children in many ways and that 'helpers' are clearly in a better position to know how to run their lives than the people themselves. The implication is, of course, logically unjustifiable. But the insinuation is inevitable.[14]

Hiding the implications of arguments is crucial because, as Orwell observes, 'In our time, political speech and writing are

12. Lewis, *Use and Abuse of Political Terms*, pp. 11–13, quoting Sir William Blackstone, *Commentaries on the Laws of England*, 1: 44, 53.
13. Ibid., p. xvi.
14. Edelman, *Political Language*, Ch. 4.

largely the defence of the indefensible.' By obscuring the full effects of the course of action we advocate, euphemisms help us gain assent to these policies nevertheless:

> Defenceless villages are bombarded from the air, the inhabitants driven out into the countryside, the cattle machine-gunned, the huts set on fire with incendiary bullets: this is called *pacification*. Millions of peasants are robbed of their farms and sent trudging along the roads with no more than they can carry: this is called *transfer of population* or *rectification of frontiers*. People are imprisoned for years without trial, or shot in the back of the neck or sent to die of scurvy in Arctic lumber camps: this is called *elimination of unreliable elements*.[15]

With these euphemisms to hide the true implications of the policies, political rhetoric can justify the unjustifiable.

American experience in Vietnam provides an excellent example. As Senator Fulbright rightly complained in 1966 hearings, 'When Chinese soldiers are described . . . as "hordes of Chinese coolies", it is clear that they are being thought of not as people but as something terrifying and abstract, or as something inanimate like the flow of lava from a volcano.' The 'technological' language policy-makers used to describe 'escalation', 'pacification', 'interdiction', etc. also served to obscure responsibilities for immoralities.

> The rhetoric is characterized by a sense of inevitability, principally because it changes verbs into nouns, so that action seems to exist independently, prior to a decision to act. A decision is made to increase firepower and man-

15. George Orwell, 'Politics and the English Language', *Collected Essays, Journalism and Letters* (New York: Harcourt, Brace & World, 1968), 4: 127–40 at 136.

power against a target: *we* hear that the war has been 'escalated' by a 'phase-up' in action. The use of the passive voice further obscures the fact that anybody has done anything.[16]

4.1.3   *Hidden Co-optation*

An important aspect of appealing to audience prejudices is the orator's claim to share their perspective. Typical stylistic devices for producing this result are simple and unsubtle instances of playing on hidden implications of a certain way of talking. The 'language of participation' in general, and the word 'we' in particular, figure importantly in this process. Use of the first person plural implies a unity between the speaker and his audience that is typically a fraud.[17] But this is really a rather clumsy trick. The implication does not seem to be at all well hidden. To explain why the trick works, the larger strategy of rhetorical appeals must be examined more closely.

The role of metaphor in rhetoric requires careful consideration. Writers from Aristotle to I. A. Richards have recognized how thick rhetoric is with metaphorical allusions and how different metaphors are from similes or straightforward comparisons, 'the resemblance being in that [latter] case stated, which in the Metaphor is implied'. The effect is that the listener must actively participate, making the connections for himself. This is hardly a mechanical process. It is not just a matter of substituting some fixed literal meaning for a metaphorical reference. Rather, it is a creative process of ex-

16. Kenneth R. Johnson, 'The Rhetoric Surrounding the Vietnamese War', mimeographed (Department of English, Indiana University, 1967), p. 8. J. William Fulbright. 'The United States and China', *Congressional Record*, 7 March 1966, p. 4938.

17. Edelman, *Political Language*, Ch. 7. Herbert Spiegelberg, 'The Right to Say "We"', *Phenomenological Sociology*, ed. George Psathas (New York: Wiley, 1973), pp. 129–58.

ploring the wide range of associations of the principal and
subsidiary subjects of the metaphor for possible points of
comparison, and these can be discovered only through (sometimes large) leaps of imagination.[18]

In this way rhetorical metaphors 'engage' the listener, requiring him to do much of the work filling in the details of the
argument. This is sometimes said to explain the psychological
power of rhetorical appeals: the listener comes to share com-
plicitly for the argument; it ceases to be the speaker's case
alone, and in some important respects has become his own as
well. Archbishop Whately, for example, advises orators that
'all men are more gratified at catching the Resemblance for
themselves, than at having it pointed out to them'.[19] This,
however, just points to an emotional truism, *viz.*, that people
are more attached to arguments they regard as their own.
The practice is obviously irrational—logically one must
evaluate arguments according to their merits, even if they are
one's own arguments—so this explanation of rhetorical co-
optation seems to point to a psychological rather than rational
model of manipulation.

With only a slight twist, this classically psychological explanation of the power of rhetorical metaphor to co-opt can
be explained in rational terms. By obliging the listener to devote more time and attention merely to decoding the message
and inferring the speaker's meaning, rhetorical metaphors
divert the energies of the listener. Resources he might have
spent on critical appraisal of the speaker's thesis, had it been
clear and straightforward, must instead be devoted to teasing
it out of the thick metaphorical overlays. Thus the strategy of

18. Aristotle, *Rhetoric*, Book 3, and *Poetics*. I. A. Richards, *The Philosophy
of Rhetoric* (New York: Oxford University Press, 1965), Lectures 5 and 6.
Whately, *Elements of Rhetoric*, Pt. 3, Ch. 2, Sec. 3. Black, 'Metaphor', *Models
and Metaphors*, Ch. 3.
19. Whately, *Elements of Rhetoric*, Pt. 3, Ch. 2, Sec. 3.

employing elaborately metaphorical rhetoric is strictly analogous to that of keeping secrets as discussed in Chapter 2. Both rely on the logic that the more people are forced to invest in discovering trivial details (obscured by metaphors in the one case or secrecy in the other) the less they will have left for making more damaging discoveries.

Another more powerful way in which metaphorical language co-opts people is by drawing them into a system of shared meanings. This is not to embrace the phenomenological position that language is all there is. On the contrary, Chapter 3 has argued that there *is* an external reality which language—political language included—often attempts to mirror. But, as Eugene Miller so persuasively argues, political language typically points to unobservables. Under such conditions, language cannot act as a simple cipher. There can be no one-to-one correspondence between the things of the world and linguistic entities. Metaphor is required: we come to understand unobservable features of our political world by analogy to observable features of our natural world; and we interact one with another on the basis of the shared understandings about our social and political worlds embodied in our shared stock of metaphors, analogies, clichés, etc. Dominant metaphors thus constitute a shared social schema which is crucial for social interaction, as discussed in Sections 3.3 and 6.1.3. Rhetoric both evokes and establishes this shared stock of metaphors, and is therefore both powerful and indispensable in shaping social experiences.[20]

The metaphors of political rhetoric might for these reasons seem to be powerful sources of political manipulation. Not only are they strong and unavoidable; they also point to 'unobservables' in ways rather reminiscent of metaphysical

20. Eugene F. Miller, 'Metaphor and Political Knowledge', *American Political Science Review*, 73 (1979): 155–70.

linguistic traps, shown in Section 3.4 to be dangerous indeed. The vital difference, however, lies in how well the two are sheltered from empirical disconfirmation. Neither metaphysical linguistic traps nor rhetorical metaphors lie on the 'experiential periphery' of a system of beliefs. But whereas metaphysical propositions lie near the core, and are only very occasionally threatened by disconfirming experiences, rhetorical metaphors lie near the surface. This is why we can so often say that metaphors are inappropriate, analogies are misleading, etc. Reality constrains our political metaphors, at least to some degree, making them a much less pliable (and hence much less threatening) tool for political manipulation.

4.2   OVERCOMING RHETORICAL TRICKS

On the orthodox model, rhetorical tricks are thought to appeal directly to the emotions, their quasi-logical form merely masking their *real* appeal. Were this the case, warnings would do no good. Knowing about the 'bandwagon' or 'big lie' techniques, for example, we would fall for them nonetheless—we could not help ourselves. Exposing logical fallacies does nothing to undermine the power of rhetoric if its basis lies outside reason. Some more serious form of therapy would be required. Thus, on the emotive model rhetorical trickery is a relatively strong source of power.

This conclusion, however, follows only from a model of rhetoric as psychological manipulation. Here I have argued that rhetoric instead misleads people who are sincerely trying to be rational, for whom the misleading arguments constitute reasons rather than rationalizations for their actions. Insofar as this is an accurate account, rhetorical manipulation is more easily overcome by simple exposure of the tricks involved.

Authors of diverse philosophical inclinations have indeed expressed faith in such a remedy. Bentham, for example, sets

great store by 'the faculty which detection has of divesting
deception of her power'. As a method of overcoming 'political
fallacies', he recommends that 'in the printed records of debates of legislative assemblies, their editor might well point
out instances of the use of these fallacies'. Bentham even fan-
tasizes that eventually legislators will learn to shout down any
of their number attempting such deceptions. The presumption that exposure deprives rhetorical tricks of their power is
nowise peculiar to philosophic radicals. Archbishop Whately
relies on the same proposition for his defence of the study of
rhetoric: 'The better acquainted one is with any kind of
rhetorical trick, the less liable he is to be misled by it. The
Artifices . . . of the Orator are,

> . . . like tricks by sleight of hand
> which, to admire, one should not understand: . . .

This is indeed one great recommendation of the study of
Rhetoric, that it furnishes the most effectual antidote against
deception of this kind.'[21]

Nothing here suggests that, in any given case, exposing

21. Jeremy Bentham, *Handbook of Political Fallacies,* ed. Harold A. Lar-
rabee (Baltimore: Johns Hopkins Press, 1952), Pt. 5, Ch. 10; cf. Orwell, 'Politics and the English Language', p. 141, remarking that 'from time to time one
can even, if one jeers loudly enough, send some worn-out and useless
phrase . . . into the dustbin where it belongs'. Whately, *Elements of Rhetoric,* p.
xl. Douglas H. Parker, 'Rhetoric, Ethics and Manipulation', *Philosophy and
Rhetoric,* 5 (1972): 69–87 at 73, writes similarly, 'I hail with enthusiasm Perelman's and Olbrechts-Tyteca's call for inclusion of the "new rhetoric" in every
man's humanistic education. This would permit a use of rhetoric that invites
weighing and evaluation of the proposition asserted while at the same time
willingly exposing and drawing attention to the technique and form employed in its presentation.' Lewis, in *Use and Abuse of Political Terms,* p. xviii,
remarks, 'There is no instrument so powerful as an accurate knowledge, and
a watchful observance of the different use of words. This often affords the
master-key which discloses the whole mystery.'

rhetorical tricks will be easy. Hidden premises and implications are typically well hidden. Of 'question-begging epithets' Bentham complains, 'The potency of this instrument of deception is most deplorable. It is only in recent years that its nature has been exposed, and the need and the extreme difficulty of such exposure have been equally made manifest.'[22] The argument here is not that the task will be easy but rather that it is possible. The point is that, if accomplished, exposure suffices to undercut the power of rhetorical trickery and that more difficult measures still (like psychological therapy) will not be required.

Furthermore, if finding and exposing rhetorical tricks is a problem, it is one that manipulators are likely to share. The 'interconnectedness of deception and self-deception' discussed in Section 2.5 reappears, this time in the form of politicians falling for their own rhetorical tricks. Narcissism—the tendency of politicians to fall in love with their own voices—is partly to blame. But the phenomenon is not altogether psychological. Politicians often forget, if ever they knew, what implications and presuppositions lie hidden in the rhetoric they ritualistically repeat. 'Not even those who *know* the ambiguity of a term are always proof against the confusion it tends to generate', Lewis complains. Vietnamese war rhetoric again proves illustrative. Top decision-makers 'did not translate their actions into these words' of technological inevitability—'escalation', 'interdiction', 'phase-up' and the like. Rather, 'this is the language they speak, creating for themselves and for us a sense of inevitable, *un*deliberate advance along a predetermined and inflexible course of action.'[23]

22. Bentham, *Handbook of Political Fallacies*, Pt. 4, Ch. 1.
23. Lewis, *Use and Abuse of Political Terms*, pp. vii–ix. Johnson, 'The Rhetoric Surrounding the Vietnamese War', p. 8.

4.3   THE DISTRIBUTION OF RHETORICAL POWER

Before considering the distribution of rhetorical power, it is important to notice what reliance upon rhetoric as a technique of rule itself implies about the distribution of social power within the society. Entrenched elites, secure in their positions of power, have little need for logical trickery to underwrite their rule. Straightforward orders are far more their style than the 'veiled' speech characteristically found in rhetorical appeals. A study of the changing oratorical styles among the Ilongot of the Philippines confirms suspicions that

> allusive styles . . . emerge in a social order based more on persuasion than compulsion. So for the Ilongots, 'crooked' speech has been linked to an egalitarian ethos; and the new 'straight' or direct kind of oratory is associated, not simply with Christianity, but with a . . . new, and increasingly authoritarian, idea of social life.[24]

Thus, use of rhetorical techniques itself implies a rather pluralistic power structure.

Still, rhetorical trickery is a mode of manipulation, and as such it is *prima facie* immoral. But it would be even more so were these opportunities narrowly available only to certain individuals or certain classes. There are two aspects to this question of how rhetorical power is distributed. First is the matter of who has the power to *use* the tricks. Second is the matter of who has the power to *expose* (and, by exposing, destroy) the tricks. Bias in the first respect is clearly less serious than bias in the second. If only certain groups can use the tricks but anyone can expose them, then there is no net long-term bias. But if anyone can use the tricks while only certain groups can expose them, a real possibility of persistent bias

24. Rosaldo, 'I Have Nothing to Hide', p. 195.

emerges: those enjoying a monopoly of power of exposure can allow those tricks working to their benefit and challenge only those working against their interests.

4.3.1   *The Distribution of Power to Use Rhetorical Tricks*

In ordinary interlocutions, one speaks and is spoken to in turn. Consequently, all the tricks available to one person will, in due course, fall available to the other. The natural reciprocity built into the speech act thus provides all interlocutors with incentives (which will typically prove rationally compelling) for honest and forthright dealings. In rhetorical harangues, this natural reciprocity is missing. These are by nature one-way exercises of power: an orator addresses an audience; his listeners have little if any opportunity to respond. Whereas the possibility of 'turning the tables' is inherent in interlocutions, the nature of the rhetorical situation virtually precludes this possibility, at least in any immediate sense.[25] In the short term, rhetorical power accrues to whomsoever holds the floor and to him exclusively.

Over the long run, it might be the case that everyone has

25. On ordinary interlocutions, see: J. G. A. Pocock, *Politics, Language and Time* (New York: Atheneum, 1971), and 'Verbalizing a Political Act', *Political Theory*, 1 (1973): 27-45; and Knut Midgaard, 'On the Significance of Language and a Richer Concept of Rationality', Quincentennial Symposium on 'Politics as Rational Action', Department of Government Skytteanum, Uppsala University, September 1977. On rhetorical situations, notice the remarks of Perelman and Olbrechts-Tyteca, *New Rhetoric*, p. 55: 'The person who takes the initiative in a debate is comparable to an aggressor.... Any society prizing its own values is therefore bound to promote opportunities for epidictic speeches to be delivered at regular intervals: ceremonies commemorating past events of national concern, religious services, eulogies of the dead, and similar manifestations fostering a communion of minds. The more the leaders of the group seek to increase their hold over its members' thought, the more numerous will be the meetings of an educational character, and some will go as far as to use threats or compulsion to make recalcitrants expose themselves to speeches that will impregnate them with the values held by the community.'

an equal chance to avail himself of the same rhetorical tricks, i.e., that everyone enjoys the same oratorical opportunities. Any such claim is implausible on its face, for as we well know access to the podium almost always seems to be restricted. Formal criteria of age, sex and social standing used by traditional societies to determine who may declaim from the speaking ground are only exaggerated forms of practices widespread throughout the 'civilized' world as well. First appearances may, however, prove deceptive. For one thing, rhetorical power is rarely as unbalanced as formal rules suggest. This is true even of traditional societies, where one would expect the rules to be enforced most rigorously. Although Maori women are usually not allowed to participate formally in rhetorical exchanges, the old women especially are respected judges of speeches and an orator's reputation is largely shaped by their reactions. 'If the speech is boring, they chatter among themselves, and when they decide that it has gone on long enough, an old woman related to the speaker may start up his *waiata* (final song), bringing his oration to a forced conclusion'.[26]

Furthermore, the formal rules can at most limit access to established channels of communication. An aspiring orator banned from the formal avenues might use informal ones instead. Keeping someone off the podium need not silence him—there are always street corners and soapboxes, and many important social movements have been inspired by ora-

26. Perelman and Olbrechts-Tyteca, *New Rhetoric*, p. 55, for example, suppose that 'group leaders will regard any attack on the officially recognized values as a revolutionary act, and, by the use of such measures as censorship, an index, and control over all means of communicating ideas, they will try to make it difficult, if not impossible, for their opponents to achieve the conditions preliminary to any argumentation'. But contrast this with the description of Maori practices in Anne Salmond, 'Mana Makes the Man: A Look at Maori Oratory and Politics', *Political Language and Oratory in Traditional Society*, ed. Bloch, pp. 45–63 at 57.

tions in such settings. The functioning of rhetorical tricks is, significantly, unaffected by the setting. Were the trick a psychological one, the loss of trappings of respectability might be a serious blow to the possibility of success. But the logical trick (of hiding premises and implications behind more agreeable arguments) works the same anywhere.

Dissident groups can derive special advantage from rhetorical tricks for hiding one's meaning. For those holding proscribed opinions, allusion is the safest method of communication. The Underground in France during World War II developed an elaborate system of code words and hidden meanings by which they could communicate news and opinions. Factions within the Soviet hierarchy have been shown to use 'veiled speech' similarly. Or, again, American slaves developed a linguistic code which 'throve on ambiguity and *double-entendre* and passed into para-language'. To describe the times of slavery, freedmen tended to say 'endurin' slavery' instead of 'during slavery', for example. Through such devices,

> slaves, in effect, learned to communicate with each other in the presence of whites with some measure of safety, and the studied ambiguity of their speech . . . helped immeasurably to prevent informers from having too much to convey to the masters beyond impressions and suspicions. If a slave informer heard a black preacher praise a runaway by calling him a '*ba-ad* nigger', what could he tell his master beyond saying he thought the preacher meant the opposite of what he had said? Even slaveholders usually required better evidence.[27]

27. Hans Speier, 'The Communication of Hidden Meaning', *Social Research*, 44 (1977): 471–501. Myron Rush, 'Esoteric Communication in Soviet Politics', *World Politics*, 11 (1959): 614–20. Eugene D. Genovese, *Roll Jordan Roll* (New York: Random House, 1974), pp. 436–37.

Rhetorical tricks for implicit argumentation are therefore peculiarly useful to oppressed groups. They must hide their meaning if they are to express it at all, whereas ordinary elites use such rhetorical tricks only to seduce listeners into occasional fallacies. Surely this more than counterbalances any distributive bias in favour of traditional elites owing to their easy access to established channels of communication.

4.3.2 *The Distribution of Power to Expose Rhetorical Tricks*

In order to describe how the power of exposing (and thereby undermining) rhetorical tricks is distributed, it is important first to describe how the mechanism works to deprive the tricks of their power. Were it necessary for such tricks to be denounced authoritatively for them to lose their strength, then the distribution of power to expose rhetorical tricks would be as biased as is the distribution of the privilege of making authoritative pronouncements. This, however, is simply an implausible account of how rhetorical tricks fall into disrepute. Whereas it is necessary to gain access to the podium in some sense to perpetrate rhetorical tricks, it is possible to expose and repudiate them from the floor. Bentham's scenario runs as follows: 'Any legislator anywhere who is so far off his guard as . . . to let drop any of these irrelevant and deceptious arguments will be greeted . . . with voices in scores crying aloud, "Stale! Stale! Fallacy of Authority! Fallacy of Distrust!" and so on.'[28] Since shouts from the audience—or quiet asides to one's neighbours—suffice to undermine rhetorical tricks, the distribution of access to established channels of communication is irrelevant to the distribution of power to expose rhetorical fallacies.

The comments introducing this Section 4.3 suggest that such a relatively even spread of power to expose rhetorical trickery goes far toward neutralizing any bias in the distribu-

28. Bentham, *Handbook of Political Fallacies,* Bk. 5, Ch. 10.

tion of power to employ such tricks. In practice, however, it must be conceded that this is unlikely to provide a complete antidote. Even if there is always the possibility of anyone exposing the fallacies, there is never a guarantee that someone will do so or that this will happen immediately. Some tricks may pass entirely unnoticed, and others may be exposed only after the passage of considerable time. This possible slippage tempts 'those shameless imposters, who seek only to produce an immediate effect without caring for subsequent detection: like the passers of bad money, to whom it is indifferent how soon the fraud is discovered, so that they escape with their dishonest gains.'[29] Thus, while the relatively uniform distribution of power to expose rhetorical tricks goes far toward correcting any biases in the power to use such tricks, it does not necessarily go all the way.

4.4   RHETORICAL EXCESSES AND THE DEBASEMENT OF POLITICAL LANGUAGE

The last chapter and the previous section argue that linguistic and rhetorical tricks respectively are, by and large, equally accessible to all. This makes them important mechanisms by which oppressed groups might challenge the hold of entrenched elites, which are at a distinct advantage with respect to other forms of social power. Given this fact, it should be clear that anything tending to undermine language itself as a political tool will have distributive biases: it will work in favour of established elites, who have plenty of other ways of getting what they want; and it will work against oppressed groups enjoying few if any other opportunities.

Rhetoric lends itself especially well to this task of debasing language. The elaborate metaphors and other stylistic affecta-

29. Lewis, *Use and Abuse of Political Terms,* p. xxi.

tions commonly associated with rhetoric are hardly incidental adornment. They are essential given the nature of the enterprise; they are necessary tools for burying premises and implications of an argument and for co-opting a listener. But, by requiring such ornamentation, rhetoric virtually invites hyperbole. These rhetorical excesses, by debasing political language altogether, work to the disadvantage of oppressed classes with few power resources other than the linguistic ones being undermined.

Ironically, rhetorical excesses often come from the very radicals against whom the consequent debasement of political language is sure to rebound. Wendell Phillips, the great American agitator for the abolition of slavery, voices the common view:

> The scholar may sit in his study and take care that his language is not exaggerated, but the rude mass of men is ... caught by men whose words are half battles. From Luther down, the charge against every reformer has been that his language is too rough. Be it so. Rough instruments are used for rough work.[30]

This is doubly in error. On the benefit side, Phillips and similarly inclined radical orators expect the gains they do because they harbour an essentially psychological model of the power of rhetoric. Here a logical understructure has been found for

30. Quoted in Ralph Korngold, *Two Friends of Man* (Boston: Little Brown, 1950), pp. 182–83. Debasement of language is a favourite theme of George Steiner, developed in *Language and Silence* (New York: Atheneum, 1967), pp. 132 ff., *In Bluebeard's Castle* (London: Faber & Faber, 1971), pp. 88 ff., and *After Babel* (London: Oxford University Press, 1975). My treatment here draws particularly upon conversations with John Pocock, whose 1976 lectures on 'Political Thought and Political Methodology' at the University of Maryland discussed 'anti-languages' as revolutionary political strategies doomed to backfire.

it instead, and in those terms it is far from clear how exaggerated phrases can boost the rhetorical force of an argument. On the cost side, Phillips fails to notice the distributive implications of debasing political language as such through the rhetorical excesses he advocates. In the long run, the very groups he hopes to benefit will be most hurt by the strategy he has chosen.

Insofar as political language is debased by the rhetorical excesses of radicals, then, the result would be better described as a mistake than as an instance of manipulation. But to a large extent the debasement of language is not caused by radicals at all but instead by the very groups whose interests it would serve. This clearly *can* count as manipulation. Bureaucrats are especially notorious for promulgating elaborate nonsense purporting to explain and justify their edicts. If their practice of speaking in code, discussed in Section 3.2 as a form of linguistic deprivation, corresponds to the strategy of withholding information (Section 2.3.1), 'gobbledygook' parallels the much more effective strategy of information overload (Section 2.5). Bureaucrats have very clear motives for engaging in this manipulation. Not only are they servants of elites who benefit from debasement of public language generally. They also have their own very special institutional interests in obscuring the real reasons for their decisions. By discouraging public debate of their actions, bureaucrats encourage the public (elites and non-elites alike) to leave them alone to carry on just as they please. This was clearly the goal of the government of the Pearce Commission: the whole point of the complex prose, particularly when directed at African populations only marginally familiar with English in its simplest form, was to stifle further discussion rather than to encourage it. Bureaucratic prose, however, is not merely complex. Worse, it is typically imprecise and often flatly inconsistent. Marcuse perceptively discusses how contradiction, 'once considered the principal offense against logic', has now become 'a principle of the logic of manipulation'. Through it, manipulative technocrats make their discourse 'immune against the expression of protest and refusal':

> How can such protest and refusal find the right word when the organs of the established order admit and advertise that peace is really the brink of war, that the ultimate weapons carry their profitable price tags, and that the bomb shelter may spell coziness? In exhibiting its contradictions as the token of its truth, this universe of discourse closes itself against any other discourse which is not on its own terms.[31]

To some extent, perhaps, bureaucrats too debase political language accidentally. Insofar as they realize what they are doing, however, their actions certainly count as manipulative. By debasing language through their rhetorical excesses, bureaucrats deprive would-be challengers of tools not only to be used against them but also to be used in discovering that they even have any grievances. Debasing language thus stifles dissent at its very earliest stage. Furthermore, this must be done deceptively if it is to succeed at all. Were people to catch on to the game, they would ignore the rhetorical excesses of bureaucrats and other would-be manipulators. Overblown rhetoric can have its intended effect only insofar as it is taken as genuine attempt at communication.

Debasing language through rhetorical excesses is a troubling mode of manipulation in many ways. It promises to have long-lasting effects which are almost certainly biased against

31. Marcuse, *One-Dimensional Man*, p. 90. K. R. Cripwell, 'Government Writers and African Readers in Rhodesia', *Language in Society*, 4 (1975): 147–54.

change. But it would be wrong to leave the impression that
there is nothing radicals could do to resist it. Were they to
recognize the conservative implications of debasing language,
they could do much to resist it. Firstly, they could curb their
own rhetorical excesses, reducing their own misguided contributions to the process. Secondly and more importantly,
they could strive to preserve a purer quasi-private language
among themselves. Orwell, in his critique of 'Politics and the
English Language', seems enthusiastic about the possibilities
of this more private strategy of purification: 'one cannot
change this all in a moment, but one can at least change one's
own habits', he writes. Elsewhere Orwell explains that 'the
process is reversible. Modern English, especially written English, is full of bad habits which spread by imitation and which
can be avoided if one is willing to take the necessary trouble.
If one gets rid of these habits one can think more clearly, and
to think more clearly is a necessary first step towards political
regeneration.'[32] Using private strategies, purifying their own
language and that of their followers, radicals could insulate
themselves somewhat from a public language rendered unfit
for political discourse by rhetorical excesses.

4.5   RHETORICAL TRICKERY AS A MODE OF
       MANIPULATION

Two fundamentally different styles of rhetorical manipulation have been identified in this chapter. One involves implicit assertions, either in the form of hidden presuppositions,
hidden implications or hidden co-optation. The second involves debasing political language. Conclusions regarding the
manipulatory potential of each can be summarized by reference to the checklist described in Section 1.6:

32. Orwell, 'Politics and the English Language', pp. 139, 128.

1. Is the interference deceptive?

In the case of implicit assertion, there can be no doubt that people are being deceived. The whole point of these rhetorical devices is to hide crucial elements of the argument. There is only a little more room for doubt with respect to debasing political language. This *might* be unintended, resulting simply from sloppy thinking and sloppy usage. But insofar as it functions as an intentional strategy of manipulation, it must be deceptive if it is to succeed. If people see clearly what is happening to them—and understand that, by debasing political language, manipulative rulers are insulating themselves from well-deserved challenges—they will immediately foil the plot by devising and using a purer form of political language among themselves.

2. Is the interference contrary to the putative will of those subject to it?

Doubtless there are some arguments which, although allowed to pass largely unexamined, would nevertheless be accepted after full and careful consideration. Thus, not all implicit assertion necessarily leads people to act contrary to their putative wills. But surely there are some instances in which they would have acted differently had they seen all the presumptions and implications of the argument motivating their behaviour, so some instances of implicit assertion must surely count as manipulative. The influence of debasing political language is probably more uniformly unwelcome. Almost everyone would prefer to be able to argue intelligently and precisely, whatever his particular policy preferences might be.

Both varieties of rhetorical trick thus meet the definitional qualifications of manipulation. The next two questions ask how serious a form of manipulation is embodied in them.

3. How persistent is the effect of the manipulation?

Implicit assertion, if it leads people to act very contrary to their putative wills, is unlikely to remain unexamined for long. Significantly, simply exposing these tricks is usually enough to overcome their power. (Hidden co-optation, insofar as it parallels the strategies discussed in Sections 2.5 and 6.1.3, is a partial exception.) Debasing language, in contrast, will have long-lasting effects. There is no quick and easy way to restore precise linguistic distinctions once the old conventions have been broken down.

4. Are any distributive biases inherent in the mechanism?

Rhetorical techniques of implicit assertion are widely available to most members of the community. So too is the power to overcome such influences. Debasing political language, while it can be accomplished by anyone (and, ironically, is often the consequence of radicals' rhetoric), is only capable of working to the advantage of entrenched interests. Debasing political language deprives disadvantaged members of the community of one of the few resources they have for forcing social reforms.

On balance, implicit assertion seems to be a pretty innocent form of manipulatory politics. It lacks either persistence or any strong distributive bias. Debasing political language, in contrast, looks really worrisome, threatening to be both persistent and strongly biased in its consequences.

CHAPTER FIVE ✠ SYMBOLIC
REWARDS

COMMENTATORS ARE UNDERSTANDABLY DIVIDED in appraising symbolic rewards. On the one hand, policy-oriented analysts are quick to notice regulatory commissions fail to regulate, political prisoners remain incarcerated, racial minorities continue to be oppressed, rent strikers fail to obtain sanitary living conditions and protesters are generally frustrated, all because the rich and powerful manage to fob off the unorganized and downtrodden with symbolic rewards. By focusing on practices of this sort, they naturally come to view symbolic rewards with contempt. On the other hand, another more sociologically aware group is far more sympathetic with demands for symbolic reassurance. No one wants to feel alienated, anomie is no fun, and symbols (along with associated myths and rituals) play a large role in defining and reinforcing group attachments crucial to preventing these unhappy conditions. Just as primitives paint their bodies and distort their anatomy to symbolize membership in the tribe, so too do members of industrial societies display their flag or cross or colour television to proclaim group attachments.[1]

Material from 'Symbolic Rewards: Being Bought Off Cheaply' by Robert E. Goodin is reprinted from *Political Studies*, vol. 25, number 3 (September 1977), pp. 383–96, by permission of the Publishers, The Oxford University Press, Ltd.

1. Offended policy analysts include: Murray Edelman, *The Symbolic Uses of Politics* (Urbana: University of Illinois Press, 1964), and *Politics as Symbolic Action* (Chicago: Markham, 1971); Ernst Haas, *Global Evangelism Rides Again: How to Protect Human Rights Without Really Trying* (Berkeley: University of California International Studies, 1978); Ira Katznelson, *Black Men, White Cities* (London: Oxford University Press for Institute of Race Relations, 1973); Michael Lipsky, *Protest in City Politics: Rent Strikes, Housing and the Power of the Poor* (Chicago: Rand McNally, 1970); and Michael Lipsky and

Present fashion dictates that we view such conflicts with a
tolerant eye, putting the dispute down to the workings of an
'essentially contested concept'. To relegate 'symbolic rewards'
to this rapidly swelling category would be to say that the very
meaning of a symbolic reward—and, inevitably, its value as
well—is something about which honest men may reasonably
disagree.[2] The theme of this chapter is that there is no need to
throw up our hands quite so quickly. It aims to discredit some
forms of symbolic gestures as unseemly manipulation but to
leave others in good standing, thus accommodating our conflicting intuitions about the value of symbolic rewards.

What is more, this is accomplished using the least sympathetic analysis of 'interests', *viz.* the classical liberal assump-
tion that men are the best judges of their own interests. Were
one to ascribe to individuals objective interests of which they
may or may not be cognizant, similar results about symbolic
rewards would follow straightforwardly: symbolic gestures
tending to further objective interests (on the Marxian
analysis, e.g., to heighten class consciousness) are truly desirable; those which are not without value, even if false consciousness leads men to demand them. Liberal methodology
blocks any such simple solution by forcing us to take a man at

David J. Olson, *Commission Politics* (New York: Trans-Action Books, 1976).
Sympathetic commentators include Edmund Burke, *Reflections on the Revolu-
tion in France* (London: J. Dodsley, 1790) and Walter Bagehot, *The English
Constitution* (London: Chapman & Hall, 1867); modern echos are cited in
Chapter 6. All this is, of course, merely a generalization of Teufelsdröckh's
Theorem, described by Thomas Carlyle in *Sartor Resartus* (Boston: James
Monroe & Co., 1836), Ch. 8, as holding that 'society is founded upon cloth',
i.e., 'that Man's earthly interests "are all hooked and buttoned together, and
held up, by Clothes."'

2. Interest in W. B. Gallie's notion of 'Essentially Contested Concepts'
originally developed in the *Proceedings of the Aristotelian Society*, 56 (1955–56):
167–98, was reawakened by Steven Lukes, *Power: A Radical View* (London:
Macmillan, 1974). For extensions and objections, see Chapter 3, especially
note 14.

his word. His demand for symbolic gratification is conclusive evidence of its value to him. The difficult task for anyone working within liberal scriptures is finding a way to discredit symbolic rewards in the first place and, having found some such argument, preventing it from condemning *all* symbolic rewards.

5.1   THE NATURE OF 'THE SYMBOLIC'

The first order of business is to distinguish symbolic rewards from tangible ones. Too often, even in professional discussions, 'symbolic reward' functions as an empty pejorative, laden with values but descriptively vacuous. For perspective on the meaning of 'symbolic rewards', that phrase should be analysed alongside other structurally similar ones: 'monetary rewards', 'material rewards', 'spiritual rewards', etc. In each of these cases the adjectival modifier serves to specify the currency in which the reward is paid. Monetary rewards are paid in cash, material ones in kind and spiritual ones in heaven. Set in this context, 'symbolic' seems to specify yet another currency.

The special features of the symbolic currency result from the more general nature of symbols. A symbol is something that 'stands for, represents, or denotes something else'. Some symbols (such as numbers or road signs) are purely neutral points of reference; but others (such as those involved in symbolic rewards) are evaluative cues as well as referential devices.[3] The obvious interpretation is that the evaluative sig-

3. Edward Sapir, 'Symbolism', *Encyclopedia of the Social Sciences,* ed. E. R. A. Seligman (New York: Macmillan, 1948), 14: 492–95, distinguishes between the sort of symbol which 'expresses a condensation of energy, its actual significance being out of all proportion to the apparent triviality of meaning suggested by its mere form' and that which is merely 'an economical device for purposes of reference'.

nificance of such symbols derives from the evaluative significance of those things to which they refer. The reason that the Battle of the Boyne is an evocative symbol for an Irishman and the Battle of Shiloh is (at best) referential is that he has a continuing stake in William of Orange's victory but only passing historical interest in General Grant's.

Hence the distinction between tangible and symbolic rewards. The tangible is, in general, that which is 'material, externally real, objective'. A reward is tangible if the actual things awarded are themselves of direct, intrinsic value to the recipient. A reward is symbolic when the value of the award is indirect, when the recipient values it only as a means to some other goods which are themselves of intrinsic value.[4] The adjective 'symbolic' has similar connotations in conjunction with other nouns such as 'symbolic gestures', 'symbolic payoffs', 'symbolic reassurance', etc. All these derive their value from those tangible goods toward which the symbols point.

Symbolic rewards rarely exist in isolation. They are typically carried on tangible goods which are themselves of some value. When a medieval prince grants a lord a fief, or a railroad executive gives a retiree a gold watch, there are tangible as well as symbolic components to the award. Forcing such examples into one category or the other simply forces the facts. We can analyse symbolic rewards as an ideal type without supposing that it ever appears empirically in a pure form.

The extent to which a reward is symbolic depends entirely on the perceptions of the recipient. An award is symbolic if—but only if and insofar as—he regards it as being of instrumental rather than intrinsic value. This, combined with

---

4. One problem with this analysis should be anticipated: food is a tangible reward while food vouchers are symbolic, because they are valued only insofar as they enable one to claim food. Ordinarily the vouchers would be thought a tangible reward, however. The reason, discussed further in Section 5.2, is that the vouchers are ordinarily *readily convertible* into food.

the fact that symbolic rewards are often carried on valuable tangible goods, opens pernicious strategic possibilities. The deft political operator will try to downplay his demands as being for merely symbolic gratification when they are in fact aimed at obtaining substantial material rewards as well. Bourgeois clamour for 'good government' seems to be an innocuous symbolic frill—recall the popular acronym 'googo'—until one notices that 'good government' is equivalent to 'government that gives business efficient service'.

5.2 THE PROBLEM WITH PROMISSORY SYMBOLS

The essential objection to symbolic rewards is that they are all too often used to buy off citizens who had been making more substantial demands. The problem is not that leaders of the protesting group betrayed their followers for narrowly personal gain. Presumably every member of the group partakes of the pleasures flowing from the symbolic rewards. Nor is the problem simply that they were bought off, that they settled for something other than what they were originally demanding. Surely it is reasonable for individuals (and, by extension, groups) to trade off all sorts of goods for one another, be they grapes and potatoes or housing and employment. Nor is the problem that they 'sold out'—that they put a price on themselves and their principles, which others came along and met. There is nothing necessarily demeaning about carrying a price tag, provided the price is sufficiently high. Georg Simmel recalls a case on point:

> Edward II and Edward III gave their friends away as hostages for the repayment of their debts and in 1340 it was planned to send the Archbishop of Canterbury to Brabant. . . . The size of the respective sums averted the

disparagement that would have affected these persons if only a negligible amount of money had been at stake.[5]

The problem with symbolic rewards is not one of betrayal, being bought off or selling out. Rather, the problem is that, by accepting symbolic payoffs instead of pressing demands for tangible goods, people are somehow being bought off *cheaply*.

Several rationales for discounting symbolic rewards in this way immediately spring to mind, but most of them are incapable of making precisely the distinctions this intuition requires. One alluring alternative, for example, turns on the proposition that tastes for symbolic gratifications are socially determined. Those desirous of symbolic rewards have acquired such tastes through the efforts of those with the power to dispense the very rewards being demanded. When the Mayor of New York walks through the streets of Harlem it is taken to be a sign that 'he cares', and the walkabout has that significance because that is the gloss put on it by Gracie Mansion press releases. A Victoria Cross would not signify bravery in action had not the Queen stipulated that meaning. 'In commonwealths', as Hobbes observes, 'they that have the supreme authority can make whatsoever they please to stand for signs of honour' which they then bestow.[6] There is something

5. Georg Simmel, *The Philosophy of Money*, trans. Tom Bottomore and David Frisby (London: Routledge & Kegan Paul, 1978), p. 374.

6. Thomas Hobbes, *Leviathan*, Ch. 10. Hobbes continues, 'A sovereign does honour a subject with whatsoever title or office or employment or action that he himself will have taken for a sign of his will to honour him', emphasising the point with an example: 'The king of Persia honoured Mordecai when he appointed he should be conducted through the streets in the king's garments, upon one of the king's horses, with a crown on his head, and a prince before him, proclaiming *thus shall it be done to him that the king will honour*. And yet another king of Persia, or the same another time, to one that demanded for some great service to wear one of the king's robes, gave him leave so to do, but with this addition, that he should wear it as the king's fool, and then it was dishonour.'

clearly self-serving in the process that offends moral sensitivities.

The argument, however, cuts equally against material and tangible goods. Galbraith and his school argue that demand for a wide range of consumer goods is determined by Madison Avenue advertising, reinforced perhaps by the 'keep up with the Joneses' syndrome. There is only a trivial difference between symbolic and material goods in this respect: basic needs for food, clothing and shelter are biologically and not culturally determined. But, then again, the types of food, clothing and shelter consumed are subject to powerful social influences. And, furthermore, might not the psychologist similarly maintain that there is a deep psychological need for some sort of symbolic reassurance? Were our scorn for symbolic rewards really rooted in objections to demand-management on the part of suppliers, it should extend to a wide range of material rewards as well. Since it does not— since we are so much more scornful of symbolic rewards in general—this argument cannot be what motivates our objections.

A more relevant argument, but still only a partial answer to the puzzle, is that symbolic rewards are cheap to offer and hence somehow less valuable to receive. Sometimes they are virtually costless to confer—how much can it cost to manufacture military ribbons or print certificates of merit or stop to pat a subordinate on the back?—but they are almost always less expensive than the tangible rewards for which they are substitutes. When a man retires, it is cheaper to give him an engraved gold watch than a good pension. It is cheaper to eulogize victims of a terrorist attack than to strengthen defences to protect their survivors, and so on. Mike Royko's objection to Mayor Daley's strategy for dealing with black riots in 1966 seems to be that it was a cheap trick. Recounting how Dr. Martin Luther King, Jr., had recommended, during a

100° heat wave, turning on fire hydrants to provide water for children to play in, Royko remarks,

> Now there was a program, and Daley liked it. Give them water. He had a whole lake right outside the door. . . . City Hall embarked on a crusade to make Chicago's blacks the wettest in the country. Portable swimming pools were being trucked in. Sprinklers were attached to hundreds of hydrants, and water was gushing everywhere. The city's department of planning mobilized to launch a long-range program of black wetness. The Chicago Park District joined in. So did the Fire Department. Suddenly the entire city administration was thinking wet. One cynical civil rights worker said, 'I think they're hoping we'll all grow gills and swim away.'[7]

The symbolic sops which politicians actually do offer are likely to be relatively cheap, of course, for the simple reason that, had it been cheaper to satisfy material demands, no symbolic gestures would have been forthcoming in the first place. But surely symbolic rewards are not always cheaper to confer than material ones. Recent American experiences with racial desegregation indicate otherwise. Myrdal discovered that the white man has a 'rank order of discrimination' in which symbolic gestures are more important than material advantages. Most important to him are bars on 'intermarriage and sexual intercourse involving white women'; next most important are 'the several etiquettes and discriminations, which specifically concern behaviour in personal relations' (e.g., barriers to social intercourse, rules as to handshaking, hat lifting, use of titles and the back door to houses); less im-

---

7. Mike Royko, *Boss: Richard J. Daley of Chicago* (New York: E. P. Dutton, 1971), p. 151.

portant are 'discriminations in law courts, by the police, and
by other public servants'; and least important are 'discriminations in securing land, credit, jobs or other means of earning a
living'. In their actions Southern whites have stuck closely to
their words, as reported by Myrdal. Under pressure from
Washington, the white community has given way on material
issues (minority employment, civic amenities in black
neighbourhoods, etc.) long before it concedes symbols of
white supremacy (most especially 'Jim Crow' practices of seg-
regating social intercourse at, e.g., lunch counters and state
schools). The point is well illustrated with a Huey Long anec-
dote:

> When a new Charity Hospital was built here, some Negro
> politicians came to Huey and said it was a shame there
> were no Negro nurses, when more than half the patients
> were colored. Huey said he'd fix it for them, but they
> wouldn't like his method. He went around to visit the
> hospital and pretended to be surprised when he found
> white nurses waiting on colored men. He blew high as a
> buzzard can fly saying it wasn't fit for white women to be
> so humiliated. It was the most racist talk you ever heard,
> but the result was that he got the white nurses out and the
> colored nurses in, and they've had the jobs ever since.[8]

Even where symbolic rewards are cheaper to confer, however, it is hard to see how that makes them any the less valuable to receive. Consider in this connection cases in which
technological advance has cut costs of producing a good but

8. A. J. Liebling, *The Earl of Louisiana* (Baton Rouge: Louisiana State
University Press, 1961), p. 23. Gunnar Myrdal, *An American Dilemma* (Lon-
don: Harper, 1944), pp. 60–61. See also William R. Keech, *The Impact of
Negro Voting* (Chicago: Rand McNally, 1968), and C. Vann Woodward, *The
Strange Career of Jim Crow* (New York: Oxford University Press, 1955).

simultaneously increased its quality. Transistor radios or calculators are far cheaper to produce than the cumbersome devices they replace. They are also improvements from the user's point of view, if only because there are no tubes to be replaced. Thus, the 'value in use' of a good does not, in general, depend upon the cost of producing it, so the fact that symbolic rewards are cheap to confer cannot explain fully why they are thought less valuable to receive.

That a man sacrifices little when offering a symbolic reward matters in a direct way only in one case: when the recipient has as one of his goals the infliction of pain on the person making the offer.[9] The emphasis here is on what *are* his goals, not what they should be. Thus, Huey Newton had every reason for rejecting symbolic rewards—they do not cause whitey enough pain. But there are no general grounds for scorning as Uncle Toms those who delight in symbolic concessions, such as a school being named after Crispus Attucks or the mayor crowning a black beauty queen, except insofar as one cares to argue that all blacks should want to inflict pain on all whites. Few political actors are so malevolent as this, and even fewer academics scornful of symbolic rewards are urging them to be, so this must be a minor component of the general argument against symbolic payoffs.

This sort of thoroughgoing bloody-mindedness should be distinguished from a perfectly plausible radical rule-of-thumb which it superficially resembles. In a world where exploitation is pervasive, and most games between oppressors and oppressed are zero-sum, it makes sense to be predisposed in favour of any policy tending to the disadvantage of the

9. Alternatively, he may value the other's sacrifice because it shows that the other has done him the honour of taking real notice of him, genuinely reflecting upon his true worth rather than just routinely signing a certificate of merit or an invoice for 'another hundred gold watches' (whose price is, in any case, written off his taxes as a 'business expense'). In this way, the other's

oppressors. The logic of the argument is that, more likely than not, anything bad for them is surely good for us. But unless *all* games are zero-sum, this will amount to no more than a useful rule-of-thumb. As is the case with all such decisional stopgaps, each case must be considered on its full merits at the earliest opportunity. It may well turn out that, in any given instance, resistance works more against the interests of the oppressed than of the oppressors. Then they should cease their resistance, and accept the symbolic rewards, however trivial their gain or slight their opponents' losses.

The indirect and contingent effects of symbolic rewards being cheap to offer could be more important. Other things being equal, scarcity begets value. A Congressional Medal of Honor is better than a Purple Heart because fewer of them are conferred; a key to the city or to the executive washroom is prized because not everyone has one. But since symbolic rewards are relatively cheap to produce, self-restraint on the part of the supplier is all that prevents him from producing a glut of them, thus diminishing the value of each one already in circulation. English history provides a striking example. Wanting to upgrade the status of the baronetcies with which he proposed to reward his courtiers, James I decreed that a baronet could sell his title to someone else. When the policy was first instituted in 1609, the notional value of the title was £ 1095 (although in the first instance all were given away and none sold); but 'owing to the excess of supply over demand ... the price fell from £ 700 in 1619 to between £ 220 and £ 250 in 1622. ...'[10] In this instance overproduction was

---

sacrifice may be a symbol of an intangible good—respect—of the sort to be discussed in Section 5.3.

10. Lawrence Stone, 'The Inflation of Honours, 1558-1641', *Past and Present*, 14 (November 1958): 45-71 at 53. Stone also provides impressionistic evidence showing that this decline in selling price was accompanied by a similar decline in the prestige of baronets.

real enough. In general, however, the perceived danger of debasement is all that it takes to put a would-be recipient off symbolic rewards, just as a cautious businessman demands payment in currencies backed by precious metals whenever he senses a danger that governments issuing softer currencies might debase them by simply turning on the printing presses. To forestall this, the supplier of symbolic rewards must exercise caution and instill in recipients confidence that the award is made only in the rarest of circumstances. Thus, the low cost of conferring symbolic rewards provides a partial explanation of the intuition that they are inherently less valuable commodities.

The most plausible general justification for disdaining symbolic rewards centres around a third argument. In many cases, symbolic reassurance amounts to an implicit promise of tangible goods to follow. The establishment of a regulatory commission is itself a symbolic gesture, but the message is that something rather more tangible (e.g., control of price-fixing monopolists) is to come. When Mayor Daley had Chicago city workers erect 'Bicycle Lane' signs along public roadways, the implicit (and subsequently unfulfilled) promise was to enforce those rules and reserve those lanes for bicyclists exclusively. So too with the election of a black mayor, appointment of a riot commission and signing of a defence pact or an equal opportunities act. All are themselves symbolic gestures, but each one also implies that some tangible goods will follow.

Such symbolic rewards are to be valued, but not so highly as the tangible rewards they promise. A promissory note is inherently less valuable than the thing promised, because there is always the chance that the promisor will default on his promise. While promises are never as good as delivery, neither should they be treated lightly. Thomas Schelling ably demonstrates how an actor's credibility gets tied up with making good on his commitments, and credibility is a very important bargaining resource.[11]

The value of a promissory symbolic reward depends on twin considerations. One factor is the intrinsic value of the thing symbolized, that which is promised. Another intimately related to the first is the strength of the symbolic link, the strength of the promise. Sometimes the promise is explicit, detailied and binding, in which case the value of the promissory symbol approaches very near to that of the actual delivery of the thing promised. This explains why money, although a symbolic reward on the analysis of Section 5.1, is rarely thought of in that way. Here our common intuition is grounded in the easy and certain convertibility of money into tangible goods. And this intuition is not nearly so firm when this relationship breaks down, as in cases of monetary payment in times of rampant inflation. There was, for example, a large symbolic component to General Washington's act of paying his troops with increasingly worthless Continental currency. The symbolic nature of the gesture is especially apparent when you notice the language of a 1776 resolution of the Continental Congress prohibiting trade with people refusing to accept Continental currency, to whom it refers as 'any person who shall hereafter be so lost to all virtue and regard for his country, as to refuse to receive said bills in payment. . . .'[12]

11. Thomas C. Schelling, *The Strategy of Conflict* (Cambridge: Harvard University Press, 1960).

12. Quoted in J. K. Galbraith, *Money* (London: André Deutsch, 1975), p. 59. In other contexts, the symbolic aspects of monetary payments are fully appreciated. Notice, with Simmel, *Philosophy of Money*, p. 387, how 'our penal code considers stealing a small amount of food and consumer goods for direct use to be only a slight violation of the law whereas the theft of an equivalent amount of money would be severely punished. It is obviously assumed that in the case of a momentary need the availability of the respective commodity is so tempting that to succumb is too human a frailty to be

That appeal is pretty clearly to symbolic rather than material interests.

The swift and certain convertibility of symbolic into tangible rewards is the exception rather than the rule. More typically, the commitment implied by a symbolic gesture is intentionally ambiguous. One trick useful to politicians in avoiding responsibility for their promises is to channel them through a third party, who symbolically assures others of the good intentions of the politician but who cannot, strictly speaking, make any promises on his behalf. Another useful trick is making tacit promises. While these tricks cause recipients to discount the promise even further, such gestures do have advantages for the individuals making them: if need be, they can always cut their losses in terms of credibility when defaulting on the promise by pleading that the promisee misunderstood the gesture. Those politicians inclined to play very safe indeed use symbolic gestures implying diffuse rather than specific undertakings. What is involved here is the politics of image, the point being that an image can persist for quite a while with little to warrant it. President Kennedy set for himself the task of 'getting America moving again', and his image of vigorous pursuit of that goal was maintained more through a full social calendar and football games on the White House lawn than through legislative triumphs. In Middle America, Nixon as President retained his image as a man 'hard on communism' even while proclaiming détente, largely through memories of his crusade against Alger Hiss. And, in the first

---

punished severely. The more the object is distanced from its immediate use and the longer the detour necessary to satisfy the need, the weaker is the attraction, and the greater is the degree of immorality involved in satisfying the impulse to steal it. . . . Money is the furthest removed from such direct enjoyments; the interest is always focused on what lies beyond it, so the temptation that, as it were, radiates from it is not a natural instinct and does not possess the force of such an instinct to act as an excuse for succumbing to it.'

few months of his Administration anyway, Jimmy Carter retained the image of an 'outsider' and a 'man of the people' through such symbolic gestures as walking in his Inaugural Parade rather than riding in an official limousine. Politicians are easily discredited when promising something specific and failing to deliver. Keeping promises vague, they run fewer risks. The use of political symbols make obfuscation much easier. A promise made through a symbolic gesture can more easily be vague because the symbol is usually connected to its referent through necessarily imprecise allusions and metaphors.

Viewing symbolic gestures as commitments to future payoffs in terms of tangible goods also helps to explain why the extent of the sacrifice of the offerer is relevant to the value of the reward. A promise is to be taken more seriously when it is accompanied by a 'good faith' sacrifice. By making such a sacrifice, the promisor invests something in the situation. Since it would be more costly for him to back out of the deal, it is more likely that he will make good on the promise.

5.3 NON-PROBLEMS WITH AFFECTIVE SYMBOLS

Section 5.1 argues that the essential nature of symbolic rewards is that they are a means of attaining something else of intrinsic value. Section 5.2 discusses symbolic rewards which are valued as a means of securing subsequent tangible goods. Logically, there is another type of symbolic reward, i.e., that valued as a means of securing intangible goods. The *Oxford English Dictionary* definition of 'symbol' suggests that this is the more standard case: a symbol is 'especially a material object representing or taken to represent something immaterial or abstract'. Social experience confirms this judgement. Meyers Fortes and E. E. Evans-Pritchard, in their classic survey of *African Political Systems,* find,

> Members of an African society feel their unity and per-
> ceive their common interests in symbols, and it is their
> attachment to these symbols which more than anything
> else gives their society cohesion and persistence. In the
> form of myths, fictions, dogmas, ritual, sacred places and
> persons, these symbols represent the unity and exclu-
> siveness of the groups which respect them. They are re-
> garded ... not as mere symbols, but as vital values in
> themselves.[13]

In our own societies, honours and titles are valued as symbols
of intangible status and respect. Flags and kings and social
rituals are valued as symbols of such abstractions as 'nation',
'community' and 'people'.

The arguments developed above apply only to promissory
symbolic rewards. When symbolic gestures are valued as
commitments to future provision of tangible benefits, the gesture is necessarily inferior to actual provision of the promised
goods. When symbolic gestures carry no such implication,
however, they are potentially as valuable as any material
commodity. Such symbolic goods fit into the individual's
preference ordering in roughly the same way as any other
good, and the process of choice involved is in principle no
different from that involved in choosing between a new automobile and a long holiday, or between a shorter life with the
pleasure of smoking cigarettes or a longer one without it. The
fact that affective symbols figure in such trade-offs is most
apparent when symbolic goods are actually bought and sold.
For example, titles of nobility have traditionally been auc-
tioned off: in the decade 1732–1742, there were 1207 payments for ennoblement or confirmation in Paris alone, and at

13. Meyers Fortes and E. E. Evans-Pritchard, 'Introduction', *African
Political Systems* (London: Oxford University Press for International African
Institute, 1940), pp. 1–23 at 17.

times when demand badly outstripped supply Frenchmen actually *rented* titles.[14] No doubt it is equally true of those symbolic gratifications which do not come under the measuring rod of money.

While symbolic gestures with expressive or affective significance are largely immune to the complaints which are properly lodged against their promissory brethren, they are subjected—unjustifiably, it will be argued—to different lines of attack. Perhaps the most obvious complaint with affective symbols is that they are susceptible to psychological manipulation for political advantage. Long before J. L. Austin lectured on *How to Do Things with Words,* politicians had discovered the power of capturing positive symbols, wrapping themselves in the flag and such like, and pinning negative symbols on their opponents. This is most effective when done subtly, preferably by passing off emotion-laden symbols as if they were purely referential ones.[15]

Basically, the complaint here seems to be that political symbols can be turned to any use, that they are utterly manipulable. But given the political power of symbols, it is

14. Robert Holt and John Turner, *The Political Basis of Economic Development* (Princeton: Van Nostrand, 1966), p. 203. Liberal economists are emphatic that we must not try to second-guess such choices. Gary Becker, *The Economic Approach to Human Behavior* (Chicago: University of Chicago Press, 1976), p. 10, notices that, 'According to the economic approach, . . . *most* (if not all!) deaths are to some extent "suicides" in the sense that they could have been postponed if more resources had been invested in prolonging life'; but the economist as such has no business telling that they should make such investments if they prefer not to do so.

15. Austin, *How to Do Things with Words* (Oxford: Clarendon Press, 1962); see also the discussions and references in Chapters 3 and 4. Examples of attempts at symbolic manipulation in politics include: Ronald D. Rotunda, 'The "Liberal" Label: Roosevelt's Capture of a Symbol', *Public Policy,* 17 (1968): 377–408; Michael Novak, *Choosing Our King: Powerful Symbols in Presidential Politics* (New York: Macmillan, 1974); and Krishnalal Shridharani, 'Symbols and Signs in the Indian Election', *Symbols and Values,* ed. Lyman Bryson *et al.* (New York: Cooper Square, 1964), pp. 405–12.

perhaps just as well that they are pliable. At least that guarantees that the deck of political symbols will never be irrevocably stacked against any particular set of players. It is encouraging that in China of the Warring State period (500 to 200 B.C.) tradition was sacrosanct but that symbol was equally accessible to rulers and challengers alike: Mo Tzu overturned the existing regime with the charge, 'You are only following the Chou not the Hsia dynasty. Your antiquity does not go back far enough.'[16] The deck of symbols will probably always be stacked in favour of some and against others. The point here is simply that there is nothing in the nature of political symbols that prevents people fron turning the tables. Indeed, the original act of stacking necessarily creates possibilities for restacking.

> The Red Square, red under the ancien regime and still red with quite another connotation, affords an interesting example of the facility with which symbolisms may be transferred from one order to another. Pulling down the memorials, especially the personal ones, of an earlier group, is an impressive opening for the new symbolism, but the conversion of the old is equally possible and frequently occurs.[17]

In practice, of course, it may be difficult either to tear down the old statues or to turn the tables. But *that* does not argue against social systems allocating symbolic rewards any more than it argues against allocating monetary rewards, which similarly tend to concentrate in the hands of a few who then use their power to resist their redistribution.

There are, in any case, limits to the possibilities for man-

16. Mo Tzu is discussed by J. G. A. Pocock in *Politics, Language and Time* (New York: Atheneum, 1971), pp. 246 ff., where he develops his larger theme of 'turning the linguistic tables'.

17. Charles E. Merriam, *Systematic Politics* (Chicago: University of Chicago Press, 1945), pp. 84–85.

ipulating affective symbols. While symbols do have a certain
tensile strength, they will surely break if bent too far. The
history of the concept of 'freedom' testifies to this fact: by
focusing on the negative implications of 'freedom as the absence of restraints', *laissez-faire* liberals left themselves open to
the challenge of reformers emphasizing the positive aspects.
In modern times, euphemisms like 'pacification' and 'defence'
have become standing jokes which serve as rallying points for
dissidents. Another example might be the way in which the
cult of R. D. Laing grew up in response to the misdeeds, linguistic and otherwise, of psychologists. In general, Charles
Frankel is surely right in saying that 'the power which symbols
have to move us is *borrowed* power. And when what they stand
for changes or disappears, they live on borrowed time.' Instances abound. 'Nothing', Merriam writes,

> is more tragic than the sight of holders of dead symbols
> invoking obedience in their lifeless names from those
> whose eyes are fixed upon the more vivid symbolisms of a
> new political or other order. The fleeing Kaiser might
> storm impotently; the pitiful shadow of the emperor of
> all the Russias in captivity at Ekaterinburg looked in vain
> for a salute from the soldiers. Mussolini reached a mo-
> ment when his scowl no longer terrified king or people.
> The symbols of power in these cases become inciting irri-
> tations and their only power is to inflame and arouse op-
> position. As with the political, so with other types of
> group symbols. They are not immortal, and their power
> holds as long as they serve vital interests and ideas.[18]

18. Ibid., p. 87. Charles Frankel, 'Liberalism and Political Symbols', *Sym-
bols and Values*, pp. 361–70 at 370. T. H. Green, 'Liberal Legislation and
Freedom of Contract', *Works* (London: Longmans, Green, 1888), 3: 365–86.
Arthur M. Schlesinger, Jr., 'Politics and the American Language', *The Ameri-
can Scholar*, 43 (1974): 553–62. Murray Edelman, *Political Language* (New
York: Academic Press, 1977).

A further limit is that these symbols cannot be manipulated too frequently or else they will lose their potency. Jonathan Swift wisely advises, 'Terrible objects should not be too frequently shown to the people lest they grow familiar. . . . It is absolutely necessary that the people of England should be frightened with the French king and the pretender once a-year; but that the bears should be chained up again until that time twelvemonth.'[19] The same is surely true of desirable objects and their symbols. Sacred values lose their power to move men when rulers are constantly appealing to them.

At a deeper level, symbols can be manipulated by being withheld. A long and respectable tradition in philosophical sociology, surveyed in Section 3.2, maintains that the set of concepts available in a language constrains the thought and hence the actions of members of that linguistic community. If citizens are deprived of the concept of radical change by the absence of referential symbols for it, then they logically cannot engage (intentionally, at least) in radical action.

Chapter 3 offers reasons for believing this to be a short-term problem only. When people's day-to-day experiences teach them the need for a concept, there is little chance that elites can long prevent them from developing it. But insofar as the problem addressed here is the lack of adequate symbolic tools, the objection to politicians engaging in symbolic discourse seems especially misguided. Surely it is likely that the needed symbols will emerge in the course of essentially symbolic debates more rapidly than they would if discourse were confined to strictly mundane topics.

Another very common motive for political leaders invoking symbols, and a very common reasons for objecting to such practices, is that these appeals distract attention from other

19. Jonathan Swift, 'The Art of Political Lying', *Works,* ed. Thomas Roscoe (London: George Bell, 1880), 2: 402–5 at 404.

SYMBOLIC REWARDS   143

matters. The Marxist analysis of religion as 'the opiate of the
people' is easily generalized to cover any and all symbolic en-
terprises.[20]

Roughly speaking, there are two main ways of playing this
symbolic distraction game. One method is to stir up trouble
along some symbolic dimension so people will forget their
other differences. The stunted growth of the Labour Party in
Ulster is usually seen to be a consequence of economic issues
being eclipsed by the religious question. Non-emergence of
distributive issues in the American South is plausibly attrib-
uted to the salience of the racial question.[21]

Outside observers might find the ensuing intercommunal
strife unsavoury, but from the perspective of the citizens
themselves it is difficult to see what is wrong with this sort of
appeal. The very fact that the symbolic issue is capable of
overpowering material ones is evidence that is popularly
taken to be the more important. And, in any case, material
issues can be displaced by other material issues as well as by
symbolic ones, so the objection is not uniquely applicable to
symbolic appeals.

The alternative distraction technique is to invoke symbols
shared by all members of the political community and thus to
quash dissent. A prime example of this might be the behaviour of Pericles during the Peloponnesian War. Twice his
leadership came under attack and twice he escaped by singing
the praises of the Athenian polity, first in the famous Funeral

20. Karl Marx, 'Contribution to the Critique of Hegel's Philosophy of
Right', *K. Marx and F. Engels on Religion* (Moscow: Foreign Languages Pub-
lishing House, 1955).
21. The displacement of conflict in general is discussed by E. E.
Schattschneider, *The Semi-Sovereign People* (New York: Holt, Rinehart &
Winston, 1960). On Ulster, see Richard Rose, *Governing Without Consensus*
(London: Faber & Faber, 1971), pp. 275–301. In these particular examples
the conspiratorial implication of the discussion may be dubious; but surely
there are some such examples in which in would be warranted.

Oration and next in an equally moving if rather more blood-curdling appeal.[22]

While the effect of this might be to sweep some contentious issues under the rug, it is significant that citizens do enjoy the feelings of solidarity thereby produced. They get something out of the gesture and, unlike promissory symbolic rewards, there is no criterion by which these feelings of solidarity can be said to be necessarily inferior to other forms of reward. Solidarity might be valued as highly as any other good on offer. This is essentially an empirical question. If it turns out that solidarity is not valued very highly, then one would bemoan the fact that citizens were denied the opportunity to put material issues on the political agenda instead. But political leaders cannot keep the lid on hot issues for long unless there are powerful gatekeepers exercising control over the political agenda; and where there are such gatekeepers the proper objection is to their existence and not to their use of symbolic gestures. Agenda-setters prevent people from getting what they want from government simply by virtue of their position, whether they work through symbolic appeals or through other channels.

The most serious worry with affective symbols would seem to be that attachment to the symbols of government might obscure the true workings of those institutions. The symbols might well serve as a blind behind which politicians can go about their sundry intrigues. Bagehot supposed that the Monarchy, House of Lords and Commons all combined to perform this function for the Cabinet in nineteenth-century Britain, and Richard Crossman observes that today the Cabinet itself simply hides the reality of prime ministerial government. In the United States, black militants maintain that the election of a black mayor, however good it makes

22. Thucydides, *History of the Peloponnesian War*, Book 2, para. 22–65.

them feel inside, only serves to obscure the real power structure within their community, which is now relocated in the suburbs. The more general point is aptly put by King Magnus, the despot of George Bernard Shaw's *The Apple Cart*, surveying his plight:

> If I do not accept the ultimatum I shall receive your resignations and his [the Prime Minister's]; and the country will learn from his explanatory speech in the House of Commons that it is to choose between Cabinet government and monarchical government: an issue on which I frankly say I should be very sorry to win, as I cannot carry on without the support of a body of ministers whose existence gives the English people a sensation of self-government. Naturally I want to avert a conflict in which success would damage me and failure disable me.[23]

Again, the factual claim is clear enough but the evaluative objection is not. Presumably citizens desire at least two types of things from government. First is the gratification to be had from the affective symbols of government, which often include certain fictions (in the sense used in Section 6.1) about the decision-making procedures.[24] Second is the material

23. R. H. Crossman, 'Introduction' to Walter Bagehot, *The English Constitution* (London: Collins, 1963). G. B. Shaw, 'The Apple Cart', *Collected Works* (New York: William H. Wise, 1930), 17: 212.

24. Jayaprakash Narayan, *A Plea for Reconstruction of the Indian Polity* (New Delhi: Wardha, 1960), argues that the unanimity rule governing deliberations of village *panchayats* (councils) serves to symbolize the cohesiveness of the community. M. N. Srinivas, 'The Indian Community: Myth and Reality', *Studies in Social Anthropology,* ed. J. H. M. Beattie and R. G. Lienhardt (Oxford: Clarendon Press, 1975), pp. 41–85, defends this model while acknowledging its limitations. Arend Lijphart, *The Politics of Accommodation* (Berkeley: University of California Press, 1968), pp. 82–88, 135–36, sees the royal House of Orange as a symbol uniting a deeply divided Dutch nation and comments upon how this symbol is bolstered by political institutions. For

output. How citizens trade off one for the other is their own business. To say that the trappings obscure the mechanics of government is to argue powerfully against evaluating policy-making exclusively by looking to the procedures seemingly involved. This is a common mistake, to be sure. The core of Lowi's critique of liberalism is his scorn for the 'ersatz political formula' which offers 'a set of sentiments that elevate a particular view of the political process above everything else. The ends of government and the justification of one policy or procedure over another are not to be discussed. . . . The process of formulation is justification in itself.'[25] But there is no logical necessity for citizens to fall into this trap. So long as they evaluate policy on the basis of outputs rather than apparent processes, there is nothing preventing them from evaluating governmental performance in an entirely coherent fashion.

There is, in summary, no complaint about affective symbols which can parallel the knock-down objection to promissory symbolic gestures. Each promissory symbolic reward necessarily corresponds to some other reward, provision of which is *ipso facto* preferable to the mere promise of delivery. No such necessary link exists between affective symbols and any other good, so they may take on any value those partaking of them care to assign. And more abstract arguments counseling caution in dealing with affective symbols in general are hardly overwhelmingly persuasive.

---

example, the constitutional fiction holds that 'cabinets are King's or Queen's cabinets, although they are all, at least after 1868, parliamentary cabinets'. To enforce this fiction, the Constitution requires that Ministers surrender either their position in the Cabinet or in the States-General (the Parliament) after three months. On the procedural consensus underlying British democracy see Ian Budge, *Agreement and the Stability of Democracy* (Chicago: Markham, 1970).

25. Theodore J. Lowi, *The End of Liberalism* (New York: W. W. Norton, 1969), p. 70.

This conclusion is well illustrated by analysis of the ordinary usage of a closely related notion, 'token'. A token is necessarily a substitute for something else, and is usually less valuable. A tradesman's token is, e.g., 'worth much less than its nominal value'. Some tokens are regarded respectfully, however, because they are symbolic of something intangible, as when a foreman gives a retiree a gold watch 'as a token of our esteem'. Calling it a token only underscores what is really of value, their deep regard. The pejorative 'tokenism' is, in contrast, used to scorn cheap substitutes for material payoffs. When employing its first woman, a previously all-male firm has been forced to acknowledge the abstract principle of sexual equality. When feminists object to such tokenism, they are really saying that their real concern is with material consequences, not limp gestures toward abstract principles, and that from this perspective a token woman employee is unimpressive. Similarly, token money is shunned because of the unsubstantiated claim that it can later be exchanged for material goods.

5.4   SYMBOLIC POLITICS IN PRACTICE

This analysis, if broadly correct, has important implications for the making of public policy. Above all, it amounts to a stern repudiation of crude realists who scorn all symbolic goods as illegitimate for pursuit in public policy, foreign or domestic.[26] The first and more trivial ground for this repudiation is that immediate delivery of material goods is often

26. Among students of international politics, the doyen of the realist school is Hans J. Morgenthau. For an especially clear statement of his position, see 'Another "Great Debate": The National Interest of the United States', *American Political Science Review*, 46 (1952): 961–88. Among analysts of domestic policy, the foremost realist is Thurman W. Arnold, *Symbols of Government* (New Haven: Yale University Press, 1935).

quite impossible, and symbolic gestures will have to suffice in
the meanwhile. By its very nature, the tangible assistance
promised in a defence pact can be delivered only after the
attack has commenced. Until then, the symbolism of the
treaty will have to do, being bolstered occasionally by further
symbolic acts such as the stationing of U.S. troops in Western
Europe as a trip wire. Decision-makers have no choice but to
act on the basis of this sort of symbolic gesture.

More damaging to the realist position, the conclusion of
Section 5.3 is that there is no reason to shun purely affective
symbolic goals and abstract ideals in making policy. One crucial proviso must be appended: provided one can afford the
luxury. It it takes all the resources one can muster simply to
survive, one can ill afford to pursue symbolic goals and ideals
that might involve compromising sovereignty. Morgenthau
seemed to believe that the West was in this precarious position
in the 1950s and his arguments for a realistic foreign policy
are couched very much in these terms.

Where empirical investigation suggests that there is some
slack, and that the individual or nation is not on the brink of
disaster, there can be little objection to pursuing symbolic as
well as material interests according to taste. Assuming Al-
bania's status as an independent nation-state is not in
jeopardy, it is entirely reasonable that it should ally with the
People's Republic of China so long as the ideological payoffs
from doing so are sufficient in Albanian eyes to compensate
for the lost material assistance from the U.S.S.R. The argument for allowing idealism to manifest itself in domestic policy or individual practice perfectly parallels this argument
with respect to foreign policy.

To argue that a nation or an individual should be exclusively concerned with safeguarding security and material
interests even when there is no foreseeable threat is to adopt a
miserly perspective on political resources. Realists are not

alone in committing this error. Both Parsons and Barry follow Pareto in defining 'interests' to consist in 'generalized means to any ultimate ends'. On that analysis, it could never be in one's interest to spend any of his money, since that would entail a reduction in one's stock of 'generalized means'. As Aquinas put the point, if the highest aim of the captain were to preserve his ship he would keep it in port forever. That surely cannot be right. Resources, after all, are valued only for what can be done with them.[27]

A second consideration raised by the present analysis of symbolic rewards concerns the complications introduced by the interaction of affective and promissory symbolic rewards. It is commonplace to suggest that much disaffection is attributable to a 'revolution of rising expectations', expectations increasing far more rapidly than they can be (or anyway are likely to be) met. Responsibility is usually ascribed to political orators who tend to make exaggerated promises from the rostrum, but it seems plausible that commitments implicit in symbolic gestures are at least as much to blame as is political rhetoric. Perhaps the black's exaggerated expectations of the Great Society were more fueled by symbolic gestures— appointment of Thurgood Marshall to the Supreme Court, the Voting Rights Act and the like—than by any proposal for social welfare legislation contained in any of President Johnson's speeches.

To some extent, these exaggerated expectations result from a simple misunderstanding. Black men surely read

27. Talcott Parsons, *The Structure of Social Action* (Glencoe, Ill.: Free Press, 1949), p. 262. Brian Barry, 'The Public Interest', *Proceedings of the Aristotelian Society (Supplement)*, 38 (1964): 1–18. St. Thomas Aquinas, *Summa Theologica*, Part I-II, Question 2, Article 5. For critiques of similar flaws in realist theories of international politics, see L. Susan Stebbing, *Ideals and Illusions* (London: Watts & Co., 1944), and Stanley H. Hoffman, 'International Relations: The Long Road to Theory', *World Politics*, 11 (1959): 346–77.

more into the Civil Rights Act than was really there in terms of the commitment of the white community to social justice. Were this the entire problem, the conclusion would simply be that politicians should be more sensitive to possibilities for misinterpretation of their words and gestures.

The problem, however, is made much more serious by the intertwining of affective and promissory symbolic rewards. The appointment of Justice Marshall aimed most immediately at the affective goal of instilling a sense of racial pride, which is a goal of considerable importance to all black leaders. President Carter's symbolic quest for human rights arguably aims principally at the affective goal of instilling a sense of 'human dignity' in oppressed peoples. Suppose for the sake of argument that no one thought there would be any material advantage flowing from either act: i.e., no one thought that Justice Marshall would ever cast a decisive ballot in cases of interest to the black community or do anything to make the American Bar Association any less hopelessly racist; and no one thought that the United States would ever come to the aid of dissident groups (such as the authors of the Czech Charter 77) demanding their human rights be respected. The point remains that, no matter how far removed from distributive issues they seem to be, such symbolic victories inevitably carry with them the implication that some material benefits will follow. The fact that the political system has been forced to grant the group symbolic rewards in the one instance implies that the group has enough power (or enough powerful friends) to carry the day again on other issues, symbolic or material. These hopes, of course, are likely to be dashed. Symbolic rewards are often cheap and, since they do not require anyone to sacrifice much, opposition to them will be milder than to material rewards. But the direct and inevitable connections are there nevertheless.

Consider, as case in point, the dramatic gesture of Lincoln

during a visit to the recently liberated Confederate capital of Richmond. During the walkabout,

> the President halted a moment to rest. 'May de good Lord bless you, President Linkum!' said an old Negro, removing his hat and bowing, with tears of joy rolling down his cheeks. The President removed his own hat and bowed in silence; but it was a bow which upset the forms, laws, customs and ceremonies of centuries. It was a death-shock to chivalry and a mortal wound to caste. 'Recognize a nigger! Fough!' A woman in an adjoining house beheld it, and turned from the scene in unspeakable disgust.[28]

The President's bow was in itself nothing more than an affective act, an affirmation of the human worth of the old black man. But the act carried with it clear policy implications. The kind of man who would bow to a black man is not the kind of man who would permit his continued exploitation and humiliation. In this way, the act also carried promises within it.

Similarly, if less dramatically, it is said that 'the Mexican revolution . . . has been a potent source of symbolic gratification; it provides many Mexicans with hope and optimism for the future, dulls existing discontents, and generally increases the legitimacy of the present regime.'[29] Peasants are proud of the revolution—in itself it is an affective symbol of considerable value. But there is also the unspoken faith that, having happened once, the revolution might someday happen again

28. *Atlantic Monthly,* May 1865, quoted by Ferdinand Mount, *The Theatre of Politics* (London: Weidenfeld & Nicholson, 1972), p. 255.

29. Dennis Kavanagh, *Political Culture* (London: Macmillan, 1972), p. 255.

and lift them out of their suffering. In this way, the revolution is a promissory symbol as well.

Promissory and affective symbols are connected indirectly but even more strongly through 'symbolic capital'. The basic idea here is that symbolic advantages which are, strictly speaking, purely affective nevertheless place one in a position to achieve dramatic material gains. As an illustration of the surprising ways in which affective symbols and especially titles can translate into practical prerogatives, consider the plight of a female guest at the LBJ Ranch. 'In the middle of the night, she felt the presence of someone in the room. She was about to scream, when this little pencil flashlight flicked on and she heard a familiar voice say, "Move over—this is *yore* President."'[30] Status *is* a good indicator of future material allocations because status (along with merit, power, need, etc.) will determine these allocations. And, since what matters on each of these criteria is one's standing *relative* to other claimants, any symbolic gesture indicating an increase in one's relative status augurs well for subsequent increases in one's allocation of material goods. 'Symbolic capital' is readily 'convertible back into economic capital.' Observers of pressure group behaviour, for example, often comment on the way in which 'an organization elevates itself in the esteem of the general public and conditions their attitudes so that a state of public opinion will be created in which the public will almost automatically respond with favour to the programmes desired by the group.'[31] The same is true of any symbolic act tending to ele-

30. Myra MacPherson, *The Power Lovers* (New York: Ballantine, 1975), p. 200.

31. H. A. Turner, 'How Pressure Groups Operate', *Annals of the American Academy of Political and Social Science*, 319 (September 1958): 63–72. See more generally Pierre Bourdieu's discussion of 'symbolic capital' in *Outline of a Theory of Practice*, trans. Richard Nice (Cambridge: Cambridge University Press, 1977), p. 119, and Fred Hirsch's discussion of 'positional goods' in *Social Limits to Growth* (London: Routledge & Kegan Paul, 1976).

vate the stature of any group or individual. Insofar as any affective symbolic reward tends to raise the esteem of the recipient in the eyes of others in the community, it necessarily tends to provide a resource he can use for promoting his long-term material interests as well.

Thus, while it is crucial to distinguish affective from promissory symbolic rewards for purposes of pure analysis, the two are inevitably intertwined in actual policy disputes. In the abstract, affective and promissory symbolic rewards must be sharply distinguished and differentially evaluated. In practice, the two are often inexorably mixed, with some of the virtues of affective symbols rubbing off onto the less reputable promissory variety and vice versa.

This does not mean that the analysis offered here is useless, only that its results must be applied with caution by policy-makers. In any given situation, the mix of affective and promissory connotations of symbolic gestures must be carefully weighed and its larger implications noted. Once all that has been done, the propositions developed here can be of considerable utility to analysts of public policy. Indeed, no practical guidance in these matters can be had without some such preliminary exercise.

5.5 SYMBOLIC REWARDS AS A MODE OF MANIPULATION

Returning in conclusion to the larger theme of manipulatory politics, this chapter has identified two distinctive symbolic modes of manipulation. One plays upon promissory symbols and the other on affective. Each of these must now be assessed in terms of the questions posed in Section 1.6.

1. Is the interference deceptive?

Both types of symbolic reward are only slightly deceptive. Promissory symbolic rewards must, by their nature, be public—no one will be influenced by promises of which he is ignorant. The only conceivable element of deception lies in the possibility for misrepresenting the strength of the promise implicit in this type of symbolic reward. Sometimes people are fooled into believing that this symbolic payoff virtually guarantees subsequent delivery of the tangible good it promises, when in fact it does no such thing. But everyone, however badly deceived on this score, must at least recognize that the promissory symbol *is* just a promise of delivery and realize that they are still awaiting delivery of the real goods. Affective symbols might be slightly deceptive in other ways. While it is immediately apparent to everyone concerned that cherished political symbols are being evoked, they are often uncertain who is doing it and why. The scope for deception through playing on affective symbols is largely limited to fooling people as regards alternative opportunities—what is being covered up or what options are being foreclosed through symbolic action. But, again, the brute fact that affective symbols are being evoked cannot be disguised.

2. *Is the interference contrary to the putative will of those subject to it?*

From the point of view of the individuals concerned, both of these types of symbolic reward are in some sense welcome. The worst that can be said about either is that, happy as people are to receive them, they would have been even more pleased to receive something else. This is always the case with promissory symbolic rewards—people would prefer having the tangible goods rather than just the promise of their future delivery. Occasionally it is also the case with affective symbols, when their evocation serves to sweep more salient issues under the carpet. More often, and almost certainly over the long run, affective symbols are played upon just because people enjoy it, there is no underlying devious motive at work.

Taken together, these first two questions define an instance of manipulation. Promissory symbolic rewards qualify—if only barely—as manipulatory on both criteria. They are slightly deceptive and necessarily inferior to some other goods people might have pursued instead. Affective symbols look even less like mechanisms for manipulation, however. While they, too, are slightly deceptive, they are not necessarily (or even likely to be, in most instances) inferior to any other goods which people might have pursued. Playing on affective symbols, then, is just too marginal a case to qualify as a mode of (rational) manipulation at all.

The next two questions focus upon the seriousness of such manipulation as is threatened by genuinely manipulatory techniques. Since affective symbols fail to qualify, they will henceforth be omitted from consideration.

3. How persistent is the effect of the manipulation?

Manipulation accomplished through promissory symbolic rewards is unlikely to be long-lived. People who value symbolic rewards only as promissory coupons will surely lose patience if they are asked to wait too long for the coupons to be redeemed. Various stalling tactics might be possible, but before long it must become apparent that the promises are empty ones. From that moment, people cease to take any further note of their promissory symbolic rewards and press instead for 'the real thing', and the manipulative influence has been overcome.

4. Are any distributive biases inherent in the mechanism?

Such slight distributive biases as inhere in the mechanism of manipulating people through promissory symbolic rewards arise from the fact that only those persons who might plausibly deliver upon their promises can make promises that will be taken seriously. You cannot promise to give someone that which is not within your power to bestow. In this way symbolic rewards contain a slight conservative bias, insofar as those who presently command the larger stock of goods and services can most plausibly promise to transfer them later. But this bias is really rather slight. There is no guarantee, especially when existing power elites are under challenge, that those in control today will be in a position to deliver on their promises tomorrow. If the revolutionaries can persuasively argue that the revolution is imminent, and come the revolution they alone will be able to deliver on their promises, then promissory symbolic rewards will work to their advantage. Even in less favourable circumstances, when they cannot guarantee that the revolution is upon us, revolutionaries are often forced to rely upon promissory symbolic rewards. Being desperately short on resources in the present, they have little choice but to mortgage the future, which is what promissory symbols allow them to do. Thus it seems that such symbolic rewards are as, or more, useful to revolutionaries, and certainly do not display any clear distributive biases.

On balance, symbolic rewards do not seem to threaten serious political manipulation. Affective symbols hardly qualify as manipulative at all. Promissory symbols do qualify, but only barely. And they fail to display either the persistence or the distributive biases that might make them really worrying instances of manipulatory politics.

CHAPTER SIX ❦ RITES OF RULERS

ALLUSIONS TO 'POLITICAL RITUALS' ARE now rather common. Elections, Murray Edelman, Richard Rose and Harve Mossawir assure us, essentially serve ritualistic fuctions. Similarly with budgeting and social planning, Aaron Wildavsky, Johan Olsen and Herman van Gunsteren concur.[1] Quite what is being claimed is unclear, however, given a certain vagueness in the meaning of 'ritual'. In contemporary language, deriving indirectly from Latin through Middle English, the word 'rite' implies 'a formal procedure or act in a religious or other solemn observance'. Since 'rite' straddles religious and other solemn activities, political analysts can, in referring to 'political rituals', allude to quasi-religious aspects of politics without actually saying so. Some clearly do intend the religious analogy: Robert Bellah and Sidney Verba talk explicitly of 'civil religion', David Apter of 'political religion' and Wildavsky of planning as an 'act of faith'. Most, however, are content to hide noncommittally behind the looseness of language.[2]

Material from 'Rites of Rulers' by Robert E. Goodin is reprinted from *The British Journal of Sociology*, vol. 24, number 3 (September 1978), pp. 281-99, by permission of the Publishers, Routledge & Kegan Paul, Ltd.

1. Murray Edelman, *Symbolic Uses of Politics* (Chicago: Markham, 1971), Ch. 1. Richard Rose and Harve Mossawir, 'Voting and Elections: A Functional Analysis', *Political Studies*, 18 (1967): 173-201 at 176-77. Aaron Wildavsky, 'If Planning is Everything, Maybe It's Nothing', *Policy Sciences*, 4 (1973): 127-53. Johan Olsen, 'Local Budgeting, Decision-Making or a Ritual Act?' *Scandinavian Political Studies*, 5 (1970): 85-118. Herman van Gunsteren, *The Quest for Control* (London: Wiley, 1976).

2. Indeed, the vagueness of the word 'ritual' seems to be its charm for very many. Jack Goody, 'Religion and Ritual', *British Journal of Sociology*, 12 (1961): 142-64. observes that social anthropologists shifted over to talking of 'ritual' so as to sidestep the troublesome question of whether the performance in question was religious or magical. Sidney Verba, 'The Kennedy Assassination and the Nature of Political Commitment', *The Kennedy Assassination and the American Public*, ed. B. S. Greenberg and E. B. Parker (Stanford: Stanford

These theological residues in the notion of 'ritual' get in the way of understanding—and especially of evaluating—political rituals. We tend to misunderstand political rituals by supposing that they are necessarily appeals to supernatural powers; and we tend to judge them too harshly by supposing them necessarily irrational. We are misled to concur in Thurman Arnold's analogy between running a country and running an insane asylum and, along with it, his suggestion that governments emulate that 'government which civilized nations impose on savage tribes, . . . utilizing taboos instead of trying to stamp them out as unsound.'[3]

I propose to develop here a two-fold typology especially but not uniquely applicable to the analysis of political ritual. Its most striking feature is the exceedingly limited role accorded to religious aspects of ritual behaviour. A great many political rituals can, it is suggested, be analysed far more plausibly as illustrations of other categories. This richer understanding of the varieties of political ritual, in turn, allows us to see traditional objections to such practices as being narrowly applicable to the religious variety almost exclusively.

6.1   VARIETIES OF RITUALS

A rite is by definition 'a formal procedure or act in a religious or other solemn observance' (*Oxford English Dictionary*). Since the aim here is to produce a general analysis, the broader al-

---

University Press, 1965), pp. 348–60. Robert N. Bellah, 'Civil Religion in America', *Daedalus*, 96 (1967): 1–21. David E. Apter, 'Political Religion in the New Nations', *Old Societies and New Nations*, ed. Clifford Geertz (New York: Free Press, 1963), pp. 57–104. Wildavsky, 'If Planning is Everything.'

3. Thurman Arnold, *The Symbols of Government* (New Haven: Yale University Press, 1935), p. 233, echoing Vilfredo Pareto, *Treatise of General Sociology*, trans. A. Livingston (London: Jonathan Cape, 1935).

ternative is adopted: a formal procedure will be called a ritual if it merely involves a solemn performance. Of course, the reason for the solemnity is usually that the rite refers to or reaffirms an important theory of some sort or another. But sometimes the rituals persist long after the theory is forgotten. Indeed, one might argue that rituals arise only once the theory has been forgotten, so their operationalizations and rules-of-thumb can no longer be modified by reference back to the underlying theory and have rigidified instead. Thus, it is far better to tie the definition to solemnity.[4]

Two conditions, solemnity and activity, are individually necessary and jointly sufficient for a formal procedure to be ritualistic. The analysis offered below must be understood as an attempt to catalogue the several varieties of ritual. The import of the dimensions to be discussed is that they separate one variety of ritual from another, not that they separate ritual from non-ritual. Neither, it must be added, is there anything in the typology to suggest a developmental sequence or to reflect in any way on the historical origins of ritual.

4. Anthropologists disagree over the definition of 'ritual'. E. E. Evans-Pritchard, *Witchcraft, Oracles and Magic Among the Azande* (Oxford: Clarendon Press, 1937), Monica Wilson, *Rituals of Kinship among the Nyakusa* (New York: Oxford University Press, 1957), and Max Gluckman, 'Les Rites de Passage', *Essays on the Ritual of Social Relations,* ed. Gluckman (Manchester: Manchester University Press, 1962), pp. 1–52 at 22, all would save the term 'ritual' for situations in which participants suppose that mystical powers are involved, suggesting that 'ceremony' be used otherwise. However useful this may be as an act of linguistic legislation, such a restriction is not even faithful to conventional usage among anthropologists themselves. S. F. Nadel, *Nupe Religion* (Glencoe, Ill.: Free Press, 1954), suggests a more useful general definition, paralleling the *Oxford English Dictionary* definition quoted in the text, construing ritual as 'formalized stylized behaviour made repetitive in that form'; and in this he is supported by Goody, 'Religion and Ritual'. This more general analysis is certainly nearer the meaning of those talking of 'political rituals', as demonstrated in Steven Lukes, 'Political Rituals and Social Integration', *Sociology,* 9 (1975): 298–308.

In the two-fold typology of rituals I propose, the first dimension distinguishes rituals according to the character of
the powers to which they are thought to appeal, whether they
are natural or non-natural. For present purposes I shall take
this distinction as given within any particular society at any
particular time. But just as people's perceptions of what is
'natural' are shaped by their society, so too are they occasionally reshaped by the same forces. The boundary between the
'natural' and 'non-natural' is a shifting one. And, in light of
the power found below in rituals appealing to supernatural
forces, one of the better meta-manipulative tricks might be to
persuade people of the existence of supernatural entities
through which you can manipulate them. Against this
strategy people have only the rather inadequate recourses described in the analysis of 'metaphysical traps' in Section 3.4.

The supernatural is included in, but does not exhaust, the
category of the non-natural. That class also includes what
might be called 'sub-natural' powers, those owing entirely to
human contrivance. Hence, the term 'non-natural' (suggesting merely something 'deviating from the natural order') is
favoured over the stronger 'unnatural' (with its implication of
something 'contrary or doing violence to nature; monstrous').

The second dimension of the typology concerns the truth
value of the claims entailed in the ritual. This distinction is
inspired by the anthropological commonplace that rituals
consist in reenactments of important social myths.[5] The defining characteristic of a myth is its 'fictitious' quality. The second fold of the present typology, then, distinguishes rituals
which evoke fictions from those which evoke non-fictions.
Either, clearly, is capable of inspiring solemn performances.
Orange Day parades in Ulster are utterly solemn events

5. Edmund R. Leach, 'Ritual', *International Encyclopedia of the Social Sciences,* ed. D. L. Sills (London: Collier-Macmillan, 1968), 13: 520–26.

VARIETIES OF RITUAL, WITH POLITICAL ILLUSTRATIONS

Appeals to powers which are:

		natural	non-natural
Makes claims which are:	non-fictional	schematizing rituals	magico-religious rituals
	fictional	representational rituals	constitutive rituals

commemorating an utterly non-fictional occurrence, William's victory at the Battle of the Boyne. Anglicans celebrate Easter equally solemnly, even though many celebrants, when surveyed, agree that the Resurrection is pure fiction.

In this second distinction, I use the word 'fiction' in rather an unfamiliar way. The altogether too common supposition is that non-fiction is necessarily true and that fiction is necessarily false. But Urmson, in analysing fiction as a literary form, shows that this is not at all the distinction embodied in ordinary language. Non-fiction, properly termed, must indeed be true. While fictional works characteristically embody much that is untrue along with much that is not, Urmson argues that 'the essentially fictional element in works of fiction is neither true nor false.' The defining feature of fiction is not that it is false but rather that it does not matter whether it is true or false. Thus, Urmson concludes, fiction is 'a logically distinct type of utterance.'[6]

These two dimensions cutting across one another generate the four cells described in the table above. Entered in each

6. J. O. Urmson, 'Fiction', *American Philosophical Quarterly*, 13 (1976): 153–57. Fictions are not just 'alogical', in the Paretian sense that it is impossible to perform the critical experiment that would prove them right or wrong. With fictions, it makes no sense to talk in terms of true and false, whether they are verifiable or not.

cell is a politically significant illustration, each of which will be discussed at some length below. These examples in no way exhaust the categories even for political purposes, much less for sociological or anthropological ones. They are, nevertheless, profoundly important and intrinsically interesting examples from a political point of view.

6.1.1 *Magico-Religious Rituals*

The paradigm case of ritual is, of course, its magico-religious form. Magic and religion are here collapsed into a single logical category, which not only follows long-established social anthropological usage but is also warranted by the typology described in the table.[7] Both magic and religion appeal to supernatural powers. Each also depends crucially on non-fictional qualities of the claims entailed in the performance on at least two points. First, either a magical or religious ritual must appeal to supernatural powers which truly exist or else be a waste of time. Second, to be efficacious, the ritual must in each case be performed properly. The crucial elements of the ritual, whether religious or magical, cannot conceivably be arbitrary or conventional.

Magico-religious rituals clearly loom large in the political life of a primitive society. In some hunting-and-gathering societies, such as the Kuikuru of central Brazil, witchcraft and divination actually offer 'alternatives to political authority'. In the rather more complex African societies discussed by Gluckman, political rituals tap undeniably magico-religious powers. Even in the advanced Roman Empire, established myth traced the foundation of the state through Romulus and Remus to Mars himself.[8]

---

7. Evans-Pritchard, *Witchcraft;* Goody, 'Religion and Ritual'.

8. Gertrude E. Dole, 'Anarchy without Chaos: Alternatives to Political Authority among the Kuikuru', *Political Anthropology,* ed. M. J. Swartz, V. W.

The question is just how large a role, overt or covert, can plausibly be assigned to these 'primitive sentiments' in modern polities. In days past, of course, they were surely important influences. But first magic declined in favour of religion and science, and religion itself is now on the decline. As late as 1867 Bagehot could still claim, 'The English Monarchy strengthens our Government with the strength of religion', admitting that the phenomenon had long been waning. By 1901 Maitland was rudely punning the 'parsonification' of the sovereign, and in contemporary times there has been a well-documented decline in religiosity among the citizenry generally. Church attendance has dropped dramatically, and surveys reveal that growing numbers deny fundamental tenets of their professed faith. Thus, when Shils and Young suggested in 1953 that the Bible presented to the Queen in the course of the Coronation service is a 'source of continuous inspiration in the moral regulation of society', Norman Birnbaum (expressing the fashionable opinion) scoffed, 'The Gideon Society would be glad to hear this, but the rest of us doubt that this book has so much influence on contemporary life.'[9]

On this point, however, fashionable opinion seems considerably at variance with mass opinion. While established religion may wane, 'there actually exists alongside of and rather clearly differentiated from the churches an elaborate and

---

Turner and A. Tuden (Chicago: Aldine, 1966), pp. 73–87. Max Gluckman, *Politics, Law and Ritual in Tribal Society* (Chicago: Aldine, 1965). Henry Tudor, *Political Myth* (New York: Praeger, 1972), Ch. 2.

9. Keith Thomas, *Religion and the Decline of Magic* (New York: Scribner's, 1971). Walter Bagehot, *The English Constitution* (London: Chapman & Hall, 1867). F. W. Maitland, 'The Crown as Corporation', *Law Quarterly Review*, 17 (1901): 131–46. Edward Shils and Michael Young, 'The Meaning of the Coronation', *Sociological Review*, 1 (1953): 63–81. Norman Birnbaum, 'Monarchs and Sociologists', *Sociological Review*, 3 (1955): 5–23.

well-institutionalized civil religion'. The language is not in the least metaphorical—civil religion is religious in quite an ordinary sense. Bellah, commenting on the American case, writes that 'civil religion at its best is a genuine apprehension of universal and transcendent religious reality as seen in or, one could almost say, as revealed through the experience of the American people.' Lloyd Warner discusses Memorial Day as a fixture on the American civil religious calendar, observing that, 'being both sacred and secular, it is a holy day as well as a holiday and is celebrated accordingly'.[10]

Scientific operationalizations of 'civil religion' not only preserve but emphasize its transcendental character. Propositions taken to be indicative of civil religion in America include: 'America is God's chosen nation'; 'July 4th is a religious occasion'; 'the President's authority is derived from God'; 'the flag is sacred'; etc. Surveys using such indicators of civil religion in America have shown that such beliefs are surprisingly common. They show, furthermore, that the civil religious attitudinal dimension is separate and distinct from formal religious belief on the one hand and ordinary political preference on the other. Respect for the British monarchy stems from a similar civil-religious attitude, as the research of Richard Rose and Dennis Kavanagh shows. Thus, it would be wrong to conclude that the religious component has disappeared entirely from political ritual. Rather, it manifests itself in a slightly new form.[11]

10. Jean-Jacques Rousseau, *The Social Contract*, Bk. 4, Ch. 8. Bellah, 'Civil Religion in America'. W. Lloyd Warner, *American Life* (Chicago: University of Chicago Press, 1953).

11. Ronald C. Wimberly, 'Testing the Civil Religion Hypothesis', *Sociological Analysis*, 37 (1976): 341–52. Wimberley, Donald A. Clelland, Thomas C. Hood and C. M. Lipsey, 'The Civil Religious Dimension: Is It There?' *Social Forces*, 54 (1976): 890–900. Richard Rose and Dennis Kavanagh, 'The Monarchy in Contemporary Political Culture', *Comparative Politics*, 8 (1976): 548–76.

6.1.2 *Constitutive Rituals*

The powers to which magico-religious rituals appeal stand somehow above the natural order. Those to which constitutive rituals appeal are equally outside the natural order, but more below than above it. These powers exist neither naturally nor supernaturally but rather in consequence of human artifice and contrivance. Consider, for example, the powers of an umpire in cricket. Whatever his natural talents or capacities, he could not conceivably have the power of a cricket umpire in the absence of conventions and rules constituting that game.[12]

Appealing to a convention, one must necessarily be evoking a fiction, for a convention is by its very nature arbitrary. Some alternatives might be more attractive (useful, amusing, stable, etc.) than others. But it is not *truth* that leads us to choose one over another. Once a convention is concluded, of course, certain propositions can have derivative truth value within the context of the system of rules thereby established. Within the rules of soccer the proposition 'Cruyff is off-side' can have truth value in a way it cannot possibly have outside that context.[13] Nothing stands above the choice of conventions, however, to lend them a similar claim to derivative truth value. They must instead be regarded as fictions which can be neither true nor false.

Artificial systems of rules, be they formal institutions and practices of government or of cricket, must have two tiers. 'Primary rules', the most familiar form, directly guide behaviour of individuals subject to them. Another less obtrusive

12. Ludwig Wittgenstein, *Philosophical Investigations,* trans. G. E. M. Anscombe (Oxford: Blackwell, 1958).

13. In this way John R. Searle, *Speech Acts* (Cambridge: Cambridge University Press, 1969), derives 'ought' from 'is', and Evan Fales, 'Truth, Traditions and Rationality', *Philosophy of the Social Sciences,* 6 (1976): 97–113, defends the rationality of ritual.

set of 'secondary rules' is also required for the manipulation (application, change, etc.) of the primary rules.[14] The most important of these for present purposes are rules investing some individual with authority to manipulate primary rules in such a way as to be regarded as legitimate within the terms of the larger political system. In their operation, these 'secondary rules' require formal ceremonies at several steps. First, there must be some ceremony investing some individual with authority. Second, there must be some ceremony by which he invokes his authority. Since he leads a private life alongside his public one, there must be some procedure by which the authority distinguishes his private from his official pronouncements.

Much of what we have come to regard as political ritual can be seen in this light. The Inauguration of a President, the Coronation of a Queen or the swearing-in of legislators or judges are all authorization ceremonies. Similarly, many accoutrements of political ritual—the Great Seal, the Speaker's gavel and mace, the judge's gown—are instruments for invoking authority. The particular manifestations are, of course, arbitrary from an external point of view: but they are essential from an internal one. The fundamental point is that these practices, or something functionally equivalent to them, are *logically necessary* elements in the operation of any artificial system of rules.[15]

14. H. L. A. Hart, *The Concept of Law* (Oxford: Clarendon Press, 1961).

15. The Manchester School of social anthropologists maintain quite generally that *les rites de passage* serve to 'segregate roles'. Political ritual is, on this interpretation, a rite marking passage from private citizen to public officeholder. See: Gluckman, 'Les Rites de Passage'; Meyer Fortes, 'Ritual and Office in Tribal Society', *Essays in the Ritual of Social Relations,* ed. Gluckman, pp. 53–88; and, for applications, Thurman Arnold, *The Folklore of Capitalism* (New Haven: Yale University Press, 1937), and Harold Garfinkel, 'Conditions of Successful Degradation Ceremonies', *American Journal of Sociology,* 61 (1956): 420–24. Logically necessary rituals must be distinguished from merely convenient ones. Initiation rituals are logically necessary for inducting

For those performances to be properly termed 'rituals' they must be conducted with a measure of solemnity that is not, strictly speaking, logically entailed by their social function. It is, however, entirely understandable that constitutive rituals should be conducted with considerable pomp. Great events are quite fittingly accompanied by great ceremony. Marriage has a more lasting impact on one's life than paying a traffic fine, and it is appropriate that it is a more ceremonious occasion even when conducted in the Registrar's Office or Soviet Marriage Hall. Monarchs and Presidents and Chief Justices play an objectively greater role in the life of a society than do army privates and ordinary magistrates, so it is entirely proper that their swearing-in should be accompanied by greater ceremony. 'Surely if the Queen skipped down the aisle at her coronation instead of marching slowly and regally, the symbolic illusion would be destroyed', as Pitkin observes. Judicial procedures may be absurdly elaborate, but tied to them is the dignity of the court: 'oyez, oyez' may be fancy, but 'here comes the judge' is a disrespectful joke. Formal robes may be unnecessarily flowing, but one may well ask with Carlyle, 'Lives the man that can figure a naked Duke of Windlestraw addressing a naked House of Lords?'[16]

6.1.3 *Schematizing Rituals*

Schematizing rituals are often employed in constructing conceptual models of the sort discussed in Section 2.5 for

---

new members into artificial groups, for example, whereas the special handshakes and code words by which members of secret societies recognize one another are logically superfluous. The handshake does not make one a member—or even renew one's membership—but only serves a strategically necessary function of substituting for membership rolls. See E. J. Hobsbawm, *Primitive Rebels* (New York: Norton, 1965).

16. Thomas Carlyle, *Sartor Resartus* (Boston: James Munroe & Co., 1836). Hanna Pitkin, *The Concept of Representation* (Berkeley: University of California Press, 1967), p. 103. Jennifer McDowell, 'Soviet Civil Ceremonies', *Journal for the Scientific Study of Religion*, 13 (1974): 265–79.

understanding and coping with complex sets of natural facts. The goal is for the model to be true, for it to correspond in important respects to natural processes, in order eventually to manipulate natural powers successfully. In the process of attempting to understand natural truths, of course, analogies and other fictions are often employed. But it is entirely possible that a model which is unrealistic in some respects might nevertheless mirror reality accurately in other respects.[17] Thus, truth is the primary concern of schematizing rituals.

The powers involved in these rituals are strictly natural. The rituals are not themselves constitutive of any new non-natural powers, nor in schematizing does one appeal to supernatural powers. Even for the devout, who believe themselves to be operating with schemata ordained by God and revealed through His Holy Word, schemata still are merely mechanisms for manipulating natural powers which themselves have a supernatural origin.

A 'solemn performance' often is employed to establish these rather mundane schemata. Anthropological evidence suggests that much of what we immediately recognize as ritual behaviour is aimed at reinforcing quasi-scientific schemata. Robin Horton reinterprets in just these terms rituals that Max Gluckman regards as representative of social relations and that Victor Turner regards as appeals to the supernatural. And the utter earnestness with which Western scientists proceed, along with their scrupulous obsession with 'proper form' and their penchant for obscurantist terminology, suggests a strong tendency for schematizing behaviour to be a ritualistic, solemn performance.[18]

17. Hans Vaihinger, *The Philosophy of 'As If'*, trans. C. K. Ogden (London: Routledge & Kegan Paul, 1924). May Brodbeck, 'Models, Meaning and Theories', *Symposium on Sociological Theory,* ed. Llewellyn Gross (New York: Harper & Row, 1959), pp. 373–403.

18. Robin Horton, 'Ritual Man in Africa', *Africa,* 34 (1964): 85–104. Stanislav Andreski, *Social Sciences as Sorcery* (London: André Deutsch, 1972).

Why rituals need to be used in establishing such mundane schemata is somewhat puzzling. Were schematizing simply an impartial search for a natural truths, we would expect it to be both apolitical and non-ritualized. Such expectations mistake the nature of science. The construction of conceptual schemata quite generally must be seen as a highly politicized endeavour. As Thomas Kuhn has shown, ritualized normal science operates to avert 'revolutionary' paradigm-shifts. Sometimes these 'political' manoeuvres are confined narrowly to the scientific community itself, having no more import for the shape of politics in general than would similar manoeuvring in a small corporate boardroom. But in a broader sense the dominant scientific paradigm dovetails with and forms the basis of a 'social construction of reality', not just natural reality but social reality as well. A well-entrenched social construction of reality forecloses debate on all manner of questions which, given an alternative construction, might well be live political questions. Scientists and social scientists ritualistically invoke norms of 'objectivity' in the same way, and for the same reasons, as journalists: 'the term "objectivity" stands as a bulwark between themselves and critics. Attacked for a controversial presentation of "facts", newspapermen invoke their objectivity almost the way a Mediterranean peasant might wear a clove of garlic around his neck to ward off evil spirits.' So too do scientists.[19]

Claude Lévi-Strauss, *The Savage Mind* (Chicago: University of Chicago Press, 1966), makes the stronger claim that all ritual, through binary contrasts, separates the continuum of experience into discrete categories instrumental to abstract reasoning of any form.

19. Gaye Tuchman, 'Objectivity as Strategic Ritual: An Examination of Newsmen's Notions of Objectivity', *American Journal of Sociology*, 77 (1971–72): 660–79. Thomas S. Kuhn, *Structure of Scientific Revolutions* (Chicago: University of Chicago Press, 1962). Paul Feyerabend, "'Science': The Myth and Its Role in Society', *Inquiry*, 18 (1975): 167–81. Alan Ryan, "'Normal" Science or Political Ideology', *Philosophy, Politics and Society*, 4th Series, ed. P. Laslett, W. G. Runciman and Q. Skinner (Oxford: Blackwell, 1972), pp. 86–

What is more important, and less familiar, is that such expectations of scientific objectivity doubly mistake the nature
of group dynamics. Firstly, any group engaged in any col-
laborative venture, however loosely organized, naturally develops a kind of ritualized code for communicating experiences and speculations and insights and discoveries. As Basil
Bernstein and Mary Douglas rightly emphasize,

> Any structured group that is a group to the extent that its
> members know one another very well, for example in
> cricket, science or local government, will develop its spe-
> cial form of restricted code which shortens the process of
> communication by condensing units into pre-arranged
> coded forms. . . . Much of the writings and conference
> proceedings of anthropologists, or of every other body of
> scholars, would have to be classed as ritualistic or re-
> stricted code in so far as the citing of fieldwork, the ref-
> erence to (often impossible) procedures, the footnotes,
> etc., are given as pre-coded items of social interaction.

Shorthand codes and abbreviations more generally can be extraordinarily important, practically as well as politically, for
what they conceal. Marcuse is right to complain,

> NATO does not suggest what North Atlantic Treaty Or-
> ganization says, namely, a treaty among the nations of the
> North-Atlantic—in which case one might ask questions
> about the membership of Greece and Turkey. USSR ab-
> breviates Socialism and Soviet; DDR: democratic; UN
> dispenses with undue emphasis on 'united'; SEATO with

---

100. Peter L. Berger and Thomas Luckmann, *The Social Construction of Reality*
(London: Allen Lane, 1967). R. D. Laing, *The Politics of Experience* (New York:
Random House, 1967).

those Southeast-Asian countries which do not belong to it.[20]

Schemata, even if they do nothing more than generate short-hand codes, might still perform an important political function.

Secondly, as Sections 3.2 and 3.3 show, the categories people possess for coding their experiences dictate in part (if only in part and temporarily) what sorts of experiences impinge upon their consciousness. As John Searle observes in his commentaries on *The Campus War*, 'the possession of the dramatic category, falling-in-love [for example], makes possible certain sorts of experience which would not be possible or would be different without that category. In a conflict as intense as a student revolt, almost everything that happens is perceived through the filter of the dramatic categories of the participants.' Searle offers various examples. When the university administration makes concessions to student demands, the phenomenon is fitted into the dramatic category of 'oppressed-minority-wins-struggle-for-justice-against-reactionary-authorities'. In many instances a more accurate description of events would be 'oppressed-minority-engages-in-pointless-battle-with-authorities-for-something-they-are-prepared-to-give-anyhow', but this is not a permissible category, and consequently it is virtually impossible to perceive events in these terms' Similarly 'whites-oppress-blacks' is an eligible dramatic category, and events falling within it are widely reported, whereas 'blacks-oppress-whites' is not an eligible category and phenomena fitting within it are ignored. Or, again, the college administrator is always perceived in terms of the dramatic category, 'college administrator, agent of the mil-

20. Mary Douglas, *Natural Symbols* (New York: Random House, 1970), Ch. 4, drawing upon Basil Bernstein, *Class Codes and Control* (London: Routledge & Kegan Paul, 1975). Herbert Marcuse, *One-Dimensional Man* (Boston: Beacon Press, 1964), p. 94.

itary-industrial complex, tool of reaction, etc.', whatever the particular individual says or does. In the 'campus war' as Searle perceives it, these dramatic categories function just as the concepts of normal science in Kuhnian paradigms. 'In so far as these categories are hypotheses, they become self-verifying, for evidence which does not support them is not even admissible.'[21]

The primary mechanism through which schematizing rituals exert political influence is language itself, as discussed in Chapter 3. Sometimes the conceptual schemata embedded in the language are actually loaded in favour of some interests and against others, after the fashion of cage-like linguistic traps. More often and more successfully, biases will derive from omission of crucial concepts. Either way, linguistic schemata and rituals for evoking them are likely to be politically charged.

6.1.4 *Representational Rituals*

Representational rituals, too, deal with strictly natural phenomena. The paradigm case might be classic rites of passage associated with various 'life crises'—birth, puberty, death, etc. These correspond to transitions of a starkly natural sort. One is born, matures and dies (in a physical sense, at least) quite independently of ritual performances.[22]

21. John Searle, *The Campus War* (Harmondsworth: Penguin, 1972), pp. 71–77. Of course, Searle's analysis applies to the professors as well, and it would be interesting to see an analysis of the 'dramatic categories' through which he is interpreting these events for us.
22. This caveat is required because rites of passage serve a constitutive as well as a representative function. Among the Ashanti, for example, an infant is not 'deemed to be human until it has lived to the eighth day when it is named and thus incorporated into its family lineage' (Fortes, 'Ritual and Office in Tribal Society', p. 85). Similarly, the deceased does not officially pass into the world of the dead until funeral rites have been conducted, even if he long ago ceased breathing. Much the same is true of rituals inducting members into associations establishing 'professional status' as a doctor, solicitor,

Rituals marking these passages memorialize natural events without appealing (or, rather, without logically having to appeal) to anything beyond.

Unlike schematizing rituals, which also deal with natural phenomena, representational rituals do not purport to offer a true explanatory account of these phenomena. Representational rituals are, rather, symbolic of salient features of social reality. Ritual representations of social relations can no more aspire to truth value than painted representations of a bowl of fruit: in both cases, what are salient features of the object to be represented must remain a matter of taste. Symbols such as these 'are neither true nor false, because they assert nothing.... But they are, like laughing, lyrics and music, expressive'.[23] Representational rituals are, therefore, classified as 'fictions'.

Social rituals in general typically have a representational aspect.[24] This is perhaps most apparent with respect to

---

etc. The rituals are in part representative of one's accomplishments in professional training and in part constitutive of professional status. See Everett C. Hughes, *Men and Their Work* (Glencoe, Ill.: Free Press, 1958).

23. Susanne K. Langer, *Philosophy in a New Key* (Cambridge: Harvard University Press, 1942), p. 84.

24. The argument is put most forcefully by Bronislaw Malinowski, *Freedom and Civilization* (New York: Roy, 1944), p. 160, who sees rituals as reenactments of a myth which serves as 'a charter for social action'. J. H. M. Beattie, 'Ritual and Social Change', *Man*, 1 (1966): 60–74, similarly emphasizes the 'expressive' aspect of ritual behaviour. Elements of this interpretation are found in Jane Harrison, *Ancient Art and Ritual* (New York: Oxford University Press, 1913), p. 49, who observes that in ritual primitive man 'tends to re-enact whatever makes him feel strongly; any one of his manifold occupations, hunting, fighting, later ploughing and sowing, provided it be of sufficient interest and importance, is material for a *dromenon* or rite.' This may also be what Durkheim had in mind when calling rituals 'collective representations', provided we follow Steven Lukes in understanding his 'sacred/profane' dichotomy as merely a manifestation of the distinction between collective and individual *consciences;* see Lukes, *Émile Durkheim* (London: Allen Lane, 1973), pp. 24–28.

ritualized play. Consider Orlando Patterson's discussion of 'The Cricket Ritual in the West Indies'. There, 'a test match is not so much a game as a collective ritual—a social drama in which almost all the basic conflicts within the society are played out symbolically'. Class distinctions are mirrored starkly in the seating arrangements: whites and light-skinned blacks in the comfortable pavilion; the black masses on the hard wooden bleachers exposed to the hot sun and 'fenced off from the rest of the ground with chicken wire'; and middle class blacks in relatively less uncomfortable covered stands with concrete seats and lower chicken wire. The game itself encapsulates the colonial experience. 'Cricket is the Englishman's game. The very name, cricket, has become a byword. Its vocabulary is a pool of stock images for Tory statesmen. No better symbol of English culture could be found. . . . It is the game, deep down, which we must hate— the game of the master. So victory—victory against the Englishman—is a matter of great moment.' Drawing on the representational and ritual aspects of the game, Patterson plausibly explains the deep emotion and frequent rioting accompanying so many test series between Britain and the West Indies.[25]

Discussing a very different locale, Geertz shows how the Balinese cockfight is likewise a representational ritual. 'Drawing on almost every level of Balinese experience . . . and binding them into a set of rules which at once contains them and allows them play', the cockfight ritual 'builds a symbolic structure in which, over and over again, the reality of the inner affiliations can be intelligibly felt'.[26]

25. Orlando Patterson, 'The Cricket Ritual in the West Indies', *New Society*, 352 (1969): 988-89.
26. Clifford Geertz, "Deep Play: Notes on the Balinese Cockfight', *Daedalus*, 101 (1972): 1-38.

More conspicuously political rituals likewise often purport to represent certain salient features of the polity. Gluckman, surveying research growing out of Evans-Pritchard and Fortes's seminal work on *African Political Systems,* concludes that, in political rituals, 'major loyalties are affirmed through the dramatic representation both of many bonds of unity and of the conflicts that lie within these various bonds'. Take the Shilluk coronation ritual as an example: 'The mock-battle between the king and Nyikang's [the medium between God and man] effigy symbolized the fundamental conflicts from one prince occupying a position representative of all Shilluk unity'; finally, 'the king is forcibly separated from his own relatives and lieges to be placed at the head of the nation, above sectional loyalties'. Western society affords abundant parallels. The Elizabethan doctrine that, in the person of the English Sovereign, 'the Body natural and the Body politic are . . . united, and as one Body' suggests identical symbolism. Public ceremonies of the Soviets, May Day parades in Red Square and the like, are similarly dramatic depictions of the cohesion of the proletariat worldwide.[27]

These examples happen to demonstrate how rituals, in representing social reality, reflect and reinforce social integration. But this is in no way a necessary connection. Representational rituals often produce social cohesion by depicting external threats, as in the political witch-hunts so common in

27. Meyer Fortes and E. E. Evans-Pritchard, *African Political Systems* (London: Oxford University Press, 1940). Gluckman, *Politics, Law and Ritual in Tribal Society,* pp. 265, 251-52, 132. E. E. Evans-Pritchard, *The Divine Kingship of the Shilluk of the Anglo-Egyptian Sudan* (Cambridge: Cambridge University Press, 1948). Ernst H. Kantorowicz, *The King's Two Bodies* (Princeton: Princeton University Press, 1957). McDowell, 'Soviet Civil Ceremonies'; and Chistel Lane, 'Ritual and Ceremony in Contemporary Soviet Society', *Sociological Review,* 27 (1979): 253-78. Consensual and differentiating rituals are found even in schools, as shown by Bernstein, 'Ritual in Education', *Class, Codes and Control,* 3: 54-66.

'corporate' societies. And in seriously divided societies there
are representational rituals that mirror those divisions.
Orange Day parades around the perimeter of Catholic quar-
ters of Belfast are graphic dramatizations of the siege under
which that community lives. May Day marches in capitalist
countries similarly provide ritualistic portrayal of deep class
divisions. The functional model of political ritual, then, errs
in overlooking dysfunctional rituals in divided societies.[28]

The implication to be drawn is that the representational
character of these rituals is what truly lies at their core, and
that whether they have integrationist or disintegrationist results depends entirely on how people react to what they see
depicted. On this more general model, it would be entirely
possible for a representational ritual to have no implications
whatsoever for social integration. One such example might be
the U.S. Supreme Court's ritualistic evocation of constitutional principles of, e.g., limited government. The point of
the ritual is more to make a statement about how the American government is organized than to stir up citizens either in
support of or opposition to the arrangements.[29]

A particularly striking application of this theory of representational rituals is to the analysis of public response to political corruption. Many purely utilitarian objections—inefficiency, waste, arbitrariness—could be raised against corruption.
But in some places, such as Ghana, Nigeria and India,
the public reaction is less strong than the gross inefficien-

28. Albert James Bergesen, 'Political Witch Hunts and Subversion in
Cross-National Perspective', *American Sociological Review*, 42 (1977): 220–32.
Lukes, 'Political Ritual and Social Integration'; but Elliott Leyton, 'Opposition
and Integration in Ulster', *Man*, 9 (1974): 185–98, shows that both types of
ritual are at work there, keeping bloodshed down.

29. Max Lerner, 'Constitution and Court as Symbols', *Yale Law Journal*,
46 (1937): 1290–1319. William Y. Elliott, "Constitution as the American Social Myth', *The Constitution Reconsidered*, ed. Conyers Read (New York: Columbia University Press, 1938), pp. 209–24.

cy would warrant. In other places, such as America, reaction is far stronger than the simple inefficiency of corruption warrants. Indeed, survey research suggests that Americans regard as most corrupt practices which are relatively cheap. The driveway of a mayor's private residence being paved by the city crew is regarded as corrupt by 96 percent of respondents. A member of Congress attempting to win a weapons contract for a firm in his district (although it may be less efficient than competitors) or save the oil depletion allowance for an oil company in which he holds substantial stock (although it costs the Treasury dearly) is regarded as corrupt by only 32 and 55 percent of respondents respectively.[30] The fairly trivial inefficiency of paving the mayor's drive seems to evoke a much stronger reaction than the relatively large potential inefficiency of awarding a contract to an uncompetitive firm.

The definition of and reaction to political corruption can more plausibly be understood by analysing the political process as an important representational ritual. In rural British mores, continuing into the early years of the past century, it was not thought corrupt for landlords to dictate the votes of tenants. This was only appropriate given the character of the society the electoral ritual represented: the landlord 'was head of a community towards which he [the tenant] had recognised duties and obligations, and with which he shared a community of interest'. In Nigeria, nepotism is regarded not as corrupt but rather as obligatory. On the representational ritual model, the nonchalance of former colonials toward

30. Victor T. LeVine, *Political Corruption: The Ghana Case* (Stanford: Hoover Institution Press, 1975). Ronald Wraith and Edgar Simpkins, *Corruption in Developing Countries* (London: Allen & Unwin, 1963). Samuel J. Eldersveld, V. Jagannadham and A. P. Barnabas, *The Citizen and the Administrator in a Developing Country* (Glenview, Ill: Scott, Foresman, 1968). John G. Peters and Susan Welch, 'Political Corruption in America', *American Political Science Review*, 72 (1978): 974–84; cf. Hazel Erskine, 'Corruption in Government: the Polls', *Public Opinion Quarterly*, 37 (1974): 628–44.

political corruption is explained by the alien character of the
institutions defining the practices as corrupt. The definition
of corruption was imposed from without rather than growing
up as representative of any salient features of the existing society. In many nations, however, the political process has indeed emerged as a representational ritual meant to capture
important features of the social process. Corruption of these
rituals is typically, and understandably, regarded as a very serious matter indeed. Americans might be obsessed with fair
practices in electoral competition, for example, because
through that ritual they are reassured of the fairness of the
economic competition pervading their society. This, in turn,
might help to explain the reaction to the Watergate scandal,
which Theodore White perceptively analyses as a 'breach of
faith'. 'The true crime of Richard Nixon', White writes, 'was
simple: he destroyed the myth that binds America together,
and for this he was driven from power'.[31]

6.1.5   *Mixed Modes*

For the purpose of cataloguing the varieties of political
ritual it is important that each type be described in pure form.
In practice, few actual rituals fit exclusively into a single category. Religious ritual is primarily an appeal to the supernatural, but not exclusively. Durkheim observed long ago that
it takes one particular form rather than another because, in
addition to appealing to the supernatural, religious ritual
must also serve as a representational ritual depicting certain

---

31. H. J. Hanham, *Elections and Party Management* (London: Longmans,
Green, 1959), p. 8. Wraith and Simpkins, *Corruption in Developing Countries.*
LeVine, *Political Corruption.* Bayless Manning, 'The Purity Potlatch', *Federal
Bar Journal,* 24 (1964): 243–49. Theodore H. White, *Breach of Faith* (New
York: Atheneum, 1975). Ronald Dworkin, 'The Man and the Office', *Sunday
Times* (London), 5 October 1975, p. 38, properly chastizes White for focusing
too narrowly on myths about the President and his character.

rather mundane features of the society in which it is found. In medieval Europe, 'The peasantry were symbolically separated from the official mysteries of the Church by liturgical rituals; whereas in the early Church the priest had celebrated Mass facing the people, in the medieval period "he turned his back on them and retreated to the fastness of the sanctuary, separated from the people's part of the Church by a forbidding screen."' Rituals such as this serve to emphasize the extent to which feudalism imposed status hierarchies in everyday life. Important constitutive functions are served by religious rites, such as baptism naming the child or the coronation installing a monarch. Many also serve schematizing ends, providing what Peter Berger calls a *Sacred Canopy* of meaning for events in this world.[32]

Consider, again, the Presidential Inauguration or the Coronation. These are primarily constitutive rituals. Through them, ordinary mortals are transformed into presidents and monarchs. But they also have rather important magico-religious overtones. The Coronation is a religious ceremony, held in Westminster Abbey and conducted by the Archbishop of Canterbury; and the incoming President swears his oath on the Bible. Much about the ceremonies also serves representational ends. Shils and Young trace these connections for the Coronation ritual, and much the same can be said for the Presidential Inauguration. Notice, for example, the supportive role of the new First Lady holding the Bible while her husband is sworn into office.

Similar intermingling is found in Erik Erikson's discussion of the essentially representational rituals whereby Americans

32. Nicholas Abercrombie and Bryan S. Turner, 'The Dominant Ideology Thesis', *British Journal of Sociology*, 29 (1978): 149–70 at 154, quoting in part from Friedrich Heer,*The Medical World* (New York: Mentor, 1963), p. 199. Peter L. Berger, *The Sacred Canopy* (Garden City, N.Y.: Doubleday, 1967).

of Jefferson's era constructed their new identity. Erikson postulates that 'any true identity is anchored in the confirmation
of three aspects of reality. One is *factuality*, that is, a universe
of facts, data and techniques that can be verified with the ob-
servational methods and the work techniques of the time.'
The first element clearly involves what have been termed
schematizing rituals in the above discussion. 'Then', Erikson
writes, 'there is an inspiringly new way of experiencing history as unifying all facts, numbers and techniques into a *sense
of reality* that has visionary qualities and yet energizes the participants in most concrete tasks.' In light of his earlier comments about the way in which all men through history 'have
entertained systematic illusions regarding the God-given
superiority of their own kind', this might most plausibly be
interpreted as involving magico-religious elements. 'And, finally,' Erikson concludes, 'there must be a new *actuality*, a new
way of relating to each other, of activating and invigorating
each other in the service of common goals.' For this purpose,
primarily representational rituals are required.[33]

From these examples, it must be surmised that each of the
foregoing categories offers only a partial explanation of any
actual ritual. Furthermore, it must be conceded that each
ritual also fits into a larger package of social practices likely to
contain rituals of all sorts. But components in such a package
are separable, logically and often practically as well: Italian
Communists participate as fully as priests allow in Catholic
religious ritual while eschewing representational and
schematizing aspects of Church ritual.[34] What is important is

33. Erik H. Erikson, *Dimensions of a New Identity* (New York: Norton,
1974), pp. 27, 33. Mary Douglas, 'Self-Evidence', *Implicit Meanings* (London:
Routledge & Kegan Paul, 1975), pp. 276–318 at 314, similarly finds that 'our
schemes of the world are determined by . . . the logical patterning deployed
in social behaviour' (p. 314), judging from research on the Israelites, the Thai
and the Karam of New Guinea.

34. David I. Kertzer, 'Participation of Italian Communists in Catholic
Ritual', *Journal for the Scientific Study of Religion*, 14 (1975): 1–12.

that, taken together, these four categories constitute a complete and coherent account of the complex behaviour involved in ritual performance. The following section demonstrates how making such distinctions helps us to reach a more balanced evaluation of political ritual in general.

6.2 EVALUATING POLITICAL RITUALS

Having explored these several varieties of ritual, we are now in a position to evaluate their impact on the political system. The focus will be on two broad categories of complaint. One holds that ritual necessarily perpetuates lies about the nature of man and his society. The other holds that ritual necessarily inhibits social change. When each of these complaints is considered in turn, we find that each applies primarily (if at all) to magico-religious rituals.

6.2.1 *Do Rituals Lie?*

The model of ritual as a mechanism of misrepresentation is well ensconced in conventional wisdom. Ritual, it is commonly agreed, evokes myth; and the *Oxford English Dictionary* defines 'myth' as 'fiction' and 'fiction' as 'deceit, pretense'. Bentham is particularly pointed in his objections to legal ritual evoking legal fictions:

> It has never been employed but to a bad purpose. It has never been employed to any purpose but the affording a justification for something which otherwise would be unjustifiable. No man ever thought of employing false assertions where the purpose might equally have been fulfilled by true ones. By false assertion, a risk at least of disrepute is incurred: by true ones, no such risk.

Even sympathetic commentators convinced of the functional necessity of such lies can manage no better apology than to call them 'rationalizations'. The taint of falsehood lingers. As Thurman Arnold argues more boldly, 'Institutional creeds must be false in order to function effectively.... They must authoritatively suppress any facts which conflict with their ideals.'[35]

Ironically, this allegation is levelled most often at forms of ritual which by nature evoke fictions, incapable of being true or false. Bentham's wrath is directed at legalistic rituals evoking legal fictions. But those, as Lon Fuller shows, are primarily constitutive rituals establishing and governing an artificial system of rules.[36] Judges, in holding that corporations are persons in the eyes of the law, are simply establishing a rule for subsequent applications of the law. They obviously are not intending to deceive anyone by suggesting that IBM is really a mammal with human characteristics. Working within a system of legal rules, the deduction that corporations count as legal persons may be true or false, of course; but truth or falsehood is confined to that narrow context. There is no more reason, on grounds of truth, for preferring a legal system deeming corporations not to be persons than there is for preferring the axioms of Euclidean geometry.

Similarly, it is often argued that representational rituals lie, most especially about the history of a society they represent. Levellers and Diggers, for example, fastened on the

35. Jeremy Bentham, 'Constitutional Code', *Works*, ed. J. Bowring (Edinburgh: William Tait, 1843), 3: 241. D. H. Munro, 'The Concept of Myth', *Sociological Review*, 42 (1950): 115–32. Arnold, *Folklore of Capitalism*, pp. 356–57. See further Christian Bay, 'Foundations of the Liberal Make-Believe', *Inquiry*, 14 (1971): 213–43.

36. Lon Fuller, *Legal Fictions* (Stanford: Stanford University Press, 1967). Geoffrey Marshall and Graeme C. Moodie, *Some Problems of the Constitution*, 5th ed. (London: Hutchinson, 1971), p. 20, similarly complain, 'The legal omnipotence of Parliament, for example, is not exactly a "pretence", though it is often called a legal "fiction". But it is no more and no less "fictitious" than any other legal rule.'

Myth of the Norman Yoke, the belief that all Englishmen had been free and equal before the Conquest. Histories as such can be true or, as in the case of the Myth of the Norman Yoke, false. The more important role of that myth, however, was in connection with a representational ritual. There historical accuracy is beside the point. Just as, to some eyes, van Gogh's impressionistic rendering of sunflowers is a more satisfactory representation than a neo-realist's, so too might myths build on inaccurate histories that better capture the spirit of the social group. The Myth of the Norman Yoke, though historically untrue, did indeed capture the profound egalitarianism motivating the Leveller and Digger movements. Geertz, in his comparison of Islam in Indonesia and Morocco, relates the legends of Sunan Kalidjaga and Sīdī Lahsen Lyusi, pointedly adding, 'These men are metaphors. Whatever they originally were or did as actual persons has long since dissolved into an image of what Indonesians or Moroccans regard to be true spirituality.'[37] Since the point of the legends is to represent spiritual bonds underlying the communities, the historical inaccuracies are of no moment.

Surely it is true that 'the myths and rituals which a regime has allowed or, more usually, encouraged to grow up around itself often reveal something significant about the real nature of that regime.' But the 'realities' such representational rituals reveal pertain to values, aspirations, goals and preferred self-images. When Macmillan projected an image of 'populist, good-humoured, consensual Toryism' or John Kennedy one

---

37. Christopher Hill, *Puritanism and Revolution* (London: Panther, 1968). Castro similarly described a mythic golden past ended by Batista's tyranny: 'Once upon a time there was a republic. It had its constitution, its laws, its civil rights, a president, a Congress and law courts. Everyone could assemble, associate, speak and write with complete freedom. . . .' Hugh Thomas, *Cuba* (New York: Harper & Row, 1971), p. 848. Clifford Geertz, *Islam Observed* (New Haven: Yale University Press, 1968), p. 25.

of 'aristocratic, activist liberalism', they were just drawing out
what were to them the most salient features of their governments.[38] It is interesting and important to know how
politicians see themselves, but we must not confuse self-image
with reality. Whether this self-characterization fits well or ill—
whether the implicit claims are true or false—is a question which
representational rituals themselves simply cannot settle.

Where fictional rituals (be they representative or constitutive) are concerned, the only possible lie is that they can have
truth value at all. In light of the discussion introducing Section 6.1, such a trick might be thought absolutely transparent.
But where the fiction/non-fiction distinction is mistaken, as it
so often is, for a false/true distinction the error is not only easy
but also inevitable. Failure to appreciate the distinctive nature
of fictions is doubtless the source of the tendency, especially
common among primitive peoples, for rituals which began as
mere representations of important features of daily life to
evolve into schematizing and, ultimately, magico-religious
rituals. The gods and goblins which serve so usefully as creative fantasies in fictional representational rituals get shifted
into non-fictional rituals where such fantasies are grossly inappropriate. Lest this tendency be thought to be confined to
primitives, notice parallels in Erikson's discussion of the process by which the founders of America constructed a new
identity, which he analyses as a process of 'pseudospeciation'.
'The *pseudo* means that, far from perceiving or accepting a
human identity based on a common specieshood, different
tribes and nations, creeds and classes (and, perchance, political parties) consider themselves to be the one chosen species
and will, especially in times of crisis, sacrifice to this claim
much of the knowledge, the logic and the ethics that are

38. Ferdinand Mount, *The Theatre of Politics* (London: Weidenfeld &
Nicholson, 1972), p. 9.

theirs.' Maurice Bloch argues that social structure quite generally is an 'invisible system created by ritual' which 'only becomes stable when its origins are hidden. . . . This is done by
the creation of a mystified "nature" consisting of concepts and
categories of time and persons divorced from everyday experience.' But, as Bloch goes on to acknowledge and as Section 3.4 has elaborated, no such concepts are ever really entirely independent of experience and disconfirming empirical
data will soon enough undermine social structure based on
such mythic fictions alone.[39]

Logically speaking, the only types of ritual that admit of
lies are those purporting to make non-fictional statements.
The danger of falsehood, while still present, is mitigated
when the rituals refer to natural forces. Such schematizing
rituals, be they linguistic or scientific, tend toward self-correc-
tion: the natural facts being misrepresented are experienced
independently of the schema, and their insistent intrusion
eventually forces its revision. When reference is to non-
natural forces, be they intellectual abstractions or magico-
religious powers, there is no obvious way in which mundane
experience might decisively discredit the ritual evoking them.
Hence rituals lie, if they do, mostly about matters of non-
natural fact just as linguistic traps can long succeed only on
the metaphysical plane, as Section 3.4 has shown.

6.2.2 Do Rituals Inhibit Social Change?

Ritual, primarily in its magico-religious form, is commonly
thought to constitute a powerful barrier to social change. This
claim has only limited validity as applied to magico-religious
ritual and even less as applied to other forms.

---

39. Maurice Godelier, 'Myth and History', *New Left Review,* 69 (1971);
93–112. Erikson, *Dimensions of a New Identity,* p. 28. Maurice Bloch, 'The Past
and the Present in the Present', *Man,* 12 (1977): 278–92.

Where political myth and ritual are located in the realm of the sacred, subjects display obsessive deference and rulers intolerant self-righteousness, and these attitudes work hand-in-glove to block social change. The deference of subjects is wholly understandable: with salvation at stake, one naturally hesitates to offend those who must mediate with supernatural powers. For those persuaded of the efficacy of magico-religious ritual under a politician's control, 'the power of ritual is just as actual as the power of command'. Bagehot observed how 'the divinity which doth hedge a king' prevents him from serving as an ordinary adviser to his Ministers. He recalls the example of Lord Chatham, 'the most dictatorial and imperious of English statesmen, and almost the first English statesman who was borne into power against the wishes of the king and against the wishes of the nobility—the first popular Minister.' Far from treating the king as brusquely as his personality and politics would seem to demand, Lord Chatham 'was in the habit of kneeling at the bedside of George III while transacting business. Now no man can argue on his knees.' The self-righteousness of rulers thus blessed is equally understandable. 'Whoever lays hands on the prevailing myth is guilty of sacrilege, a blasphemer of the law and of the gods, and has to be struck down.'[40]

What this model crucially overlooks is the fact that the divine edict conferring authority on rulers also limits their authority. When one defers to the will of the Sovereign because he is in some sense keeper of the faith, one's deference ceases immediately when the ruler demonstrably loses faith. This is

40. Leach, 'Ritual', p. 525. Bagehot, *English Constitution*, pp. 113-14. Francis Delaisi, *Political Myths and Economic Realities* (London: Williams & Norgate, 1925), p. 386. See also Lewis Lipsitz, 'If, as Verba Says, the State Functions as a Religion, What Are We to Do Then to Save Our Souls?' *American Political Science Review*, 62 (1968): 527-35, and Reinhard Bendix, 'The Mandate to Rule', *Social Forces*, 55 (1976): 242-56.

the distinction Michael Walzer traces through English history between 'regicide and revolution', offering various examples of non-revolutionary dissidents who swore allegiance to the Crown even whilst severing the head upon which it was then resting. Among primitive African tribes, it is similarly the Kingship rather than the king which is divine. When, owing to his physical failings or ritual impurities, the king is deemed responsible for some natural disaster, rebellion against the king is justified in the name of the Kingship.[41]

A ritual ruler's power is usually limited by his need for followers. Ritual power, even if it derives from magico-religious sources, can often be exercised only with the collab-oration of a certain number of other people. Even sorcerers need their apprentices. By refusing this necessary coopera-tion people can, if not actually deprive him of his magico-religious power, at least deny him any opportunities to use it. And by threatening to withhold this necessary cooperation people can secure significant concessions from magico-religious rulers. A case in point concerns the supposed power of medieval kings to heal scrofula through the 'royal touch'. 'There was no more signal "confirmation" of an "indubitable

41. Michael Walzer, *Regicide and Revolution* (Cambridge: Cambridge University Press, 1974). Fortes and Evans-Pritchard, *African Political Systems*, p. 18. Evans-Pritchard, *Divine Kingship*. Fortes, 'Ritual and Office in Tribal Society'. Exercising power through rituals, whatever their form, tends to re-strict the options of the ruler. Maurice Bloch, 'The Distinction between Power and Rank as a Process: An Outline of the Development of Kingdoms in Cen-tral Madagascar', *Archives Européennes de Sociologie*, 18 (1977): 107-48 at 140, observes, 'If a ruler totally adopts the mode of communication of ritual for carrying out his will he at the same time loses his ability to affect events for his own *personal* ends as opposed to the ends of his office. He must therefore continually switch from the mode of communication of ritual to a secular mode of communication using the one for statements concerning his unchal-lenged role as "father of his people", the other in order that he may play the astute politician.' See also Bloch, 'Symbols, Song, Dance and Features of Ar-ticulations', *Archives Européennes de Sociologie*, 15 (1974): 55-81.

title" [to the throne] than the gift of miraculous healing,' so during succession struggles 'each of the claimants ... sought to attract to himself by all possible means those who were suffering from scrofula and seeking to be cured.' Pretenders to the throne needed scrofula sufferers to step forward, and this gave ordinary people considerable leverage over magico-religious rulers. As evidence of this power, consider the 'astonishing rise in the rate of alms in England' from Edward III to Henry VII: gold began to be given to scrofula-sufferers who received the royal touch, instead of the more traditional silver tokens, as 'a lure to those who might have hesitated to come forward for the royal touch ... when rivals for the throne were mutually denying each other the power to work healing miracles. ... In France, where no such internal struggles took place, the sum handed to the beneficiaries of the royal touch remained fairly small.'[42] Thus ordinary people can often have much leverage over their magico-religious rulers by virtue of their power to repudiate their faith in the rulers' magic, thereby undercutting its potency.

Even more revolutionary possibilities arise in the not uncommon case in which rulers do not enjoy a monopoly of magico-religious ritual power. If political dissidents have their own avenue of ritual appeal to the gods, they might well use it against the existing regime. Sometimes this solidifies into actual 'religions of the oppressed'. Often it manifests itself in less organized magical ju-ju attacks on political elites, ranging from arousing 'spirits of protest' in Zimbabwe to reassuring soldiers that magical water will protect them from bullets, as during Mulele's 1963 Congo rebellion.[43] Magico-religious ritual can, then, serve the cause of change as well as opposing it.

42. Marc Bloch, *The Royal Touch* (London: Routledge & Kegan Paul, 1973), pp. 66–7.

43. Vittorio Lanternari, *The Religions of the Oppressed*, trans. Lise Sergio (New York: Knopf, 1963). Peter Fry, *Spirits of Protest* (Cambridge: Cambridge

Representational rituals erect even fewer barriers to social change. Generally, they only amplify whatever sentiments would have existed in their absence. If people like what they see represented, the ritual will reinforce their natural tendency to be allegiant. If, on the contrary, they are distressed by what is depicted, the ritual will only intensify their dissatisfaction. Geertz offers an example from Java illustrating precisely this point. Performing a *slametan* (a ritual feast emphasizing the homogeneity of rural peasants) upon the death of a youngster in the urban *kampong,* where homogeneity is conspicuously lacking, only served to create further social tension and to accelerate breaks from the rural past. When a self-consciously revolutionary community emerges, it devises appropriate new rituals—Sorel's General Strike, May Day parades, rearrangement of communal fiesta schedules, etc.— to represent the new social reality. And once a social revolution has occurred, new rituals are adopted or old ones overlaid: when Shaka unified the Zulus into a military state, the ritual of national ceremonies was retained but militarized to represent the new social form.[44]

Moreover, the need for wide segments of the community to participate in representational rituals to enable them to represent what they are meant to represent gives people a measure of control over their rulers. They might simply refuse to participate in the rituals of an unacceptable regime. Consider the example of

---

University Press, 1976). H. Jon Rosenbaum and Peter C. Sederberg, 'The Occult and Political Development', *Comparative Politics,* 4 (1971): 561–76.

44. Clifford Geertz, 'Ritual and Social Change: A Javanese Example', *American Anthropologist,* 59 (1957): 32–54. Georges Sorel, *Reflections on Violence,* trans. T. E. Hulme (New York: P. Smith, 1941), Lukes, 'Political Ritual and Social Integration'. Paul Friedrich, 'Revolutionary Politics and Communal Ritual', *Political Anthropology,* ed. Swartz, Turner and Tuden, pp. 191–220. Max Gluckman, 'The Kingdom of the Zulu of South Africa', *African Political Systems,* ed. Fortes and Evans-Pritchard, pp. 25–55 at 31.

A Korekore chief whose autocratic inclinations were checked when he discovered that the cooperation he needed for traditional community rituals was not forthcoming. The general belief of his people that the chief had no right to force them to do anything against their will was supported by communal rituals in which the cooperation of a number of commoner families who had ritual roles to play, and of a significant number of village headmen, was required.... Anyone could, and many did, show their dissatisfaction with the rule of a chief by failing to attend the communal rituals he organized.[45]

Far from inhibiting popular control of autocratic rulers, such rituals can give people great leverage to reform their rule.

Representational rituals do narrow attention to a few selected aspects of social relations. This might help preserve the status quo if the focus is on the agreeable and away from the disagreeable aspects. It might equally well facilitate change, providing reassurance by directing attention to continuities with the past and thereby freeing other areas for radical change. Bagehot's theme was that the 'dignified' elements of the English Constitution—myths about checks and balances, the power of the Monarch and the Lords and the Commons—enable the system to adapt 'efficient' responses (i.e., the Cabinet) to demands of mid-nineteenth century political realities. Similarly, Maine's analysis of the development of ancient Roman law suggests that 'legal fictions' and the juristic rituals surrounding them facilitated innovation by preserving the appearance of continuity and stability.[46] Even

45. M. F. C. Bourdillon, 'Knowing the World or Hiding It', *Man*, 13 (1978): 591–99 at 596–97.

46. Bagehot, *English Constitution*. Henry Sumner Maine, *Ancient Law* (London: John Murray, 1861), Ch. 2. Marshall and Moodie, *Some Problems of the Constitution*, p. 21, assert that in Britain there still 'exist potential dishar-

though representational rituals do direct attention to selected aspects of the society, then, they are as likely to do so in a way facilitating as inhibiting change.

Schematizing and constitutive rituals each contribute only slightly to inhibitions on social change. In both cases, the contribution amounts to little more than inertia. It is always easier to stay with routines (schemata or rules) already in existence than it is to negotiate and establish new ones. Beyond that, however, there is nothing sacrosanct about the existing arrangements. In both cases they are obviously creations of men for the convenience of men, and there is no strong reason not to shift from one to another even more convenient one. Groups opposed to the status quo soon enough organize themselves, devising new systems of rules constitutive of 'anti-societies' and new 'anti-languages' appropriate to the new reality they have created for themselves.[47]

6.3   RITUALS AS MODES OF MANIPULATION

Politics is indeed ritualized, but in many different ways. This chapter has isolated four distinct classes of political ritual: (1) magico-religious; (2) constitutive; (3) schematizing; and (4)

---

monies between a way of describing the Constitution which is not yet regarded as completely false or outdated, and a way of describing it which has not yet become quite acceptable or comfortable.' As an example, they discuss the 1953 proposal 'that certain divisions should not follow immediately upon the debate in the House but after an adjournment, during which it was said Members might read the debate in *Hansard*.' To this proposal Herbert Morrison objected mightily: 'While it is perfectly true that the debate may proceed, and three-quarters of the Members taking part in the division may not have heard a word of it, nevertheless it is respectable on the face of it.' Morrison, for one, was not quite ready to admit the 'new' reality of party-line voting!

47. Possibilities for transcending the ritual are discussed in M. A. K. Halliday, 'Anti-Languages', *American Anthropologist*, 78 (1976): 570–84, and in Chapters 3 and 4 above.

representational. Respecting these distinctions is crucial to a balanced evaluation of the phenomenon, since familiar objections to ritualized politics actually apply to the magico-religious variety quite narrowly. Summarizing the conclusions of this chapter by reference to the checklist proposed in Section 1.6:

1. Is the interference deceptive?

Magico-religious rituals may well be deceptive. The more trivial—and the less common—deception lies in politicians appealing to gods which they do not themselves believe to exist. The more serious deception lies in putting words in the mouths of gods. Rulers often manipulate their people by manipulating their gods. For this trick to succeed, it probably must be concealed. Were people to see that rulers were manipulating the gods, they might well wonder whether the gods would be pleased. Concluding, as they probably would, that gods do not like being used in this way, the discovery of this sacrilege provides the basis for a rebellion of the faithful against the manipulative ruler. Similarly, schematizing rituals must probably be deceptive if they are to succeed in being manipulative. Were people to notice the biases being introduced through the schemata being established through these rituals, they would probably reject them, or at least begin searching for alternatives. While both magico-religious and schematizing rituals can and often will be deceptive, constitutive and representational rituals properly understood are incapable of being either true or false. These rituals can be deceptive only insofar as they purport to make truth claims to which they may not legitimately aspire.

2. Is the interference contrary to the putative will of those subject to it?

Insofar as either magico-religious or schematizing rituals are deceptive in these ways, they quite probably cause people to act contrary to their putative wills. Unless they did, there would be no reason for the deception. The conclusion with respect to constitutive and representational rituals is less clearcut. It is an undeniable advantage for people to have some such rituals available, so it seems impossible for all such rituals to be necessarily contrary to the people's putative wills. Still, it is entirely possible that in any particular instance the rituals misguide people.

Both these defining features of a manipulatory act are likely to be present in magico-religious or schematizing rituals. It is rather less likely that constitutive or representational rituals would even qualify as manipulatory. Usually they lack the necessary element of deception. But since that might occasionally be present, perhaps it is better to regard them as extremely marginal instances of the phenomenon. Two further criteria are useful in determining how serious a form of manipulation each variety of ritual embodies.

3. How persistent is the effect of the manipulation?

Magico-religious rituals probably have long-lasting effects. They can be overcome—people can turn the gods against the rulers, or they can renounce the gods—but these are long-term recourses. Constitutive rituals might, for simple reasons of institutional inertia, persist for long periods. The effects of schematizing rituals will probably be much less long lived. Empirical evidence not fitting happily into the schema will probably soon appear to force its revision, and those engaged in simple schematizing have no supplementary strategies (such as information overload, discussed in Section 2.5) to shore up their schema in case of such a challenge. Representational rituals, too, are likely to have short-lived effects. As the community they represent changes, the rituals themselves will have to change as well.

4. Are any distributive biases inherent in the mechanism?

Magico-religious rituals are initially biased in favour of established authorities who are officially empowered to perform them. But grants of ritual power typically carry with them heavy responsibilities, legitimizing opposition to authorities who have abused their ritual offices. Furthermore, when embodied in 'religions of the oppressed', magico-religious ritual can also form the basis for explicitly revolutionary movements. While the initial bias of magico-religious ritual is conservative, then, this bias is not absolute and such rituals might also be used for revolutionary ends. Constitutive and schematizing rituals contain few distributive biases at all—anyone can use them. Representational rituals are only slightly more biased, insofar as they might be used to distract attention from unsavoury aspects of the society they depict. Otherwise, they too display few distributive biases, and any social group can—and a great variety of them do—employ such rituals to represent their most salient features.

Overall, magico-religious ritual seems to be the only form which poses any very worrying manipulatory potential. Its effect is both persistent and biased, at least in the first instance. The other three forms display only slight distributive biases, and at least two of them (schematizing and representational) probably also lack persistence.

CHAPTER SEVEN ❡ THE POLITICS
OF THE OBVIOUS

Nothing is so treacherous as the obvious.
Joseph Schumpeter[1]

There is room for a more detailed analysis of the *logic of situations*.... Beyond this logic of the situation, or perhaps as a part of it, we need ... studies, based on methodological individualism, of the social institutions through which ideas may spread and captivate individuals, of the way in which new traditions may be created, and of the way in which traditions work and break down.
Karl Popper[2]

WHEN SOMETHING IS SEEN AS the obvious solution to a shared social problem, it is naturally the alternative which is chosen. In politics just as in *Modern English Usage*, 'the obvious is better than the obvious avoidance of it.'[3] We take as serious criticism of a politician that he consistently opts for cute and contrived solutions over the more conspicuous ones. And, on the face of things, there seems to be nothing political in this predisposition toward the obvious. This is not because such solutions are distributively neutral—on the contrary, the obvious solution typically demands heavier sacrifices from some than from others. But so too does cruel fate. What puts both providence and obvious solutions beyond the pale of the political in the popular mind is the presumption that their biases

1. *Capitalism, Socialism and Democracy*, 3rd ed. (New York: Harper, 1950), Ch. 20.
2. *The Poverty of Historicism* (London: Routledge & Kegan Paul, 1957), Sec. 31.
3. H. W. Fowler, *Modern English Usage* (Oxford: Clarendon Press, 1926).

are somehow natural, built into the 'logic of the situation' rather than being imposed by anyone standing to profit from them.

This is a fiction I hope to expose by showing how the obviousness of political solutions can be manipulated through social—and indeed political—processes. Thus, my theme is one of the *rigging of the obvious*. And this is a political theme insofar as successful manipulations at this stage can take the place of more blatant power plays later. After discussing a few cases to demonstrate that obviousness can be manipulated to political effect, I turn in the next three sections to alternative explanations of how the strategy works. The power and biases of each strategy are then examined. In the final section I illustrate the range of the favoured alternative, interpreting the politics of the obvious as a rational reaction to coordination problems, by reference to examples grand (the genesis of traditions) and mundane (policy choice).

Before proceeding, however, troublesome terminology must be clarified. A solution may be 'obvious' in either (or both) of two senses. In the one I employ in this chapter, obviousness is a function of perceptions. 'X is obvious' is equivalent to 'Some individual(s) $A,B, \ldots$ *regard* X as obvious', which is to say they accept X as the self-evident and commonsensical answer to their problem. This is distinct from the sense in which 'obviousness' refers to some essential property of the proposal. There are, arguably, some schemes which *really are* obvious solutions even if no one notices them: if the problem is saving starving children, they obviously should be fed; if the problem is siting a new road, it obviously should run through the valley rather than over the mountain. Whether any proposals are truly obvious in this larger sense is debatable. My purposes are served, however, simply by distinguishing the two senses and by observing that there are many more proposals which are regarded as obvious (first sense) than which really are obvious (second sense). This gap between perceptions and reality defines the possible scope of any politics of the obvious.

7.1 THE OBVIOUS CAN BE POLITICIZED

One might suppose that, by now, political decision-making has been fairly thoroughly investigated. Specialized case studies abound; generalized treatises are by no means scarce. Yet obviousness as an influence upon political decisions merits comment only in passing, if at all. Typical is E. J. B. Rose's remark on British immigration control policy in his classic study of *Colour and Citizenship:*

> In the early 1950s control could be discussed across the floor of the House by Members of all shades of opinion as an element in a programme designed to promote the welfare of the newcomers. If, as ministers of both parties indicated, control could not be introduced, this was for reasons that were largely technical. After the Eden Government's decision not to introduce control, technicalities were erected into a principle, to which each party in turn adhered. This principle was increasingly held as prohibiting any measure of interference in the process of migration, at any stage.[4]

Or consider the comment, made in passing by Heclo and Wildavsky, on the way the British learnt their lessons from the Suez debacle:

> The spending implications of most events are not self-evident; men have to give them meaning. Take, for

4. E. J. B. Rose, *Colour and Citizenship* (London: Oxford University Press for Institute of Race Relations, 1969), p. 220. See also Ira Katznelson, *Black Men, White Cities* (London: Oxford University Press for Institute of Race Relations, 1973), Chs. 8 and 9.

example, the Suez crisis. A good case might have been made for sharply increasing the amount of air-sea lift capacity as well as generally enhancing the state of readiness of the armed forces. But this is not what happened. ... Instead of convincing political leaders that the nation had not done enough, the humiliation of 1956 apparently demonstrated to their satisfaction that it had tried to do far too much. Suez thus began a process of disengagement that led to still further cuts in defence expenditures. Regardless of whether the post-Suez minister of defence was conservative or socialist, he knew what he was up against. 'I could not raise the ceiling on defence,' recalled one ex-minister, 'because the climate was against raising it. Therefore I was left with the choice of priorities within existing totals.'[5]

With casual asides such as these, commentators do occasionally acknowledge that perceptions of 'obvious' obstacles constrain decision-makers in certain ways or that perceptions of 'obvious' solutions lead them unthinkingly in others. But this phenomenon is accorded little place in studies of *political* decision-making, for we reserve the term 'political' for affairs which are somehow contentious; and obvious solutions tend to be accepted on the nod. Obviousness is always taken as part of the natural and objective background against which political action is set. Nowhere in the policy-making literature is there explicit recognition of the possibility of these perceptions being manipulated in such a way as to structure political debate in favour of certain interests and outcomes.

It takes an extraordinary event to shake our faith in the alluring logic holding the obvious to be apolitical. Here I shall

5. Hugh Heclo and Aaron Wildavsky, *The Private Government of Public Money* (London: Macmillan, 1974) p. 32.

focus upon one such extraordinary event, the threatened impeachment of President Nixon. My rationale is the same as J. L. Austin's: 'As so often, the abnormal will throw light on the normal, will help penetrate the blinding veil of ease and obviousness that hides the mechanism of the natural successful act.'[6] The impeachment campaign against Nixon is, in many ways, a paradigm case of the politics of the obvious. When a President is discredited and disgraced and driven from office, there is no way those events can be characterized as anything but political. Yet in standard political parlance they would qualify as profoundly apolitical. Indeed, had they not been (or more precisely been perceived to be) nonpolitical they would have never come to pass. Ever mindful of the scandalous 1868 precedent, impeachment organizers constantly shunned anything smacking of another political lynching. The drive must be bipartisan, they were forever intoning. In a two-party system, bipartisan equals nonpartisan; and where 'party political' is the only accepted sense of 'political', nonpartisan is tantamount to nonpolitical.

More remarkable was the way in which this bipartisan majority emerged. Ordinarily bipartisanship comes through a long series of tough negotiations between parties with divergent viewpoints, making the 'compromise' status of the resultant policy clear enough. In the case of impeachment, however, negotiations and frank compromises were conspicuous by their absence. There was instead the widespread perception that impeachment was inevitable, not just in the political sense that the votes were there to carry the motion, but, more important, because that result seemed somehow inexorable in the logic of the situation. House Republican leaders seemed to share this illusion. On 1 April 1974, well before the 'smok-

6. J. L. Austin, 'A Plea for Excuses', *Proceedings of the Aristotelian Society*, 57 (1956-57): 1-30.

ing gun' appeared, Rep. John Anderson was saying, 'I think
the vote is going to be to impeach. I feel the pass of inevitability.' In retrospect, Rep. John Rhodes agrees, 'The beginning
of the end came before the Supreme Court decision. I don't
know quite what triggered it. But the feeling had permeated
the House that the Judiciary Committee had a lot stronger
case than had been imagined.' Even in the White House during 'the final days', the story was one of aides manoeuvring to
persuade the President of what they had themselves come to
regard as obvious—the President had to go.[7]

A model of 'the natural unfolding of events' seemed to
predominate among the participants themselves. But much in
the history of the impeachment story makes us wary of this
model. What makes us especially dubious of any 'external obviousness' at work is the sheer speed with which perceptions
of the obvious were altered. Elizabeth Drew usefully draws
attention to one narrow example, Congressional reaction to
the House Judiciary Committee voting Articles of Impeachment:

> It is odd how quickly the perception of reality has
> changed again. There was a time when it was said that the
> Judiciary Committee, being 'stacked' liberal, would, of
> course, vote for impeachment but that it did not follow
> that the House would do so; it was not just the opponents
> of impeachment who discounted in advance a possible
> recommendation by the committee that the President be
> impeached. Now the general perception is that a vote to

7. Elizabeth Drew, *Washington Journal: The Events of 1973-1974* (New
York: Random House, 1974), p. 219. James M. Naughton, 'Persuading the
President to Resign', *The End of a Presidency* (New York: Bantam Books,
1974), pp. 57-72 at 59. The White House story is depicted in Bob Woodward
and Carl Bernstein, *The Final Days* (New York: Simon & Schuster, 1976).

impeach is a foregone conclusion in the House and that the President's fortunes are slipping rapidly in the Senate.... There was a time when some said that the committee's deliberations were just the preliminaries—... but it seems now that the Judiciary Committee's action was the defining one.[8]

We must also reflect more generally upon the rate at which the antecedent consensus against impeachment of any President melted into a new consensus that impeachment was the only adequate remedy for Nixon's princely pretensions. In the fifteen months between the first fall of Senator Ervin's gavel and the final fall of Nixon, 54 million Americans actually changed their minds. The largest landslide in American electoral history had changed, in only two more years, into an equally unstoppable coalition in favour of subjecting Nixon to the nearest thing to capital punishment a sitting President can know. On average, the movement acquired converts at the astonishing rate of 118,000 a day.[9]

This contrasts sharply with the more ordinary pattern in which nothing is obvious at the outset and in which the obviousness of some solution or another emerges at a much more

8. Drew, *Washington Journal*, p. 381.

9. *The Gallup Opinion Index: Political, Social and Economic Trends*, no. 111 (September 1974): 8, reports the following poll results:

	June 1973	August 1974
pro-impeachment	19%	57%
anti-impeachment	69	31
no opinion	12	12

The actual numbers mentioned in the text presuppose a constant voting age population of 142 million, reported in the *Statistical Abstract of the United States*, 95th ed. (Washington, D.C.: Government Printing Office, 1974).

measured pace. In such cases we are apt not even to notice
that obviousness is serving as a policy guide, much less that
this guide is being manipulated for partisan advantage. Even
with regard to that other great American national trauma, the
Vietnamese war, the politics of the obvious worked slowly
enough to remain inconspicuous. From the high point of
support for the war effort just after the Gulf of Tonkin inci-
dent to its ebb the day the American Embassy in Saigon was
evacuated, the obviousness of withdrawal struck only 20,000
Americans on average daily, one sixth the rate of conversion
to the impeachment cause.[10]

Instances in which obviousness emerges more gradually
are no less instances of the politics of the obvious, of course.
By the time of the final fall of Saigon, it had become obvious
to a vast majority that the United States must not intervene to
postpone the inevitable; and that climate of opinion forcefully
constrained would-be jingoists in the Pentagon and White
House. The significance of the speed with which the obviousness of impeachment emerged is simply that it made conspicuous what is typically unobtrusive, viz., the *political*
character of obvious solutions. What was eventually accepted
as the obvious answer to a nasty predicament—impeaching
the President—had so very shortly before topped the list of
unthinkable political taboos. Put that way, it is clear that the
process by which something emerges as the obvious solution
can substitute for orthodox political processes for imposing
the selfsame policy as a contentious alternative. Semantic

10. George Gallup, *The Gallup Poll, Public Opinion 1935 -71* (New York:
Random House, 1972), 3: 1899, reports an August 1964 poll showing 71%
approving, 16% disapproving, 13% with no opinion of U.S. handling of affairs in South Vietnam. *The Gallup Opinion Index: Political, Social and Economic
Trends*, no. 119 (May 1975): 4, reports an April 1975 poll showing further
military aid to South Vietnam being opposed by 79%, favoured by 15%, with
6% expressing no opinion.

quibbles aside, what substitutes for politics must itself count as political, at least for the purposes of a positive political theory attempting to explain how the system actually works.

7.2   OBVIOUSNESS AS FACT-FIDDLING

Once the possibility of political manipulation of the obvious is recognized, theoretically compelling questions become how the strategy works and why. The first model I shall examine represents the politics of the obvious as a consequence of the fiddling of facts and their interpretation. One way to shape behaviour is to persuade people that certain facts are true—indubitably, obviously true—when actually they are quite untrue. People might be manipulated in this way even if they are perfectly rational, in the sense of always evaluating alternatives carefully and always opting for the one which on balance seems to hold the preponderance of advantage. The potential for manipulation arises out of constraints individuals naturally encounter in choice situations. Section 2.1 has shown how, given the strictly limited information one possesses at the outset and the cost of acquiring and interpreting more information, it is perfectly rational to make decisions on the basis of incomplete information.

Rationality leads us to act partially in ignorance, and politicians play on this 'rational ignorance' for partisan advantage. Occasionally they try to make their preferred outcome seem to be the obvious one through the big lie or by squelching or distorting damaging information (as in the case of Agnew's harassment of the media). More often the strategy is simply to release a plethora of information favourable to their case, pursuant to the propaganda strategy analysed in Section 2.4. Then the decision will virtually make itself: it is not that everyone feels some compulsion to agree on the same solution; it is just that, given the preponderance of evidence, no reasonable man could differ with the 'obvious' solution. As often, the obviousness of a solution is made to emerge by 'putting the problem in context'. The strategy here is to impose an interpretive framework in terms of which the advocate's favourite policy figures centrally, making it the obvious solution to the problem. With this strategy, fact-fiddling shades into concept-rigging, which is the subject of Section 7.3 below.[11]

It is passé among both economists and philosophers to discuss how information-management techniques can instil in the most rational of men false beliefs which prevent them from efficiently fitting means to ends. If subjected to enough advertising, we may actually come to believe that Wheaties will enable us to run the four-minute mile or that STP will enable our broken-down auto to drive it. More fundamentally, the same techniques can be used to fudge the choice of our goals in life, a choice that also seems to be based on information. It is softer, more impressionistic evidence of how a life directed at these ends would compare with one directed at some others instead, to be sure. But this sort of information is just as (and maybe more) susceptible to fiddling as any other, and the techniques for fiddling are identical. The reason most members of any given society aim at the same ends probably is less that they have made identical informed choices among alternatives than that they know so much about the one option and so little about the others.

11. See Chapter 2 and sources cited there. On the manipulative possibilities of information-management, see especially: William A. Niskanen, Jr., *Bureaucracy and Representative Government* (Chicago: Aldine-Atherton, 1971); Randall Bartlett, *Economic Foundations of Political Power* (New York: Free Press, 1973); Tibor Scitovsky, 'Ignorance as a Source of Oligopoly Power', *American Economic Review (Papers and Proceedings)*, 40 (1950): 48–53; and Aaron Wildavsky, 'Analysis of Issue-Contexts in the Study of Policy-Making', *Journal of Politics*, 24 (1962): 717–32. On the 'setting the problem in context' strategy, see Sections 2.5, 3.4 and 6.1.3 above.

The tactical concerns facing politicians hoping to carry the day by information-management have been discussed at length in Chapter 2. Roughly speaking, they must devote equal attention to two considerations. First is to make certain that the evidence favourable to their cause is always far the weightier. But they must get these glowing reports onto the table without arousing so much suspicion that others are motivated to investigate the seamy side of their proposal. Several tactics, many amounting to no more than rhetorical gimmicks, are useful in this connection. Among the more important is the tactic of preserving the anonymity of the source of information in order to prevent it from being dismissed as biased propaganda.[12]

The information-fiddling perspective on political obviousness offers one way of reading the impeachment story, our paradigm case. The dramatic popular conversion to the impeachment cause came on the heels of some pretty dramatic revelations, more about the sordid presidential character than about any particular actions. On this reading, antecedent quiescence was maintained mainly through cover-ups and the cataclysm was inevitable once the true facts of the matter leaked out—it is somehow 'obvious' that any President caught cheating on his income taxes or bending the rules to keep his cronies out of jail must be removed from office. But this analysis of the situation runs directly counter to some powerful and widely shared intuitions. For those of us touched by the imperial wrath in connection with anti-media or anti-protester crusades or his host of other Holy Wars, revelations about Nixon's role in Watergate came as only superfluous reinforcement of prior character judgements. Already

12. Robert Axelrod, 'Schema Theory', *American Political Science Review*, 67 (1973): 1248–66. Brian Sternthal, Lynn W. Phillips and Ruby Daholakia, 'The Persuasive Effect of Source Credibility', *Public Opinion Quarterly*, 42 (1978): 285–314.

knowing that Nixon was the sort of man who would (if he could) muzzle the opposition press, conduct military adventures of dubious legality and (if his own CIA is to be believed) of even more dubious efficacy and condone random shootings on the campus, what more does it really tell us of his character to discover that he spies on opponents, tape records visitors without their permission, curses and cheats on his taxes? From the opposite end of the political spectrum, Nixon's staunchest supporters always voiced equally strong doubts that the simple release of information about the President's role was in any way decisive. They maintain—quite reasonably, I believe—that had Nixon come clean at the outset the whole thing would have blown over in no time.[13]

7.3   Obviousness as Concept-Rigging

In a second model of the politics of the obvious, 'obviousness' refers to the location of a notion in the shared conceptual structure of a society. Certain notions are obvious because language is well-equipped to deal with them, while others are obscure merely because it is difficult to get a linguistic handle on them. Mary Douglas analyses the parallel notion of 'self-evidence' in similar terms: 'knowledge in the bones, a gut response, answers to a characteristic in the total pattern of classification. . . . Each category of thought has its place in a larger system. Its constituent elements are there because of rules which distinguish, bound and fill the other categories.' For example, among the Karam of the New Guinea highlands, the relation of the bird called

---

13. In Woodward and Bernstein, *The Final Days*, Nixon aides are constantly offering this advice, albeit in ignorance of how much Nixon really had to hide. Even now, however, some still argue this case. See, e.g., Raymond Price, *With Nixon* (New York: Viking, 1978).

cassowary to wild plants and animals has the same patterning of logical forms as the relation of the cassowary to human and non-human beings and this is of the same pattern as the relation between a woman's brothers and her children. For the Karam, all these instances are true in the same unchallengeable way.... But it is they themselves who have created the order of their universe so that the statements they make about it in this form are self-evidently true.[14]

Even methodologically inclined social scientists can appreciate the workings of this mechanism to rig political outcomes. Anyone familiar with Hempel or Kaplan is accustomed to regarding 'concepts' as 'data containers'.[15] And, to press the analogy egregiously, data for which there is no container are likely to get lost. On a more pedestrian level, one plausible explanation for the failure of Marxism to catch on in America is that the English language and the patterns of thought it molds are ill-suited to any such Teutonic metaphysic. A further case in point is Pocock's *Politics, Language and Time*, which expertly traces the way in which conceptual gaps can cause people to overlook action opportunities.

In a way, the impeachment inquiry provides a case in point. The concept of impeachment, having been embodied in the Constitution, was always with us. But it had long lived at the conceptual fringes of constitutional law—and even fur-

14. Mary Douglas, 'Self-Evidence', *Implicit Meanings* (London: Routledge & Kegan Paul, 1975), pp. 276–318 at 312–13.

15. Carl G. Hempel, *Fundamentals of Concept Formation in Empirical Sciences* (Chicago: University of Chicago Press, 1952). Abraham Kaplan, *The Conduct of Inquiry* (San Francisco: Chandler, 1964), Pt. 2. The phrase is from Giovanni Sartori, *The Tower of Babel*, International Studies Occasional Paper No. 6 (Pittsburgh: International Studies Association, 1975), p. 20.

ther removed from the centre of the popular mind and ordinary language. One result was that, at the outset of the investigation, there was not a very rich vocabulary—betraying a
considerable impoverishment as well—as regards impeachment of a President. As the proceedings progressed, as
lawyers faced the daily need to discourse on impeachment
matters, a rather rich conceptual schema arose to meet the
felt need.[16]

This model fails to account adequately for the events surrounding the impeachment inquiry in two ways, however.
Firstly, given a strong sense of linguistic determinism, it is difficult to explain how anyone got the idea of impeachment in
the first place. Secondly, and more damaging, even after the
conceptual rehabilitation of 'impeachment' the course of action associated with that concept was *no more* obvious than
that of letting sitting Presidents rule. In terms of conceptual
centrality, these alternatives were on an equal footing, so no
account of the politics of the obvious can explain how one
won out over the other.

7.4 OBVIOUSNESS AND COORDINATION PROBLEMS

Fact-fiddling and concept-rigging offer rather unsatisfactory
explanations of the political power of obviousness, especially
with regard to the impeachment of Nixon. A far more insidi-
ous form of the politics of the obvious connects it to coordination problems and the peculiar difficulties surrounding their
solution. This model is strongly suggested once we have set

16. Milestones included publication of: Raoul Berger, *Impeachment* (Cambridge: Harvard University Press, 1973); and U.S. Congress, House, Committee on the Judiciary, *Impeachment: Selected Materials*, 93rd Cong., 1st sess.,
1973. Notice also discussions of the notion of an 'impeachable offence', and
the distinction from a 'criminal offence', reported in Woodward and Bernstein's *The Final Days* and Drew's *Washington Journal*.

our paradigm case, impeachment, in its larger politico-historical context.

Two classes of related cases merit attention here. One is deposing a tyrant. The impeachment moves against Nixon clearly fall under this head while nowise exhausting the class. The British doctrine of 'collective responsibility' was devised in the eighteenth century as the obvious way for the Cabinet to counter divide-and-conquer tactics and to assert its power over an all-powerful Sovereign. Countless dry constitutional histories detail background to this development, but its essential logic is best captured in the injunction of Shaw's Prime Minister Proteus to his Cabinet just before confronting the despotic king: 'If you start quarrelling and scolding and bawling, which is just what he wants you to do, it will end in his having his own way as usual, because one man that has a mind and knows it can always beat ten men who havnt and dont.'[17]

A second class of cases concerns defence, be it of the nation or of the group and its traditions. Whenever a group is seriously threatened, internal differences tend to be set aside and all members coalesce against the common enemy. Thus, during both World Wars, Governments of National Unity formed in Britain and nonpartisanship (at least on war policy) prevailed in the United States.[18] Traditional theories of the prerequisites for nonpartisanship and group cohesion are surely wrong to focus exclusively on external threats to the nation. Imminent civil war provokes the same defensive non-

17. G. B. Shaw, 'The Apple Cart', *Collected Works* (New York: William H. Wise, 1930), 17:212. Cf. E. A. Freeman, *The Growth of the English Constitution* (London: Macmillan, 1876), and A. V. Dicey, *The Law of the Constitution* (London: Macmillan, 1885).

18. Georg Simmel, *Conflict and the Web of Group Affiliations*, trans. Kurt Wolff and Reinhard Bendix (New York: Free Press, 1955). Lewis A. Coser, *The Functions of Social Conflict* (New York: Free Press, 1956). Alan Beattie, 'British Coalition Government Revisited', *Government and Opposition*, 2 (1966): 3–34.

partisanship, except of course among those instigating the threat—partisans in the gun-toting sense. Recalling that colonies were always regarded as part and parcel of the mother country, nonpartisan approaches to decolonization can be regarded as cases in point.[19] Nor need the threat be strictly human. Grand Coalitions have often formed in defence against the ravages of cruel fate. In 1931 British Labour Prime Minister Ramsay MacDonald invited Tories and Liberals to join a unified National Government to fight the depression, and one suspects that military coups are welcomed in many banana republics in hopes they will bring a nonpartisan attack on inflation.[20]

The politics of the obvious has a role, although perhaps not a unique one, in the solution of both types of problem. Set in this context, it becomes clear that the strategy is one for enabling a group of individuals with a common interest to turn back a threat from a cohesive enemy. By virtue of the 'united we stand, divided we fall' logic apparently characterizing core applications, the politics of the obvious can be seen as a response to a coordination problem. Within some broad

19. See esp. Gary Wasserman, 'The Politics of Consensual Decolonization', *African Review*, 5 (1975): 1-15, on the manipulative aspects of the process.

20. The politics of the obvious is not coextensive with nonpartisanship in all forms but is rather a special case. When all parties perceive some obvious solution to collective problems, like equipping an army to turn back the Red/ Fascist Tide, they all join in backing that solution without haggling over the substantive details. But in some cases nonpartisanship reflects the ordinary processes of coalition-building writ large, with all parties supposing their diverse interests are best served at least in the short term through a marriage of convenience. Gabriel Almond, Scott Flanagan and Robert Mundt, *Crisis, Choice and Change* (Boston: Little Brown, 1973), provide many examples of such oversized coalitions in crisis situations. The nonpartisan Belgian line on the Arab oil embargo might be another, with its precipitous breakdown typifying the comparative instability of nonpartisanship created through the politics of coalition-building rather than through the politics of the obvious.

limits, which particular solution is chosen is less important than jointly settling on the same solution and presenting a united front. As Lord Melbourne pointed out to his Cabinet colleagues in defence of the principle of collective responsibility, 'It doesn't matter much what we say but we must all say the same thing.'[21]

A coordination problem is said to exist whenever there exists a solution or solutions which, if jointly pursued, produce a higher payoff for everyone involved than they could expect from acting independently. Occasionally there is a unique coordinated solution. Typically there are several, each allocating the rewards of cooperation slightly differently among various participants. Some, notably Schelling, would save the term 'coordination problem' for situations in which everyone is indifferent between all alternative possible coordinated solutions. I find it more useful to broaden the term so it applies to any situation in which each participant gains more from coordinated activity than from independent activity. In spite of the conflict of interests over *which* coordinated solution is pursued, everyone still finds it rational (i.e., it pays each of them more) to settle for *any* of the alternative coordinated solutions in preference to acting independently. As I shall show below, interesting political implications flow precisely from broadening Schelling's analysis in this way.[22]

Ordinary processes for resolving coordination problems through integration, bargaining, compromise and log-rolling presuppose a small and unharried set of actors. Where there

21. Melbourne's comment is quoted in R. M. Punnett, *British Government and Politics*, 2nd ed. (New York: Norton, 1971), p. 179.

22. Thomas Schelling, *The Strategy of Conflict* (New York: Oxford University Press, 1960), pp. 290–303. David K. Lewis, *Convention* (Cambridge: Harvard University Press, 1969), follows his lead. For a more complete analysis of the alternative I suggest, see Robert Goodin, *The Politics of Rational Man* (London: Wiley, 1976), Ch. 4.

is a very large group to be coordinated, individual bargaining and mutual adjustment as methods for reaching and enforcing joint decisions simply break down. In the absence of some authoritative leadership, individuals will be in the position of the parachutists in Schelling's classic analogy: 'Two people parachute unexpectedly into [an area], each with a map and knowing the other has one, but neither knowing where the other has dropped nor able to communicate directly. They must get together quickly to be rescued.'[23] But, since the jump was unplanned, there was no antecedent agreement on a rendezvous point. Thus, each parachutist is forced to study his own map for an 'obvious' rendezvous—the only bridge, the only house, the highest hill, or whatever—which his partner presumably will also regard as the obvious point.

As it stands, this analogy seems to deny precisely the present thesis, that of the gerrymandering of obviousness. Most obvious landmarks were provided by Mother Nature, and even those which owe their existence to human agents were hardly put there with the purpose of attracting wandering parachutists. There is much in this, and in his later discussion of the value of simple fractions (e.g., 1/2) and powers of ten (1, 10, 100) in solving allocation problems, to suggest that Schelling believes these solutions to be really obvious in some external sense and not simply perceived to be so.

To draw out the political side of obviousness, however, concentrate on the crucial role of the cartographer in Schelling's example. The key to each parachutist's strategy for second-guessing his partner is the map he knows they both share. Any points which are in some way special according to the map are likely rendezvous spots. Significantly, each parachutist might walk past several monstrous bridges too new to be shown on the map to reach the only one, old and

23. Schelling, *Strategy of Conflict*, p. 54.

decrepit through it may be, which does appear on the map. Or, for a rather more complex example, they might ignore a truly spectacular rock formation on a nearby summit and rendezvous instead at a far more ordinary stone heap which happens to be the only one named on their map. Although each sees both configurations from a distance and thinks the one a far more unusual spectacle, each would press on for the other more ordinary rock pile, fearing that perhaps from a different angle the unnamed formation might be less striking. Similarly, they might rendezvous at the summit of what their map mistakenly shows to be the highest peak, each discounting the evidence of his own eyes that some other is taller. Even if both parachutists know they are equipped with shoddy maps which may well be wrong in many particulars, the same logic holds. They will make for points which are unique according to their map, provided only that each is confident that the other has the *same* map as he does.

The political parallels are straightforward. A great many people might think of an alternative which is clearly superior to what is being offered as the 'obvious' solution to a political problem. They might even all independently (but unknowingly) come up with the same alternative. But, given the importance of coordination in beating back political opponents, none can afford to wager that his fellow citizens are as clever as he. It is safer to stick with the 'obvious' if suboptimal solution.

In all the examples discussed so far, everyone is arguably indifferent between rendezvous points just as the Schelling definition of a coordination problem demands. But the same logic works when people are not indifferent between all the alternatives. Suppose that the parachutists were not innocent civilians keen on meeting up so as to facilitate their rescue but rather companies of soldiers anxious to rendezvous in order to launch a massed attack on an enemy across the river. Both company commanders would logically march past several new and unguarded bridges perfectly suited to their strategic purposes and head instead for the one rickety and heavily guarded old bridge shown on their map because, given the sketchy map they share, each knows the other will regard that landmark as the obvious rendezvous. They prefer coordination at a bad rendezvous point to missing each other altogether.

Broadening the analysis of a coordination problem in this way creates the possibility of a political manipulation of the obvious. In Schelling's examples, the cartographer can have no motive for fudging the map, for all points are equally good for everyone. Having noticed that there can be (and typically is) a conflict of interest over which coordinated solution is chosen, we can now see motives for manipulation. Different coordinated solutions (e.g., 'obvious' points) have different distributive profiles. While everyone prefers any coordinated solution to none, everyone has his own favourite among them. And the cartographer, by biasing his map, is able to play favourites.

The methods used in making something politically obvious are, at root, the same as those of the cartographer. In both cases the strategy is to provide what is comparatively a plethora of information about some alternative, and it automatically emerges as the obvious solution. This has nothing to do with the familiar trick, already discussed in Section 7.2, of fiddling facts or simply overwhelming someone with so much positive information that further investigation seems pointless. If one's game is politics of the obvious in the coordination sense, the information need not be biased in favour of the desired alternative nor even on balance favourable. It is enough that 'everybody's talking aobut it' for an alternative to emerge as the obvious solution.

Tactically, it is important to put out the information

anonymously. In ordinary political affairs, the advantage of anonymity is that it prevents the information from being discounted in light of its source. In the context of the politics-of-the-obvious strategy in a coordination game, there is quite a different rationale. Information reported without attribution ('it is said that . . . ') tends to be interpreted as having come from somewhere deep within the social network, as having passed through so many hands that its original source has long ago been lost. In many instances this is true enough, as with old adages and ancient skills. Other times, however, this is simply the work of some adept tactician playing the politics-of-the-obvious game. Solutions get adopted in that game not because they are obvious to some particular individual but rather because they are thought to be obvious to all. Releasing information anonymously, one creates the illusion that the obviousness of a particular alternative is truly widespread throughout the population. This is a technique of bureaucratic in-fighting pioneered by Franklin Roosevelt in 'off the record' press briefings and perfected by each successive generation of political hacks. The work of Art Buchwald's 'Great Mentioner' is strikingly similar: one often hears that someone is being 'widely mentioned' for his party's presidential nomination but never who is doing the mentioning; so Buchwald, being too polite to implicate the candidate's own staff, postulates a mysterious 'Great Mentioner'.

Some versions of the impeachment story suggest that an analysis such as this might be illuminating. According to plausible accounts, the affair was stage-managed through semi-anonymous gnomes on Capitol Hill using their 'ability to create the illusion of power, to use mirrors and blue smoke'. In his modern morality tale, *How the Good Guys Finally Won*, Breslin relates how his hero, Rep. 'Tip' O'Neill, fed vague rumours of impeachment into the congressional grapevine and saw them coming back amplified several times over.

O'Neill took care to block premature votes on impeachment (e.g., the Drinan proposal) which would have failed and thereby compromised its status as the obvious choice at a later date. Once the obviousness of impeachment was widely appreciated, he took care to block alternatives (e.g., a censure motion) from entering the agenda and denying impeachment its status as the uniquely obvious solution.[24] Of course, O'Neill was just following the instincts of a savvy politician. What is significant is that those instincts led him to behave precisely as a rational player of the politics-of-the-obvious strategy in a coordination game should.

My coordination model of the politics of the obvious underlying the impeachment campaign may need clarification on at least two points. First, I am obliged to specify who is party to the coordination problem. In the abstract this class includes everyone who prefers joint pursuit of the coordinated solution to acting independently. In the case at hand it includes anyone who prefers impeaching Nixon to allowing him to complete his full term, the most likely outcome in the absence of concerted action to the contrary. There were always a certain number of people who regarded Nixon, his *persona* and his politics, as a net advantage for the country. The number constantly dwindled—eventually even Republican officeholders came to regard Nixon as a net electoral liability—but to the end there were those who thought Nixon

24. Jimmy Breslin, *How the Good Guys Finally Won* (New York: Viking, 1973), pp. 35, 30, 44, 180. 'Impeachment Lobby: Emphasis on Grass-Roots Pressure', *Congressional Quarterly Weekly Report*, vol. 32, no. 21 (25 May 1974): 1368–73. On grapevines more generally, see Eugene Bardach, 'Subformal Warning Systems in the Species *Homo Politicus*', *Policy Sciences*, 5 (1977): 415–32. Perhaps my contrast between the fact-fiddling and coordination models is overdrawn: the essence of the coordination strategy is to manipulate one crucial fact, *viz.*, that everyone else regards your own favourite option as the obvious one.

should neither resign nor be impeached. They can nowise be construed as being party to the coordination problem I have been discussing. Of course, the fact that some people were not party to the coordination problem does not mean that the situation was not a coordination problem for those who were—drivers at an intersection face a coordination problem in deciding who should go across first, even if there are some autos in the world not lined up at that crossroads.

Second, I should say something about how deep the structuring of the obvious went in the case of impeachment. Sometimes an experience results in deeply institutionalized prejudices and decision practices that persist for a very long time and define the appropriate responses to a wide range of stimuli. An example might be the lesson the British Labour Party drew from MacDonald's treachery, prejudicing it against peacetime coalitions of any sort for nearly half a century. The structuring of the obvious did not go nearly so deep with impeachment. Although it came to be regarded as the obvious, extraordinarily appropriate remedy in the case at hand, that was recognized as being a peculiar situation indeed from which no general lessons would be drawn. Impeachment is still very far from becoming the accepted way for Congressmen routinely to display displeasure with the President or his policies.

7.5 POWER AND BIAS IN THE POLITICS OF THE OBVIOUS

Three models of the politics of the obvious—fact-fiddling, concept-rigging and coordination—have now been identified. The next task must be to assess their relative importance. Assuming that the purpose of politics is bending others to your will, this resolves into a question of which is the best power resource, with the twin considerations of the strength of the power and its reliability. On both criteria, the coordination model comes out far ahead of its competitors.

From the viewpoint of conniving but myopic politicians, fact-fiddling might seem quite a good trick. Even if citizens were generally suspicious of the ruse, it would characteristically not be worth their while (individually or collectively) to expose it. But Chapter 2 shows that, from the point of view of citizens, it is not an especially dirty trick. If the issue is sufficiently important to enough people with enough resources, they can fund independent research discrediting that which they have previously been spoon-fed. (They need not rebut the substance of the evidence—it is cheaper and equally effective simply to discredit the source as biased and unreliable.) Scientific reports in praise of the anti-ballistic missile system were, for instance, effectively discredited by the series of studies commissioned by Sen. Edward Kennedy.

Where interested parties are less wealthy and more dispersed, the familiar problems associated with 'the logic of collective action' cannot be discounted entirely. Socially useful knowledge is often a public good benefitting everyone once anyone makes it available; so everyone waits for someone else to provide it. But in practice such effects tend to be mitigated by relative concentration of interest and resources among a few individuals. The more appropriate analogy is to NATO, where the public good is sufficiently valuable to a sufficiently wealthy member (the United States) that it provides the good for all practically singlehandedly, rather than to a trade union, where no single member could or would care to provide the public good in question all by himself.[25] Add to this

25. Mancur Olson, Jr., *The Logic of Collective Action* (Cambridge: Harvard University Press, 1965). Olson and Richard Zeckhauser, 'The Economic Theory of Alliances', *Review of Economics and Statistics*, 48 (1966): 266–79. Michael Taylor, *Anarchy and Cooperation* (London: Wiley, 1976).

the selective incentives for certain persons (newsmen, the politician's opponents) to expose the lies and the free-rider problem largely disappears.

Similarly, concept-rigging is neither a strong nor a reliable resource for purposes of power politics. Phenomenologists and their ordinary language fellow-travellers tend to exaggerate the importance of conceptual constraints, as Chapter 3 has shown. Wittgenstein's observation that 'the limits of my language mean the limits of my world' is fair enough as an empirical generalization.[26] People do find it difficult to think about things outside their language. But quite often these things press themselves upon people's consciousness and thereby work their way into language. Linguistic constraints are thus themselves constrained by people's need to talk about a shared reality. A social construction of reality which meshes poorly with our experience of the objectively real world will soon be revised. For this reason, conceptual schemata can rarely dictate to people for long. They can, in the short term, prevent them from noticing things; but they cannot very well cause them to perceive phantasms. The only exception seems to be with respect to 'abstract' entities (gods, principles, etc.) of which we have no direct sensory evidence. Here alone concept-rigging can work unchecked. Since most abstractions are somehow connected to large sets of facts, however, even this seems a limited opportunity.

As far as it seems reasonable to go down the phenomenological path is this: Given the sense data typically generated through everyday experiences, and given the classificatory schema ('common sense') which society conveniently provides for arranging them, few people ever bother moving beyond these shared understandings. With sufficient

26. Ludwig Wittgenstein, *Tractatus Logico-Philosophicus*, trans. D. F. Pears and B. F. McGuinness (London: Routledge & Kegan Paul, 1961), p. 6.

provocation, however they can and will.[27] This makes concept-rigging a rather unreliable mode of political domination.

What is most remarkable about the coordination model of the politics of the obvious is that there is so little citizens can do to resist it. Fact-fiddling is easily overcome: if someone in disagreement with the conventional wisdom puts out new information which is palpably correct and demonstrably useful, others will snap it up. Likewise, if one proposes a new conceptual category which clearly possesses great utility, it will surely spread. Those suffering under an 'obvious' solution to a coordination problem have no such easy recourse. All they can do is try to initiate discussion of alternatives to the obvious solution hoping that, with several remedies under discussion, none will be obvious. Success with that strategy carries a high cost, however. In the absence either of some central coordination or of an 'obvious' solution, there is great danger that everyone will work at cross-purposes and the crucial coordination will be lost.

From what has been said so far, it might be thought that neither this form nor any other of the politics of the obvious contains any inherent distributive biases—that anyone's attempts at manipulation are as likely to succeed as anyone else's. This is never strictly true, especially in the coordination model. Some people are always better situated to play the role of cartographer (e.g., those in control of the media, those in positions to command media attention). The larger worry is that some group might systematically work the politics-of-the-obvious strategy to their advantage in coordination games. In order to do this the group must possess the follow-

27. See Chapter 3 for further development of these criticisms. John Urry, *Reference Groups and the Theory of Revolution* (London: Routledge & Kegan Paul, 1973), Ch. 5, comes to similar conclusions on the basis of hints provided by Alfred Schutz himself in 'The Stranger: An Essay in Social Psychology', *American Journal of Sociology*, 49 (1944): 499–507.

ing characteristics: (1) it must be sufficiently small to allow members to coordinate among themselves a joint campaign to establish some particular alternative as the obvious one; (2) it must be sufficiently powerful for that small group to carry off the coup; and (3) it must be sufficiently insulated from the larger community that debates within the group over which alternative to offer as the obvious one will not spread to the larger community, thus undermining the attempt to establish it as the obvious choice. These, of course, are characteristics traditionally associated with established elites.[28]

Nothing I have said proves that any such elites exist or, if they do, that they have in fact availed themselves of these opportunities. Neither have I said anything to deny that non-elites can occasionally play the politics-of-the-obvious coordination strategy to advantage. What I do assert is simply this: established elites alone could systematically work the strategy to their advantage. Other groups will win and lose with it more-or-less randomly.

7.6 THE SCOPE OF MANIPULATED OBVIOUSNESS

The politics of the obvious has been shown to be an especially pernicious way of solving social coordination problems. In

---

28. Notice Nelson Polsby's interesting comment on the role of elites in the impeachment process: 'Truman was unpopular with the people when he fired Douglas MacArthur but General Marshall didn't resign, Undersecretary Lovett didn't resign, Dean Acheson didn't resign ... as a matter of fact they breathed a sigh of relief. They were delighted and MacArthur came marching back and he walked into a Senate investigation by Richard Russell and Robert Kerr which was convened for the express purpose of letting the air out of his balloon. The difference I think is in structure. Now elites who had been suffering this campaign of vilification from the Nixon administration turned on him and the masses came along afterward.... ' Demetrios Caraley *et al.*, 'American Political Institutions After Watergate—A Discussion', *Political Science Quarterly*, 89 (1974): 713-49 at 729-30.

what follows I shall show that it is, at least potentially, also a rather pervasive one. An opportunity for people to play the politics-of-the-obvious strategy exists wherever there is a coordination problem, and these are widespread indeed. I shall suggest the possible scope of politics of the obvious by showing that coordination problems amenable to such solutions range from mundane matters of policy choice to grand questions of group traditions.

Policy choices often pose coordination problems. Consider the case of residential segregation on the basis of race. Thomas Schelling suggests, quite plausibly, that the prejudices of white American homeowners are such as to make this a coordination game: each is willing to tolerate a certain number of black neighbours, but if everyone else sells their homes to blacks then he will himself abandon the neighbourhood; each would remain, but only so long as he can be sure that enough other whites will stay as well. Therefore, which course of action each homeowner pursues depends upon his estimate of what others will do. Estimates such as these are typically taken to be somehow objective perceptions of obvious features of one's society. Cooley regards the 'imaginations which people have of one another' as 'the solid facts of society'. But these perceptions are often in error, and these errors can often have grave political consequences. Katz and Allport found that a student fraternity was racially segregated because its members thought each other far more racist than any of them actually were. Similar explanations have been offered for the reluctance of department store managers to hire black sales personnel, for congregations to appoint black ministers and for whites to support 'open housing'.[29]

29. Thomas C. Schelling, *Micromotives and Macrobehavior* (New York: Norton, 1978), Ch. 4. Charles H. Cooley, *Human Nature and the Social Order* (New York: Free Press, 1956), p. 121. Daniel Katz and Floyd H. Allport, *Student Attitudes* (Syracuse, N.Y.: Craftsmen Press, 1931), pp. 152, 157.

Reforming public policy always presents another more general sort of coordination problem. There is only one *status quo*, and there are always powerful forces supporting it, whereas there are always multiple paths of reform, each having its own champions. Without coordination within the reform caucus, the unified opponents of change are almost certain to win. Reformers must coordinate their efforts and rally behind some joint programme. But typically there is no one individual or organization to provide the needed coordination, and reformers must instead rely upon 'obviousness' for coordination cues.

To some extent such cues are provided by strictly political manipulations of perceptions of the obvious, but to a large extent academics themselves structure policy debates. Policy research does much to delimit the scope of what are recognized as 'social problems' and to define the 'accepted' view of how such problems should be resolved. Fashionable opinion, even that fashionable in academic circles, is often badly in error—Moynihan's complaints about the intellectual underpinnings of the War on Poverty indicate that this is a particularly dramatic case in point.[30] Those solutions, however, became the focis of reformers' joint efforts in spite of the fact

Gerhart Saenger and Emily Gilbert, 'Customer Reactions to the Integration of Negro Sales Personnel', *International Journal of Opinion and Attitude Research*, 4 (1950): 57–76. Warren Breed and Thomas Ktsanes, 'Pluralistic Ignorance in the Process of Public Opinion Formation', *Public Opinion Quarterly*, 25 (1961): 382–92. Hubert J. O'Gorman, 'Pluralistic Ignorance and White Estimates of White Support for Racial Segregation', *Public Opinion Quarterly*, 39 (1975): 311–30. O'Gorman and Stephen L. Garry, 'Pluralistic Ignorance—A Replication and Extension', *Public Opinion Quarterly*, 40 (1976): 449–58.

30. D. P. Moynihan, *Maximum Feasible Misunderstanding* (New York: Free Press, 1969), Ch. 8. See Martin Rein and Sheldon H. White, 'Policy Research: Belief and Doubt', *Policy Analysis*, 3 (1977): 239–71, on the 'value critical' role of policy research more generally.

that many had serious misgivings about them at the time. In the context of a coordination game, it is often advisable for people to settle for what they know to be a suboptimal solution if (1) it is the only one everyone else is likely to settle upon and (2) everyone going in different directions would produce much worse results than agreeing to this suboptimal policy.[31]

While the politics of the obvious is working to manipulate such mundane matters as policy choice, it is also structuring our group traditions and the behavioural constraints they impose. The tremendous sociological and psychological urge to bind ourselves to a distinct group with distinguished traditions is widely recognized. The elements of a coordination problem implicit in the selection of group traditions is often obscured, most powerfully by the presumption that there is no selection involved. The simple view of tradition and custom as something handed down intact from time immemorial precludes any element of choice. However, admitting as little as Vico's proposition that traditions get jumbled in transmission introduces an element of choice—which is the garbled and which the true tradition? Most commentators go well beyond Vico in admitting that there is enough in the past ex-

---

31. Perhaps some solutions and ways of reaching a solution are objectively obvious and chosen without any attempt at political manipulation. An example might be the tendency for policy-makers to be forever fighting the last battle, to which Stanley Hoffman traces *Gulliver's Troubles* (New York: McGraw-Hill, 1968). The recent past, and the lessons it holds, is always the most conspicuous point for coordinated future action. Suppose we have a standing Wednesday luncheon the location of which we vary from week to week. If we forget to set a time and place for next week's meeting before you depart on holiday, the natural presumption is that next week we will lunch at the same time and place as our last meeting. There are of course many other equally *unique* alternatives—the arrangements for this date last month or last year—but none is nearly so *obvious* as the solution suggested by the immediate past. (And, notice, we may return in spite of a perfectly ghastly meal last week.) There is absolutely nothing political in this.

perience of any group to bear many alternative interpretations, to sustain claims that many different and incompatible
traditions are truly those of the group. Thus, we find historians as diverse as Oakeshott, Collingwood and Pocock agreeing with Hill's observation that 'history has to be rewritten in
every generation, because although the past does not change
the present does; each generation asks new questions of the
past, and finds new areas of sympathy as it re-lives different
aspects of the experiences of its predecessors.'[32] This choice
of group traditions, of course, is a politically charged affair
with profound implications for the distribution of power and
authority within the group.

Specifying traditions not only presents these very political
problems of choice. It also presents a coordination problem of
a classic variety: for something to be *the* tradition of a group,
all of its members must settle on the *same* tradition; and, as
we have seen, they typically have several equally plausible
alternatives from which to choose. (To some extent, we can
always redefine the group as those who *do* agree, purging

32. Christopher Hill, *The World Turned Upside Down* (New York: Viking,
1972), p. 13. R. G. Collingwood, *The Idea of History* (New York: Oxford University Press, 1946). Michael Oakeshott, *Experience and Its Modes* (Cambridge:
Cambridge University Press, 1933), esp. Ch. 3. J. G. A. Pocock, *The Ancient
Constitution and the Feudal Law* (Cambridge: Cambridge University Press,
1957), and 'Time, Institutions and Action: An Essay on Traditions and Their
Understanding', *Politics and Experience*, ed. P. King and B. C. Parekh (Cam-
bridge: Cambridge University Press, 1968), pp. 209-37. For anthropological
examples, see: Gillian Feeley Harnik, 'Divine Kingship and the Meaning of
History among the Sakaluva of Madagascar', *Man*, 13 (1978): 402-17; J. J.
Fox, 'A Routinese Dynastic Genealogy: Structure and Event', *The Translation
of Culture*, ed. T. O. Beidelman (London: Tavistock, 1971); M. Southwold,
'The History of a History: Royal Succession in Buganda', *History and Social
Anthropology*, ed. I. M. Lewis (London: Tavistock, 1968), pp. 127-51; A. F.
Robertson, 'Histories and Political Opposition in Ahafo, Ghana', *Africa*, 43
(1973): 41-58; and I. Cunnison, 'History and Genealogies in a Conquest
State', *American Anthropologist*, 59 (1957): 20-31.

dissidents—but frequent or widespread recourse to this strategy destroys the group as a viable unit.) In this coordination game there is great scope for the politics of the obvious to work.

The most conspicuous attempts at political manipulation of group traditions come in connection with attempts at 'nation-building'. Mazrui offers a very frank discussion of the strategy in *Cultural Engineering and Nation-Building in East Africa*: language, literature, electoral systems and even certain styles of economic development are recommended as mechanisms of 'cultural engineering', defined and defended by Mazrui as 'the deliberate manipulation of cultural factors for purposes of deflecting human habit in the direction of new and perhaps constructive endeavors.' Manipulating tradition for political advantage is a strategy often used by contenders vying for political power, most interestingly by dissidents to topple established elites. Recall the example of Mo Tzu successfully challenging the existing regime with the charge, 'You are only following the Chou, not the Hsia dynasty. Your antiquity does not go back far enough.' In 1911 Sun Yat-Sen moved China 'backwards toward revolution' by hauntingly reenacting this scenario. Friedman, describing the gestalt of his Revolution, writes, 'The change to a more just world is experienced as a return, setting things right again. It is doubtful if the villager sees himself as rebelling. Rather he is trying to defend what has been and is rightfully and traditionally his.' Similarly, seventeenth-century English radicals decried the Norman Yoke and urged, unsuccessfully, a return to the traditions of individual freedom and economic equality presumably prevailing before the Conquest. Indeed, wherever authority rests in whole or in part on traditions and lineages, it is always sound radical strategy to produce 'subversive genealogies'. And in principle it should always be possible to find as many scoundrels as saints in any genealogy, be it of an individual or of a regime.[33]

Traditions as well as policies, then, are politicized in several senses. They benefit some and disadvantage others; and, in the abstract, alternative traditions and policies with different distributive profiles are equally eligible. A weak form of the politics of the obvious is always at work discouraging those burdened by the existing traditions or policies from trying to shift to some more advantageous alternative—once discussion of these alternatives begins, none will appear obvious and the crucial coordination might be lost to the disadvantage of all concerned. And often a stronger form of the politics of the obvious is involved, where elites are not simply the incidental beneficiaries of biases inherent in current conceptions of the obvious, but may also have helped to structure those perceptions to their own advantage. This must be demonstrated for each case, of course, but it is a dangerous possibility that should not be ignored.

7.7 OBVIOUSNESS AS A MODE OF MANIPULATION

This theory of the politics of the obvious should be set in the larger theoretical context of pre-agenda-setting. As such,

33. Ali A. Mazrui, *Cultural Engineering and Nation-Building in East Africa* (Evanston, Ill.: Northwestern University Press, 1972), p. xv. Pocock, 'Time, Institutions and Understanding', and Edward Friedman, *Backwards Toward Revolution* (Berkeley: University of California Press, 1977), p. 211, discuss the Chinese cases and Pocock, *Ancient Constitution and the Feudal Law*, and Hill, *World Turned Upside Down*, discuss the English example. See Judith N. Shklar on 'Subversive Genealogies', *Daedalus*, 101 (Winter 1972): 129–54, and, for an example, Harry W. Basehart, 'Traditional History and Political Change Among the Matengo of Tanzania', *Africa*, 42 (1972): 87–96. James C. Scott, 'Protest and Profanation: Agrarian Revolt and the Little Tradition', *Theory and Society*, 4 (1977): 1–38, 211–46, further demonstrates that the variability of tradition is politically significant.

its conclusions are familiar ones: underlying the ordinary political system is some kind of a structure containing biases (read modestly as 'power resources', boldly as 'prejudices against certain interests') which can be mobilized to political advantage. What is lacking in most such arguments, and what the theory of the politics of the obvious provides is a bridging theory plausibly accounting for the genesis of these structures. The primary value of the notion of political obviousness lies in its power to explain how the structure underlying the ordinary political system gets rigged and biases mobilized.

Here I have identified three forms of the politics-of-the-obvious strategy, one fiddling facts, a second rigging concepts and a third playing on the need for coordination. Summarizing my conclusions with respect to each variety in terms of the questions posed in Section 1.6:

1. Is the interference deceptive?

Both fact-fiddling and concept-rigging are probably marginally deceptive, or at least they try to be. Rigging perceptions of an obvious coordinated solution does not, strictly speaking, *have* to be deceptive. Even if the wandering parachutists knew that their mapmaker only sketched in his favourite hills, they would nevertheless use his map to pick out 'obvious points' for their rendezvous. But in political contexts it is far more likely that the trick will have to be deceptive if it is to succeed. Had Congressmen immediately perceived what 'Tip' O'Neill and others were up to when they began spreading impeachment rumours, they would have discounted the reports. They would have ceased to regard these as accurate assessments of 'the mood of the House' and might well have taken other cues as to what was the most widely perceived 'obvious' solution to 'the Nixon problem'. To avoid having their signals discounted in this way, politicians playing the politics-of-the-obvious coordination game will probably have to play it deceptively.

2. *Is the interference contrary to the putative will of those subject to it?*

Both fact-fiddling and concept-rigging, insofar as they succeed in deceiving anyone, probably cause people to act contrary to their putative wills. Rigging perceptions of the obvious solution to coordination problems also diverts most people from pursuing their most-preferred solution. They gain something in the deal, to be sure: to win they must coordinate on some solution or another; and it is better to win your second choice than to lose all by holding out for your first choice. While people gain something through this trick, however, it is not nearly so much as they might have done in the absence of the interference.

All three ways of playing the politics of the obvious thus seem to possess these defining features of an act of manipulation. The coordination game variant presents these features rather less strongly than the others, since it is not necessarily deceptive and is not contrary to people's putative wills in the strongest possible sense. Still, it meets each of these requirements sufficiently to count as an instance of manipulation. And, as we shall see when turning to the next two criteria, its persistence and biases are sufficient to make it a really worrying form of manipulation when it is used as such.

3. *How persistent is the effect of the manipulation?*

Fact-fiddling, like the propaganda strategy discussed in Chapter 2, is likely to have only rather short-term effects. Neither are the effects of concept-rigging expected to be very persistent, although (as Chapter 3 shows) some forms of the strategy might have more persistent effects than others. Only the coordination variation on the politics-of-the-obvious strategy holds out any prospect for truly long-lasting effects. Once people settle, for whatever reasons, upon one solution as the 'obvious one', it is usually rational for them to stick with it. They might try to force a renegotiation of the chosen solution, but in so doing they run the risk of both undermining the old solution and failing to establish firmly any new one as 'obvious' in its place. Hence they would fail to coordinate and would lose the game as a whole.

4. Are any distributive biases inherent in the mechanism?

Fact-fiddling and concept-rigging contain only slight distributive biases. The finding here strictly parallels that in Chapters 2 and 3 respectively. The coordination variation on the strategy does, however, contain some fairly strong biases in favour of those occupying central positions in the communication network. They alone are capable of putting out persuasive rumours of the sort that go to establish an 'obvious' solution to a coordination problem.

Fact-fiddling and concept-rigging are, therefore, not really very worrying forms of manipulatory politics. Their effects are neither persistent nor biased. The politics of the obvious, played in connection with a coordination game, does pose serious manipulatory threats, being both persistent and biased.

CHAPTER EIGHT ⟨ APPRAISING AND AVOIDING POLITICAL MANIPULATION

THE LARGER GOAL OF THIS STUDY is, the Preface promised, to produce evaluatively significant empirical results. The time has come to collect the findings and to assess them according to the ethical standard embodied in my conception of manipulation as the evil core of power. This task of appraisal requires us to ask two questions of the previous descriptive chapters: Are the practices really manipulative? And, if so, how serious a form of manipulation is involved?

As a first step, each of the mechanisms of manipulation discussed in Chapters 2 through 7 must be measured against the definition of 'manipulation' offered in Chapter 1. Two necessary conditions were there identified. The practice must be (1) deceptive and (2) working against the putative will of the person being manipulated. If either of these conditions is lacking, the case cannot strictly speaking be one of 'manipulation'.

Several of the political acts we might be tempted to call manipulative fail to qualify as such on one or the other of these simple definitional criteria. A ruler might play on 'affective symbols', for example, without engaging in manipulation at all—the people involved actually welcome this practice as a means of reaffirming their symbolic attachments to the community. Or, again, rulers cannot deceive anyone by manipulating 'constitutive' or 'representational' rituals if the nature of these rituals is properly understood. These rituals are strictly incapable of being either true or false, so the only way any ruler can deceive anyone with them is to claim for such rituals a truth status to which they cannot rightfully aspire.

In many other places careful investigation reveals that, although manipulation is clearly underway, it is not of an especially worrying form. Such a conclusion might rest on either of two types of judgement. Firstly, an act of manipulation will be less worrying the less persistent it is. Lies and secrets cannot be sustained for very long, for example. Linguistic traps are dismissed in Section 3.3 as tricks that can only work in the short term, at least as regards non-metaphysical propositions. Rigging perceptions of the obvious solution to a political problem through fact-finding can succeed for a time, but there is every reason to suppose that this trick can and will be successfully challenged in due course. Secondly, a mechanism of manipulation will be less menacing if it displays no distributive biases, i.e., if it is equally available to everyone. Anyone can lie, keep secrets or lay cage-like linguistic traps. The rhetorical trick of hiding premises and implications of an argument can work to the advantage of the oppressed as well as to that of the oppressors. This makes these mechanisms of manipulation less worrying than they might otherwise be.

The table below lists the twenty mechanisms of manipulation discussed in Chapters 2 through 7. Drawing on admittedly impressionistic evidence, it attempts to appraise each of them along these four evaluative dimensions. Really firm conclusions must, of course, await further and more detailed empirical investigation. These are at best rough-grained estimates—of what is possible and what is impossible, of what is likely and what is unlikely—and in certain cases the finer texture might well matter. A caveat is especially required as concerns my estimates of distributive bias. All I have usually been able to conclude with confidence is that there are possibilities for the downtrodden to turn manipulatory techniques to their advantage. It may well turn out that, while this is always *possible,* it is usually extraordinarily difficult and hence extremely improbable. Such a finding might make several mechanisms of manipulation look more menacing than I have suggested. But such a finding can come only from a more relentlessly empirical form of investigation than this first cut at the problem could have hoped to offer.

These caveats notwithstanding, the general pattern of the conclusions, presented in summary form in the table, is truly striking. It indicates how very little cause for concern most of the tricks surveyed in Chapters 2 through 7 provide. Most of them are not necessarily manipulative at all, either because intentional deception is not necessarily involved (I-B-2, I-C, III-B, IV-A, IV-B, V-A, V-B, V-C, V-D, VI-B) or else because the interference is not necessarily contrary to the putative will of the person affected (I-B-2, I-C, III-A, IV-A, IV-B, V-B, V-D, VI-C). Even when these manipulative possibilities are realized, their effects are often easily overcome (I-A, I-B-1, I-B-2, I-C, II-A-1, II-B, III-A, IV-A, V-C, V-D, VI-A). Of the twenty, only the five mechanisms marked with an asterisk seem to present much of a threat at all. The pair marked with a single asterisk seem only slightly worrying. The information overload strategy (I-D), although possibly persistent, is only slightly biased; and cage-like linguistic traps on a metaphysical plane (II-A-2), although similarly persistent, are not necessarily the result of intentional deception and are not the exclusive province of any particular segment of society. Overall, there are only three strategies (III-B, V-A, VI-C), marked in the table with multiple asterisks, which seem altogether worrisome. Debasing language, magico-religious political rituals and rigging perceptions of obviousness in coordination games are all strategies likely to involve sustained and distributively biased forms of political manipulation.

These conclusions are broadly reassuring, but they also have a disquieting aspect. This arises from the fact that the list of manipulatory techniques in the table is nowise exhaustive.

SUMMARY OF EVALUATIVE CONCLUSIONS

| | Dimensions of Evaluation | | | |
| | Is manipulation involved? | | Seriousness of Manipulation | |
Mechanism of manipulation	deceptive?	unwelcome?	persistence	distributive bias
I. Untruth				
A. Lying (Section 2.2)	yes	yes	brief	slight
B. Secrecy (2.3)				
1. Withholding information	yes	yes	brief	slight
2. Co-optation	perhaps	probably not	probably brief	slight bias in favour of policy-makers
C. Propaganda (2.4)	slightly	slightly	probably brief	slight
* D. Overload (2.5)	probably	probably	possibly long	slight
II. Linguistic Traps				
A. Cage-like traps (3.2)				
1. Real-world (3.3)	probably	probably	brief	slight
* 2. Metaphysical (3.4)	probably	probably	possibly long	slight
B. Linguistic deprivation (3.2)	probably	probably	probably brief	some bias in favour of teaching classes
III. Rhetorical tricks				
A. Implicit assertion (4.1)	probably	possibly	probably brief	any biases counterbalance

** B. Debasing language (4.4)	perhaps	probably	long	strong conservative bias, although often unintended consequence of radical rhetoric
IV. Symbolic rewards A. Promissory (5.2)	slightly	appreciated, but not as much as actual delivery	brief	slight bias in favour of those who might be able to deliver
B. Affective (5.3)	slightly	no	——	
V. Rituals ** A. Magico-religious (6.1.1)	perhaps	if so, probably	probably long	biased in favour of established authorities, but radical possibilities
B. Constitutive (6.1.2)	not if properly understood	possibly	possibly long	slight
C. Schematizing (6.1.3)	perhaps	if so, probably	probably brief (as IIA1 or IIB)	slight
D. Representational (6.1.4)	not if properly understood	possibly	probably brief	slight
VI. Obviousness A. Fact-fiddling (7.2)	probably	probably	brief (as I)	slight (as I)
B. Concept-rigging (7.3)	perhaps	if so, probably	as in II	as in II
** C. Coordination (7.4)	probably	no, but some alternative probably more preferred	possibly long	biased in favour of those occupying central positions in communications networks

Asterisks (*) denote especially worrying forms of manipulation; the more asterisks, the more ethically worrisome.

It cannot be: the subject simply does not lend itself to such treatment. As Chapter 1 argues, manipulation is essentially a matter of tricking people, and this effectively precludes any attempt at deducing a complete and exhaustive list of all political tricks that might work. Indeed, Chapter 7 has revealed one very troubling form of political manipulation which has long gone unrecognized. One only wonders how many more might be at work without our recognizing them. Any comfort we take in finding the much-discussed modes of manipulation (of language or rhetoric or symbols or rituals) to be largely innocuous must, therefore, be balanced by our unease in the knowledge that we might be subject to many serious forms of manipulation without ever noticing.

Given the fact that the list of manipulatory techniques is necessarily incomplete, the task of avoiding manipulation requires far more than knowing counterstrategies specifically tailored to each of the mechanisms of manipulation discussed above. Insofar as we can anticipate the tricks, it is of course important to discuss ways of resisting them, as previous chapters have done. But since we know that we cannot anticipate all possible tricks, it is also important to explore in a more general way the sources of manipulative power and ways of countering it. As a first step, we might examine the trio of especially worrying mechanisms of manipulation more closely to see what properties they share.

Troublesome tricks all seem to share two very significant properties. First, all three are to a great extent *impersonal* strategies of domination.[1] They are not strategies targeted

---

1. 'In cases involving manipulation ... compliance is forthcoming in the absence of recognition on the compiler's part either of the source or the exact nature of the demand upon him.' Peter Bachrach and Morton S. Baratz, *Power and Poverty* (New York: Oxford University Press, 1970), p. 28. While this is not necessarily true of all forms of manipulation, as Bachrach and Baratz imply, it is true of all the really serious forms.

narrowly *against* any particular individual or group. Language is debased for everyone. All are subject to the same commandments of the same gods. Obviousness must be a widely shared perception if it is to function effectively in a coordination strategy. Furthermore, these are not perceived to be strategies deployed *by* any particular individual or group. Insofar as they are perceived in this way the strategies stand that much less chance of succeeding. Seeing that someone is trying to debase your language as a means of preventing you from carrying on meaningful discussions, you attempt to develop or maintain a purer form of language among those of you he is trying to prevent from talking together. Seeing that rulers use magico-religious rituals to their personal advantage, one wonders whether the gods would be pleased. Seeing that someone has rigged perceptions of obviousness tempts one to play spoiler, although the high costs associated with that counterstrategy might make one reconsider.

Second, all three really worrying forms of manipulation tend to be *self-perpetuating*. With some modes of domination, 'the means eat up the end.'[2] This is the case with the tyrant ruling by brute force alone, where the mechanisms of coercion (armies, police, spies, etc.) require constant upkeep and regular renewal of investments. Such modes of domination are less worrying because, other things being equal, the higher cost of sustaining them makes them less long-lived. What makes the three mechanisms of manipulation identified above so worrying is that they, in contrast, tend to be self-perpetuating. Debasement of language proceeds of its own

2. Pierre Bourdieu, *Outline of a Theory of Practice,* trans. Richard Nice (Cambridge: Cambridge University Press, 1977), p. 184. Routines display similar properties, as seen in Geraint Parry and Peter Morriss, 'When is a Decision Not a Decision?' *British Political Sociology Yearbook,* ed. Ivor Crewe (London: Croom Helm, 1974), 1: 317–36.

momentum once the process is underway, as Orwell complains bitterly.[3] Magico-religious rituals increase adherence to the system of beliefs from which they derive their power—unlike ordinary economic goods, the power of such rituals tends to accrue rather than diminishing with use. Similarly, an alternative once installed as the obvious solution to a political problem tends to be self-reinforcing: as one person sees that others regard it as the obvious solution, its obviousness becomes that much more compelling for him; and others react similarly to his new perceptions in turn.

These are plausibly features not just of the three mechanisms identified here but also of any truly worrying mode of manipulation. If so, certain fairly general conclusions for avoidance of political manipulation follow. Recognizing manipulation is, presumably, a necessary precondition for overcoming it. People on their guard for manipulation usually look out for nasty actions by nasty people. But now that we have seen that the really troublesome forms of manipulation tend to be impersonal and self-perpetuating, we know better. In the cases here discussed, manipulation cannot be traced to the activities of anyone in particular but only to the relentless workings of systemic bias.

A more reliable strategy for detecting (and thereby helping us to avoid) manipulation more generally would focus attention first upon the biases of the political system. Once we have seen who wins regularly, our task is to investigate the source of these biases and the mechanisms by which they are perpetuated. Some biases will, no doubt, turn out to be purely accidental—the work of no one—but often in the course of such an enquiry we will work our way back to some manipula-

3. George Orwell, 'Politics and the English Language', *Collected Essays, Journalism and Letters* (New York: Harcourt, Brace & World, 1968), 4: 172–40.

tive act of some particular individual or group. Had we started looking for manipulation *per se,* however, it is likely that we never would have noticed the trick. Indeed, that is the essence of a really good political trick. It is also the foundation of all the really worrying forms of political manipulation.

NAME INDEX

SUBJECT INDEX

DATE DUE